Jonathan Lethem

Manchester University Press

Contemporary American and Canadian Writers

Series editors
Nahem Yousaf and Sharon Monteith

Jonathan Lethem

James Peacock

Manchester University Press
Manchester and New York
distributed in the United States exclusively by Palgrave Macmillan

Published by Manchester University Press
Oxford Road, Manchester M13 9NR, UK
and Room 400, 175 Fifth Avenue, New York, NY 10010, USA
www.manchesteruniversitypress.co.uk

Distributed in the United States exclusively by
Palgrave Macmillan, 175 Fifth Avenue, New York,
NY 10010, USA

Distributed in Canada exclusively by
UBC Press, University of British Columbia, 2029 West Mall,
Vancouver, BC, Canada V6T 1Z2

British Library Cataloguing-in-Publication Data
A catalogue record for this book is available from the British Library

Library of Congress Cataloging-in-Publication Data applied for

ISBN 978 07190 8267 2 hardback

First published 2012

Edited and typeset
by Frances Hackeson Freelance Publishing Services, Brinscall, Lancs
Printed in Great Britain
by CPI Group (UK) Ltd, Croydon, CR0 4YY

For my mother

Contents

Series editors' foreword

This innovative series reflects the breadth and diversity of writing over the last thirty years, and provides critical evaluations of established, emerging and critically neglected writers – mixing the canonical with the unexpected. It explores notions of the contemporary and analyses current and developing modes of representation with a focus on individual writers and their work. The series seeks to reflect both the growing body of academic research in the field, and the increasing prevalence of contemporary American and Canadian fiction on programmes of study in institutions of higher education around the world. Central to the series is a concern that each book should argue a stimulating thesis, rather than provide an introductory survey, and that each contemporary writer will be examined across the trajectory of their literary production. A variety of critical tools and literary and interdisciplinary approaches are encouraged to illuminate the ways in which a particular writer contributes to, and helps readers rethink, the North American literary and cultural landscape in a global context.

Central to debates about the field of contemporary fiction is its role in interrogating ideas of national exceptionalism and transnationalism. This series matches the multivocality of contemporary writing with wide-ranging and detailed analysis. Contributors examine the drama of the nation from the perspectives of writers who are members of established and new immigrant groups, writers who consider themselves on the nation's margins as well as those who chronicle middle America. National labels are the subject of vociferous debate and including American and Canadian writers in the same series is not to flatten the differences between them but to acknowledge that literary traditions and tensions are cross-cultural and that North American writers often explore and expose precisely these tensions.

The series recognises that situating a writer in a cultural context involves a multiplicity of influences, social and geo-political, artistic and theoretical, and that contemporary fiction defies easy categorisation. For example, it examines writers who invigorate the genres in which they have made their mark alongside writers whose aesthetic goal is to subvert the idea of genre altogether. The challenge of defining the roles of writers and assessing their reception by reading communities is central to the aims of the series.

Overall, Contemporary American and Canadian Writers aims to begin to represent something of the diversity of contemporary writing and seeks to engage students and scholars in stimulating debates about the contemporary and about fiction.

Nahem Yousaf
Sharon Monteith

Acknowledgements

I would like to thank the editors of this series, Sharon Monteith and Nahem Yousaf, for their astute reading and for their critical but kind comments. Thanks are also due to Matthew Frost and Kim Walker at Manchester University Press for patient advice on all the administrative and contractual things that I am no good at.

Thanks are certainly due to friends and colleagues who have supported me during the writing of this book, read and given feedback on various sections and indulged my desire to talk about Lethem all the time. Special thanks to Oliver Harris and Tim Lustig at Keele University and to Joe Brooker at Birkbeck. Thanks also to those members of the Research Institute for the Humanities at Keele who granted me Research Fellowship time to complete the manuscript. I would like to thank Adam Gearney, whose excellent paper on *As She Climbed* at the Lethem symposium (10 July 2010 at Birkbeck, London) showed me the relevance of Nietzsche's work to the novel.

As usual, Sheena, Bonnie and Ruby deserve the highest love and respect simply for putting up with me. And, of course, I would like to thank Jonathan Lethem for granting me an interview, for his encouraging comments and for his walking tour of the neighbourhoods that inspired *Motherless Brooklyn* and *The Fortress of Solitude*.

The author gratefully acknowledges permission to reproduce in altered form portions of 'Jonathan Lethem's Genre Evolutions' published in *Journal of American Studies* 43.3 (December 2009) and portions of '"New York and yet not New York": Reading the Region in Contemporary Brooklyn Fictions' published in *European Journal of American Studies* 2008.2. The full interview I conducted with Lethem is cited as 'Personal Interview, 2009' in order to distinguish it from the version published in *The Adirondack Review* and cited as 'Peacock, 2009'.

Introduction: genre collisions and mutations

'Of course it's weird,' said Don. 'That's why we love it, right Paul?
It's from another dimension, it's fucking weird, it's science fiction.'
(Lethem, 2002: 94)

What do you get if you cross detection and science fiction? What happens when you stage a sci-fi picaresque inside an animal's body? And what happens when a kangaroo develops the power of speech and starts wielding a gun? The punchlines are all to be found in Jonathan Lethem's writing, and they are only partially comic. This book proceeds from the broad and frequently rehearsed observation that Jonathan Lethem's novels and short stories subvert established fictional genres in some way, and that the frequent intermingling and clashing of genres is reflected in the bizarre characteristics displayed by many of the characters. For example, 'Light and the Sufferer' (1996), from which the prefatory quotation is taken, is a gritty urban drama of fraternal bonding, drug addiction and robbery which just happens to feature mysterious aliens tracking the main characters. *The Fortress of Solitude* (2003) disrupts a semi-autobiographical coming-of-age narrative by investing some of the neighbourhood Brooklyn kids with superheroic powers. *As She Climbed Across the Table* (1997) is billed as 'campus comedy', yet allows science fiction to infiltrate and eventually colonise its witty satire on academic life. *Girl in Landscape* (1998a) is a coming-of-age Western set in space and introduces American frontier loners to alien races.

Given some of Lethem's early key influences, writers such as Philip K. Dick and Charles Willeford who 'had embattled careers because of genre prejudice', it is unsurprising that Lethem is vocal about his antipathy toward 'bankrupt categories' (Gaffney, 1998: 51, 50). If he feels, touchingly, that 'Philip K. Dick died for my sins' (Gaffney, 1998:

51), it is because Dick's posthumous recognition as someone able to fashion the generic stuff of pulp science fiction into profoundly literary meditations on reality, religious thought and the alienating potential of technology paved the way for a writer like Lethem who is similarly resistant to labels like 'high' and 'low', 'canonical' and 'marginal'. (Indeed, it was partly the Library of America's publication in 2007 of his *Four Novels of the 1960s*, edited by Lethem, that helped salvage Dick's reputation, and welcomed him, somewhat ironically, into the American canon.)[1] For Lethem, argues Andrew Hoberek, there is no meaningful distinction to be made between 'high' and 'low' or between 'literary fiction' and 'popular fiction'. Rather than indulging in a postmodern 'appropriation of popular genres' by more 'literary' forms, he treats genres as serious literature in themselves (Hoborek, 2007: 238). In truth, Lethem's engagement with genre is much *more* serious than some other contemporary 'postmodern' writers, notably Paul Auster, who are also known for subverting genres. Auster is similarly self-conscious about his employment of genre conventions, but ultimately sees little value in them at all. His starting point in a text such as *City of Glass* is the assumed redundancy of the detective genre and its disassociation from reality, whereas Lethem, for all his talk of 'bankrupt categories', does appreciate their value in the first instance, recognising that they have more of a connection with the ways we structure reality than a writer like Auster might care to acknowledge.

So throughout the theoretical sections of this introduction and the chapters that follow, this is the underlying assumption: genres reflect and frequently dramatise the human need to shape and make sense of a complex and shifting world. They help us organise and understand reality but, it should be stressed, are not themselves reality: as John Frow says, they 'create effects of reality and truth' (Frow, 2006: 2). Neither are they reducible merely to sets of stylistic devices or tropes, however. In mediating between the lived experience of social situations and their textual representations, genres become central to 'human meaning-making and to the social struggle over meanings' (Frow, 2006: 10). Genres are not just useful, according to Frow, they occupy a 'privileged' (Frow, 2006: 12) position within cultural analysis precisely because they always assume that meaning is inseparable from formal considerations, as well as questions of enunciation – that is, the position from which one speaks – and social, political and historical context. Moreover, genres participate in and help to establish particular discourse communities by assuming schematic knowledge on the part of readers. Whether this knowledge is intertextual, that is, gleaned from previous similar examples, or real-world, it is necessary in order to decipher the textual clues which would proclaim a text *as* generic and thus confirm the expectations readers inevitably bring to any text they encounter. It is in this sense that genres create and perform 'worlds' or, in Alfred Schutz's evocative phrase 'finite provinces of meaning' (Schutz, 1970: 252).

What is important about these worlds or provinces is that they are shared, and that they therefore presuppose and contribute to the formation of communities of readers, critics and writers. Although other aspects of genre theory are examined in subsequent chapters (its historical connection to taxonomic evolutionary theory in Chapter 1, for instance), it is the community-building aspect of genre upon which I focus in this introduction, because it is the most pertinent to Lethem's real-world preoccupation with subcultural identity as well as, of course, his attitude to literary and popular cultural genres. Rick Altman's work in *Film/Genre* (1999) is especially useful for this argument, because it persuasively navigates a path between what Thomas Pavel dubs the 'two temptations' of genre theory: the desire to 'freeze generic features, reducing them to immutable formulas' and the desire, exemplified by Maurice Blanchot (1959), 'to deny genres any conceptual stability' whatsoever (Pavel, 2003: 201). In the following analysis of Altman's work, as well as the references to Dick Hebdige's classic work *Subculture: the Meaning of Style* (1979) which accompany it, the distinctively ethical implications of Lethem's genre treatments emerge.

While there is a common assumption that '[g]enres have clear, stable identities and borders', Altman argues, such an assumption invariably masks ideological or political views. The maintenance of clearly delineated genres helps shore up critical or disciplinary positions. Thus, and Lethem's satirical take on critical genres such as deconstruction and social anthropology in *As She Climbed Across the Table* clearly illustrates this, 'genres are never entirely neutral categories. They – and their critics and theorists – always participate and further the work of various institutions' (Altman, 1999: 6, 12). Altman also rejects the idea that genres are 'transhistorical', that they can 'be lifted out of time and placed in a timeless holding area as if they were all contemporaries' (Altman, 1999: 19). Once again, such an idea stems from a desire to make a historically defined theoretical or critical perspective appear universal and definitive. Yet 'there is no place outside of history from which purely "theoretical" definitions of genre might be made' (Altman, 1999: 9). Genres evolve and mutate, and their critical reception is historically determined. The consumer of genre fiction sees genres interacting and changing over time in the process of reading, and is forced to consider the historical, cultural and political circumstances contributing to these changes.

For Altman there is a 'constant category-splitting/category creating dialectic that constitutes the history of types and terminology' (Altman, 1999: 65–6) in which critics, producers and fans all participate. Producers, for example (and although Altman's focus is cinema, it is not difficult to imagine a parallel process occurring in the publishing industry), are engaged in a critical process 'that actually precedes the act of production' (Altman, 1999: 44) in that they assay past products and cherry-pick successful elements for future products which in turn might form recognisable new genre types. Although such an assaying impulse is clearly tied to the 'capitalist need for product differentiation' (Altman, 1999: 64), it just as clearly contributes to the inconsistency and fluidity of genre definitions and to Altman's fundamental conception of genre-as-process.

All of which is not to suggest that Altman advocates an anarchic view of genre or that he indulges in a romantic fetishisation of the text as ineluctably unique object. He would surely concur with Catherine Schryer's contention that despite the relatively unstable relation between texts and genres, it is at any given moment 'stabilised-enough' to facilitate formal identification (Schryer, 1994: 107). Hayden White's reflexive view of 'periodization', through which 'a synchronous moment is marked out for examination' and which infers genres of 'historical reality' itself (White, 2003: 605), also presupposes this stability.

It is in the concept of '*constellated communities*' (Altman, 1999: 161) that instances of stability can best be located in Altman's work; indeed, his emphasis on the role of the spectator or reader of genre texts is his most important contribution to genre theory. Although genre consumers occasionally participate in actual groups, the sci-fi comic convention in *The Fortress of Solitude* being a good example, Altman argues that 'genre spectatorship more often involves constructing an image of such a group out of fragments gleaned from every possible field', including 'industry discourse ... critical language, passing comments and chance encounters' (Altman, 1999: 161). With an obvious reference to Benedict Anderson's 'imagined communities', Altman dubs these groups 'constellated communities' because 'like a group of stars their members cohere only through repeated acts of imagination' (Altman, 1999: 161). Simply to view a movie or to read a novel is to engage in 'lateral communication' (Altman, 1999: 162), to speak symbolically with like-minded consumers; acts of spectatorship and acts of reading reinforce the feeling of community and thus the sense of stability. Altman goes on to call the relationship between one spectator and another (or for my purposes one reader and another) 'secondary discursivity' (Altman, 1999: 172).

Evidently genres and constellated communities have a symbiotic relationship: the existence of genre texts creates communities in repeated acts of reading and secondary discursivity but, importantly, it is that very discursivity which keeps genres splitting and evolving. For Altman, the inevitable inconsistency of genre definitions between members of a community is 'a basic component of genre reception' (Altman, 1999: 175). Each member of a group characterises and defines each text or genre differently and, as Altman explains: 'Only through inconsistencies of this type can a genre be redefined through one of its subsets, thus giving rise to a new genre. It is precisely because there are no master systems but only diverse system-building paths that new generic categories remain constantly possible' (Altman, 1999: 176). Gary K. Wolfe puts it another way: 'a healthy genre, a healthy literature, is one at risk, whose boundaries grow uncertain and whose foundations grow wobbly' (Wolfe, 2002: 27). Moreover, this same subjectivity and diversity applies to community participation itself. Even though stability is perceived or imagined in the shared enjoyment of genre texts, it is also the case that participants are far from 'limited to a single generic community. The same individual may, at different times, be part of a screwball comedy community, a musical community, an exploitation community and a gay porn community' (Altman, 1999: 161).

Here one arrives at a crucial intersection of generic behaviour – 'not the real world, but a game we play with moves and players borrowed from the real world' (Altman, 1999: 157) – and real-world behaviour in Lethem's writing. To participate in genre communities is effectively to join subcultural or counter-cultural groupings. Precisely because a genre text can temporarily suspend normative societal rules and offer 'a break with social standards' in the form of outlandish or transgressive behaviours, 'it also creates an implicit tie among those who find pleasure in breaking this particular cultural norm in this particular manner' (Altman, 1999: 158). This view of

generic community as countercultural impulse is consistent with
Dick Hebdige's famous articulation of youth subcultures' challenge
to hegemony as rooted in the interruption of the 'process of normali-
zation', the repudiation of that which is taken for granted (Hebdige,
1996: 18). What is key on both generic and real-world planes is that a
particular subcultural identity emerges and is only viable through acknowledgement of other groupings with which it comes into contact.
Hebdige's complex analysis of punk's deliberately constructed 'frozen
dialectic' with black forms of expression such as reggae persuasively
makes this point (Hebdige, 1996: 69). John Frow, alluding to Rosalie
Colie's conception of genres as 'tiny subcultures' (Colie, 1973: 116),
says something very similar: 'Genres frame the world as a certain
kind of thing, and we notice this framing only at its intersection with
other subcultures of meaning' (Frow, 2006: 93).

We are now in a position to explain precisely why Lethem's use
of genre is primarily ethical. First and foremost, it is intrinsic to his
thematic preoccupation with 'the fragility, beauty, and importance of
subcultural life' (Personal Interview, 2009). Most explicitly in *The
Fortress of Solitude*, with its graffiti writers, sci-fi enthusiasts and soul
fans, but also in the rock and roll novel *You Don't Love Me Yet* and,
more obliquely, in *As She Climbed Across the Table*, which satirises
academic and theoretical discourses, Lethem's fascination with subcultures is an enduring element of his work. Attendant upon this fascination there are always underlying questions of an anthropological
kind, which Lethem articulates in this way: 'can you make a meaningful zone of operation and declare it sufficient unto itself?' (Peacock,
2009) and 'what's the right size of group to set up your little utopia
with?' (Personal Interview, 2009). Examples of such little utopias
would include the eccentric family unit formed at the close of *Amnesia Moon* (2009), the rock band in *You Don't Love Me Yet* (2007a)
and the group of pot-smoking chaldron enthusiasts at the centre of
Chronic City (2009a).

William Deresiewicz, in his somewhat scathing review of the latter
novel, uses the phrase 'self-enclosed adjacencies' to describe these
groupings (Deresiewicz, 2009: 49), and his formulation perhaps
gets closer to revealing what is ultimately most important about them
– their contiguity with other groupings. For if subcultural utopias are
contiguous with others, then presumably they will occasionally over-
lap. In fact, this overlapping, the occasional intervention or intrusion
of one zone of operation into another, is essential for Lethem: it

forces members of a subculture to consider alterity, to understand that regardless of how possessively committed one is to one's own idiosyncratic cultural curation and identity, there are other people with widely disparate interests nonetheless just as committed to theirs, no matter how outlandish they may appear to non-adherents. So when science fiction intervenes in hard-boiled detection as it does in *Gun, with Occasional Music* (1994), or when it enters the bildungsroman, as it does in *Girl in Landscape*, the surprising intervention makes a statement about the flexibility of generic categories and simultaneously 'becomes a parallel interrogation into the question of what happens to a human existence when fantastic elements intrude' (Kelleghan, 1998: 228). It is representative of Lethem's self-professed fondness for 'writing metafictionally about genre' (Kelleghan, 1998: 227), for self-consciously interrogating the genres in which his writing participates, but it also asks a fundamentally human question about how the individual behaves when confronted with what is perceived as exotic or out of context and with the realisation that one is connected to others whether one likes it or not.

To bring genres into collision is thus, to reprise Dick Hebdige's idea, to challenge the processes of normalisation but it is also to resist what Lethem repeatedly refers to as 'amnesia'. Perkus Tooth's attack on Chase Insteadman in *Chronic City* succinctly captures Lethem's somewhat idiosyncratic use of the term: 'You're like the ultimate amnesiac American, Chase. You can never imagine anything actually happened before you wandered along' (Lethem, 2009a: 217). 'Amnesia' denotes willed ignorance, a kind of solipsism resulting from a refusal to acknowledge the diverse alternative lives of others. Although this study does not primarily approach it from a trauma theory perspective (ably covered by theorists such as Cathy Caruth (1996) and Dominick LaCapra (2001)), it is worth observing that amnesia in Lethem's work frequently does have traumatic causes. As subsequent chapters elucidate, the death of Lethem's mother when he was fourteen has informed the fundamental lack at the heart of all his writing. In 'The Beards', the author offers his most honest admission of this: 'Each of my novels, antic as they may sometimes be, is fueled by loss. I find myself speaking about my mother's death everywhere I go in this world' (Lethem, 2005: 149). While the death of Judith Lethem can hardly be avoided, especially when discussing *Girl in Landscape*, there is little to be gained, given their fabulous qualities, from treating Lethem stories as romans à clef; it is much more fruitful to explore the ways in which a national or global feeling of bereavement and lack can be extrapolated from personal loss. Chapter 2, for example, explores the larger traumatic consequences of the unspecified cataclysmic event in *Amnesia Moon*. The analysis of one of Lethem's recent short stories, 'Procedure in Plain Air', which closes this introduction, distils the generic and ethical questions touched on so far and reveals the lack in this instance to be, materially and metaphorically, the holes in New York made by the attacks on the Twin Towers. Inclined throughout his writing toward the concretisation of metaphor, Lethem in 'Procedure' makes manifest LaCapra's idea that trauma 'creates holes in existence' (LaCapra, 2001: 41).

What links these two examples and many others is their depiction of a retreat into increasingly localised concerns as an amnesiac reaction to traumatic events. Psychologically, as I have suggested, this takes the form of a solipsistic denial of others' experiences and a stubborn adherence to familiar, repeated patterns (genres) of behaviour. However, what Lethem describes as 'the ethical treacherousness of local preserves' (Personal Interview, 2009) is also enacted spatially in his novels, particularly those such as *Motherless Brooklyn* (1999) and *The Fortress of Solitude* set in his home borough of Brooklyn. Describing the gentrification drive of the 1970s which is so central to *Fortress*, Lethem says: 'These neighborhoods were attempts to divide middle class brownstones from the surrounding poverty, and that attempt was full of ethical disasters. The only way to sustain those assertions was through amnesia, blindness, blinkers, a kind of exaggerated, distorted perceptual field' (Personal Interview, 2009). Without wishing to be too schematic, I would argue that this geographical specificity, coupled with the microscopic attention to urban regional detail and its attendant danger of regional amnesia, is one of the features that distinguishes Lethem's New York novels from the earlier stories written when he was still living in California (having left Bennington College without finishing his degree). Set either in a surrealised California, or in 'a sort of cartoon desert, a Nowheresville' (Schiff, 2006: 126), the first three novels have in common ostentatious collisions of genre in which a narcotic kind of science fiction tends to rise to prominence. From *Girl in Landscape* (which is classed as a New York novel for reasons made clear in chapter four), the emphasis is on genres arguably more amenable to explorations of community, subcultures and questions of regional identity – detective fiction, coming-of-age, fictionalised biography.

Perhaps, then, there is some inherent characteristic of Brooklyn which facilitates a more humanistic and realistic regionalism; perhaps, also, the ironic distancing of the author's early science fiction is partly a side effect of the West Coast exile from his birthplace. Certainly, upon first reading *Motherless Brooklyn* and *The Fortress of Solitude* one might be inclined to agree with their author that they are novels much more preoccupied than their predecessors with 'real stuff – sandwiches, sidewalks, the subway' (Schiff, 2006: 126) and less overtly built upon an intertextual '"exoskeleton" of plot or concept' (Weich, 2003) such as the playful clashing of Raymond Chandler and Philip K. Dick. However, it is precisely in the obsessive curation of geographical and cultural minutiae in the Brooklyn novels (later affectionately satirised in the figure of Perkus Tooth) that Lethem runs the risk of succumbing to the same localism he warns against. As Chapters 5 and 6 suggest, there is an irony inherent in the mining of childhood Brooklyn experience: the more one remembers, the more one attempts to focus on and make sense of the tiny details of local culture and architecture, the more one is tempted toward atomisation, fetishisation, nostalgia and, indeed, amnesia.

Nonetheless, Lethem's entire career so far can be read as an elaborate exercise in amnesia avoidance. The diversity and prolificacy of his output attests to the 'frantic compensation' for parental loss creative activity affords (Lethem, 2005: 148) and also enacts at the level of cultural production the same category-crossing and rupture of formal and generic boundaries seen in individual texts. A brief list of some of Lethem's projects reveals an almost pathological need for cross-fertilisation between text types. Lethem regularly contributes liner notes and commentaries to the Criterion Collection's reissues of classic movies such as *The Killers* and *Bigger than Life*; he has edited the Library of America's Philip K. Dick anthologies, the *Da Capo Best Music Writing 2002*, as well as, appropriately enough, *The Vintage Book of Amnesia* (2000); he has collaborated with Walter Salas-Humara, lead singer of The Silos, to create the 'floating workshop or lab for making music' known as I'm Not Jim (www.imnotjim.com); he has ventured into graphic novels with *Omega the Unknown* (2008); and he has set up the 'Promiscuous Materials' project which allows writers, musicians and filmmakers freely to take his work for adaptation. All of which excursions testify to a sincere desire to see cultural forms and genres bleed into, enrich and transmogrify each other in a constant evolutionary process.

Such a desire is also reflected in Lethem's frequent employment in recent works of ekphrasis, which he defines as 'the novel's capacity for extensive descriptions of other art forms' (Lethem, 2005b: 55). Given that ekphrasis in texts such as *The Fortress of Solitude* and *Chronic City* often instantiates a remediation of childhood or traumatic experience, however, it is tempting to view it as both a treatment for and a symptom of amnesia: as both an attempt to recognise alterity (specifically, alternatives to novelistic discourse) and a reaffirmation and fetishisation of the novelist's rhetorical power and hence of his supreme ability to capture, in various modes, the myriad fragments of pre-traumatic experience.

Another of my contentions about Lethem's more recent writing in this book is this: though it is still indebted to genre and imbued with a pulpish sensibility even as the author ceases to be an 'outsider' and becomes 'a middle-aged novelist writing bloated, ambitious books' (Barber, 2009), it is less likely than older works such as *Gun, with Occasional Music* to bring genres so violently, fantastically and ostentatiously into collision. Early stories repeatedly question the effects of sudden fantastic events and deploy diverse genre tropes in the service of that question. Examples of such fantastic elements would include the grotesque concretised metaphor of the recidivists literally built into the structure of the prison in 'Hardened Criminals' (1996) and, on a global level, the catastrophe which precipitates the action of *Amnesia Moon*. Later works have been less inclined to ask the same question. Indeed, they frequently seem to ask instead, 'what happens when the fantastic becomes ordinary?' One finds in a novel like *Chronic City* the demotic and the fantastic held in precarious balance, and consequently a subtle recalibration of the very notion of the fantastic. In a Manhattan occasionally suffused with a 'weird pervasive chocolate smell' (Lethem, 2009a: 158) and at the mercy, possibly, of a giant escaped tiger, a city as much a 'fragile ... projection' as a material place (Lethem, 2009a: 309), the fantastic becomes the texture of the everyday.

Against this background, the story of Janice Trumbell, the astronaut girlfriend of narrator Chase Insteadman who finds herself 'trapped in orbit with the Russians' (Lethem, 2009a: 10), represents not an incursion of the fantastic, the sci-fi into the normal run of things, but rather a factitious element of cosmic tragedy delivered in manageable chunks. Rather than jolting citizens out of complacency and forcing them to reassess their lives, it exists as 'daily newspaper fodder' (Lethem, 2009a: 10) and as 'soap opera' (Lethem, 2009a: 68) to provide reassurance and familiarity. Janice's plight, whether or not it is real, functions as a mass 'entertainment' (Lethem, 2009a: 308), a collective spectacle which nonetheless symbolises and testifies to each individual's entrapment in increasingly localised roles. Science fiction it might be, but here the term 'generic' clearly assumes some of its common pejorative senses: sci-fi in this context becomes ordinary, anodyne, banal.

This is not to say that Lethem's own treatments of genre have recently ceased to be engaging or fun, only that the relative subtlety of their integration allows for nuanced examinations of Lethem's recurring preoccupations: alienation, responsibility to others, the viability of 'little utopias' and the dangers of retreat into local conditions. Though still meta-generic, recent stories have swapped bold and self-conscious stagings of genre clashes for explorations of the ways in which human instincts, if left unexamined or untested, can bring about a descent into easy conventionality, familiarity or tribalism and the stolid rejection of difference from one's little world. So a story such as 'Procedure in Plain Air', published in *The New Yorker* in 2009, worries about the ease with which genre can become stale but does so allegorically, by means of a disquieting tale about human behaviour, and specifically about the dangers of compliance. The reading of the story which closes this introduction provides a more detailed example of the ways Lethem merges generic and real-world concerns and of the ways his writing shrewdly responds to historical circumstances.

The title is a variation on 'hiding in plain sight', another of Lethem's recurrent ideas; it neatly captures the mood of a story concerning the dispassionate performance of mundane tasks in full public view, tasks which nonetheless lead to sinister ends and are made all the more sinister for their apparent oblivious openness. An unemployed man referred to only by his surname, Stevick, watches from the bench outside a typically 'fancy' and pretentious Manhattan coffee shop (Lethem, 2009b: 79) as two men in matching jumpsuits park an 'unmarked' truck in front of a fire hydrant on the opposite side of the street and proceed to dig, first with tools 'notably quiet and efficient' and secondly with jackhammers (Lethem, 2009b: 79), a small hole in the road next to the kerb. Strangely 'enthralled by the activities that had commenced with the truck's arrival' (Lethem, 2009b: 79), Stevick wanders over to inspect the hole after the men have left. What he sees is an excavation 'steep and accurate ... an inverted phone booth of emptied dirt and rubble' with three 'fitted planks ... stacked beside the hole' awaiting the fulfilment of their role (Lethem, 2009b: 79).

Holes in the middle of New York City have become a preoccupation for the author. Clearly, Stevick's hole is a decocted version of Laird Noteless's monumental *Fjord* in *Chronic City* (Lethem, 2009a: 109), and equally clearly both are indebted to the cartoonist Saul Steinberg, who is, according to Lethem, 'always drawing skyscrapers that are inverted, that are holes in the ground' (Peacock, 2009). Yet it is the echoes of September 11 2001 that reverberate most powerfully. For Lethem, the Ground Zero site functions as a symbolic reminder of the losses incurred during the attacks, and therefore joins the long list of 'lacks' at the heart of his novels and short stories.[2] But 'the gigantic hole at the bottom of Manhattan now, where those buildings were effectively reversed' (Peacock, 2009) has a material power which goes largely unacknowledged; this is precisely why Stevick's close inspection of the hole itself is significant. Lethem continues: 'We all live a stone's throw from this chasm which just has this horrible authority and also invisibility. It's deeply meaningful but we're always just thinking, "What are they going to put there?" or "I can't believe they haven't put something there yet." You know, we don't grant any reality to the hole in the ground, even though it's been with us for pushing toward a decade' (Peacock, 2009). Symptomatic of the neurotic drive for newness characteristic of Manhattan in novels such as *Motherless Brooklyn* and *The Fortress of Solitude*, the giant hole is robbed of its historical and physical impact in being regarded as, in Lethem's phrase, 'only a delayed plan' (Peacock, 2009).

When the plan for Stevick's hole is finally enacted, 'Procedure' ceases to be a realist, lightly comic tale of inertia and the dull lives of ordinary New Yorkers, and rapidly turns into a mini-dystopia, a Kafkaesque parable of inscrutable authority and bovine complicity. The two men return in the truck, open it up and drag out a third man, gagged and bound, whom they proceed to place standing in the hole. Suddenly the function of the boards becomes clear: 'the captive nestled just underneath the three fat boards when these were fitted over his head' (Lethem, 2009b: 80). The hole is a bespoke prison, then, yet it is the 'narrow specialization of their tasks' which makes the two men impervious to the prisoner's suffering. As the clean-shaven one puts it when questioned by Stevick, 'We're on installation and delivery ... Pick-up's another department' (Lethem, 2009b:

80). Excessive localisation is one of Lethem's chief preoccupations, as subsequent chapters make clear, and here it reveals itself in the purely perfunctory carrying out of small tasks with no understanding of the complete punishment and incarceration process, or most importantly, its ethical consequences. In passing, it is worth noting that this is a concern shared by other contemporary authors. In Chuck Palahniuk's *Fight Club* (1997), for example, the narrator's job as 'recall campaign co-ordinator' (Palahniuk, 1997: 31) for a car manufacturer reduces people to statistics and elements within a larger process that they and he cannot perceive or understand. In a novel obsessed with complete processes – film projection, making explosives – the breaking down of a process into its constituent parts becomes alienating and dissociative in a way which mirrors the narrator's neurological condition. Tyler Durden's proud claim that in Project Mayhem 'each guy is trained to do one simple job perfectly' ignores the fact that each guy thereby becomes a drone with no conception of the political or ethical implications of his micro-task (Palahniuk, 1997: 130).

'Procedure', like *Fight Club*, suggests that the compartmentalisation of one's activities leads to a breakdown in human relations. Moreover, the dispassionate, businesslike way in which the men go about their allotted tasks serves to anaesthetise the strangeness of the incident. Whereas the characters in 'Light and the Sufferer' readily acknowledge that the presence of aliens is 'fucking weird', here there is no sense of a sudden intrusion of the surreal or fantastic, only the apparent continuation of a banal reality which goes unchallenged by all but Stevick. If people wished to demonstrate some ethical awareness, they would surely consider these events weird. Even Stevick's questions, rather than, as one might expect, proceeding along the lines of 'What the hell are you doing?', focus on mundane, practical matters: 'How long are you going to leave him in there?', he asks. Any feeling of civic or ethical responsibility on Stevick's part is shown to be vague, already diminished, something merely residual; he presses the men on the question out of 'some faint civic courage, a notion that he'd absorbed certain duties as a local witness to the open-air procedure' (Lethem, 2009b: 80). His question, he recognises, 'was perhaps a feeble one, but, for anyone observing, the fact that he'd stood up from the bench and begun some stalling interrogation could be seen as crucial, either in a deeper intervention to be conducted by more effective and informed members of the community or in some later accounting of Stevick's comportment and behavior' (Lethem,

2009b: 80). Such provisional and pusillanimous thoughts serve only to make the reader wonder if anyone is observing and, if they are, do they care? In fact there is no evidence in the story that 'more effective and informed' citizens or an appreciable 'community' even exist. Stevick finds himself standing above the hole, and when he turns to look back at the café, 'no one in fact [is] regarding him from the window' (Lethem, 2009b: 80).

As I have said, the hole in the ground is unmistakably an image inspired by 9/11; the fact that there is now a prisoner inside, 'knees wedged in dirt' (Lethem, 2009b: 80) and dressed in a jumpsuit, only serves as further confirmation. With its visual echoes of the notorious yet iconic Guantánamo Bay uniforms, 'Procedure' offers a disturbing vision of public indifference to punishment, cruelty and, above all, the demonisation of difference. The attack on the Twin Towers, it implies, constituted the sudden interruption of the fantastic into reality; what follows the unimaginable event is inevitable division and the banality of everyday cruelty.

My contention, of course, is that such ethical concerns are invariably approached via genre concerns in Lethem's writing, and 'Procedure' is one of the most subtle recent examples. Central to the relationship between ethics and genre in the story are the jumpsuits, and Stevick's observations upon first seeing the captive are particularly revealing:

> The man was dressed in the same uniform, as though recently demoted from their company. But his skin, Stevick noted wearily, as if this fact beckoned to outrage he ought to feel rising within him but didn't, was darker than theirs. His head shaved, where their hair was intact; his two-or-three day beard rough, where theirs were, in one case, trimmed into a goatee and, in the other, shaved clean. So the jumpsuits, rather than suggesting equivalence between the three, framed difference. (Lethem, 2009b: 79–80)

Yet again, Stevick gestures toward a feeling of moral disgust that has already been thoroughly dessicated. Whether or not the colour of the victim's skin is the principal reason for his rejection from the unspecified 'company', however, Stevick's observations reveal a number of crucial aspects of what can be regarded as generic behaviour. In treating the man this way, the two 'operatives' (Lethem, 2009b: 80) are enacting a theory of strict genre definition and function which regards any minor deviation from accepted norms as a dangerous and punishable transgression of categories. They are, in a sense, behaving like those critical and academic institutions which, Rick Altman observes, try and eradicate contradictions and inconsistencies in the development of genre communities (Altman, 1999: 175). In so doing they remind us that genre is always bound up in questions of power, and, as Jacques Derrida famously maintains, of 'law' (Derrida, 1980: 56).

What the operatives fail to realise (or most likely choose to ignore in their eagerness to fulfil their assigned roles) is that the jumpsuits, rather than simply marking the undesirable difference of the third man, *necessarily* and *invariably* frame the difference, the variety intrinsic to all categories. As Derrida insists, if genre presupposes laws, limits, 'norms and interdictions' (Derrida, 1980: 56), it must also presuppose 'a law of impurity or a principle of contamination' (Derrida, 1980: 57). This is because any element of a genre can be lifted and placed in a different generic context (what Derrida dubs 'citation') and because the mark or label applied to a genre (for example 'novel' or 'science fiction') exists both 'outside' the genre 'without belonging' to it (Derrida, 1980: 59) and sometimes within it, as an idea that can be remarked upon reflexively by a text within the genre set. (An example of this paradox, what Derrida calls 'invagination', would be the knowing reference to 'science fiction' in 'Light and the Sufferer'.) With a typically deconstructive flourish, Derrida goes on to insist that '[t]here is no madness without the law. Madness cannot be conceived before its relation to law' (Derrida, 1980: 81). Thus the imposition of boundaries presupposes madness, unruliness, contamination.

This madness can be attributed in large part to readership and perception. As Altman emphasises, the inconsistency of genre definitions between readers and fans is productive of new genre labels. Genre is a process of citation, constantly evolving and mutating along different paths. As Stevick takes up his position above the hole, this crucial question of perception and reception is dramatised and given an ethical inflection in the interpretations of the various spectators who wander up and talk to him. First the counterman leaves the café for a cigarette and says to Stevick, 'So you're in charge now, huh?' (Lethem, 2009b: 80). Evidently he reads Stevick's function as guard or warden, someone complicit with the jumpsuited operatives. Clinging on to his vestigial sense of moral responsibility, Stevick replies 'I didn't want to leave him completely alone' (Lethem, 2009b: 80), before tacitly acknowledging his own status as cipher, or indeed as metaphorical hole, by adding, 'I'm something of a stopgap or placeholder, really' (Lethem, 2009b: 80). Later in the afternoon a café customer armed with a briefcase and an umbrella aggressively offers another reading of Stevick's vigil: 'You artists need to grow up and learn the difference between an installation piece and a hole in the ground' (Lethem, 2009b: 82). What is up for debate here, then, is the genre of the situation: is it an act of policing, of sympathy, or of conceptual art?

Stevick's anaclisis means that he is constantly troubled by the question of whether 'his relation to the man beneath the boards qualified as a human transaction' (Lethem, 2009b: 80). It becomes 'a kind of personal situation' for him because of the 'gravity and authenticity' he ascribes to the man and the hole and his craving for 'a shared undertaking' (Lethem, 2009b: 82), or a relationship stronger than the 'passing connections' embodied in the figures of the counterman and Stevick's ex-wife (Lethem, 2009b: 83). Yet his desire to establish what Altman would call a 'constellated community' is always under pressure from disparate, externally imposed readings of his situation. Despite his best intentions, his function appears to alter over time. When the mysterious 'inspector' arrives with a clipboard and gives him a sandwich, Stevick falls further toward collusion with the operatives. In the duffelbag left by the inspector, Stevick eventually finds a set of jumpsuits, identical to the ones worn by the operatives and the captive. His ex-wife, Charlotte, who has stopped to talk to Stevick with her customary ironic tone, gleefully proclaims, 'You're hired! ... You've been promoted from a temp position to staff' (Lethem, 2009b: 83).

It is a beautifully ambiguous conclusion to the story. Faced initially with what appears to be a dilemma – whether to don a jumpsuit and finally accept his role in the punishment process, or whether to try and maintain his sense of human connection – Stevick suddenly comes to understand that '[t]he beauty of the uniform was that it settled nothing' (Lethem, 2009b: 83). Framing difference as much as similarity, the jumpsuit serves as a symbolic reminder of Derrida's axiom, 'participation never amounts to belonging' (Derrida, 1980: 65). Dependent on one's perspective, Stevick's vigil remains either an act of banal cruelty (after all, he never thinks to let the man out of the hole) or a show of solidarity. The final lines therefore become deliciously tense: 'Success in an endeavor like this one lay in the details. Stevick was certain he was going to do a good job' (Lethem, 2009b: 83).

'Procedure' takes Lethem's ongoing concerns with genre categories and re-contextualises them with renewed urgency in a post-9/11 tale of fading community. Whilst not advocating a kind of moral relativism – incarcerating people in holes is shown to be at least unpleasant – it nonetheless indicates the extent to which human behaviour, like generic behaviour, is largely a matter of perception. Yet it also constitutes a warning, to pick up on one of Lethem's favourite ideas once more, against amnesia, the wilful forgetting or ignorance of other people's experiences. Let us not forget that the jumpsuits mark both difference and similarity; they are a reminder that however much we try and isolate ourselves in ever smaller sub-groupings, there are contiguous or overlapping groupings which, no matter how different they might at first appear, are likely experiencing similar emotions and difficulties. It is only recognition of this fact that allows communities to evolve in positive, empathetic ways and to embrace difference. Finally, as the next two chapters show, Lethem's interest in 'Procedure' in the way individual roles and communities evolve recalls the more hyperbolic treatments of evolution in the early novels.

Notes

1   Lejla Kucukalic dubs Philip K. Dick a 'canonical writer of the digital age' (Kucukalic, 2009: 23) in light of his prescience in describing the ontological uncertainties engendered by human interaction with machines, for example. Yet she still acknowledges the fact that contemporary critics all too often display a bias against his work and science fiction in general (2009: xi).

2   Lethem tends to conflate the ideas of 'loss' and 'lack', postulating the former in the latter; that is, suggesting that the felt need implies something that was once there. As Dominick LaCapra stresses, the two terms are frequently used interchangeably, though strictly speaking a lack may refer to something that was never there in the first place (LaCapra, 2001: 53).

1

Private dicks: science fiction meets detection in *Gun, With Occasional Music*

The paratextual features of Lethem's debut novel, *Gun, With Occasional Music* (1994) enact their own ambiguous evolutions, and this chapter begins by unpacking sets of significances from these features that will then be applied to the novel as a whole. Patterned with cross-hairs, the cover of the most recent Faber edition unashamedly declares the hard-boiled, noir credentials of the narrative within. Indeed the cover design, visually indebted to the famous shot in John Huston's film adaptation of *The Maltese Falcon* in which Sam Spade's partner Miles is murdered, can be regarded as a distillation of noir into some of its most iconographic elements: a dame, a shadow, a gun. Nino Frank's description of noir as offering an '*impression* of real life, of lived experience and – why not? – of certain disagreeable realities that do in truth exist' (Frank, 1996: 23, italics added) is revealing: if the gun, eponymous hero of Lethem's novel, is the hard, material signifier of those disagreeable realities, it is also, as in this cover image, stylised to such a degree that one can no longer ascribe much reality to it, only, perhaps, the reality effects discussed in the introduction. In conjunction with the words 'a novel' inserted just above the title, the cover picture expresses nothing if not knowing self-consciousness about the interplay of reality and representation inherent in any generic acts, and about the novel's status as representation.

Further evidence for reflexivity is provided by the back cover blurb. However, in calling *Gun, With Occasional Music* 'part dystopian sci-fi, part noir detective story – a dark and funny postmodern romp' the blurb raises more questions than our protagonist Conrad Metcalf might have licence to ask without forfeiting all his karma points and finding himself in suspended animation ('the freeze'), questions that this chapter nevertheless sets out to answer. Is it simply the collision of sci-fi and noir that warrants the label 'postmodern'? Do postmodern genres exist (to borrow a question from Ralph Cohen), and what might a postmodern analysis of genres, or more accurately in this case, an analysis of depictions of established genres put under pressure in postmodern environments, entail? If, as Brian McHale proposes, detective fiction is the 'epistemological genre *par excellence*' and science fiction its ontological counterpart (McHale, 1987: 16), does the modification of the former by the latter in Lethem's novel represent some kind of evolution of the detective genre, equipping it to navigate its way through and speak more eloquently to a world characterised by hybridity, fluidity, uncertainty, simulation and multiple subjectivities? This is a world, as Adam Roberts observes (Roberts, 2006: 28), increasingly colonised by science fiction ideas that are no longer prophetic as such, but have become 'a mode of awareness about the world' in its present condition (Csicsery-Ronay, 1991: 308). Brian Attebery goes further and argues that theorists of the postmodern such as Fredric Jameson, Jean Baudrillard and Donna Harraway frequently couch their ideas 'in science fictional terms' (Attebery, 2002: 91): the postmodern, therefore, is the world made sci-fi.

Central to any discussion of *Gun*'s Dickian, dystopian sci-fi tropes and its preoccupation with evolution must be, as will become evident, the malevolent marsupial who steals several scenes in the novel. Lethem's fondness for talking animals can initially be located in what he dubs his 'ground zero' reading experience – *Alice in Wonderland* (Sussler, 2008) – but the epigraph to *Gun* specifies another influence, one dense in evolutionary connotations:

> There was nothing to it. The Super Chief was on time, as it almost always is, and the subject was as easy to spot as a kangaroo in a dinner jacket.

These are the opening lines of Chapter 2 of Raymond Chandler's final Philip Marlowe novel *Playback* (1958) and the most obvious thing to say about them is that they constitute explicit acknowledgement of the author's debt to the hardboiled tradition and more particularly to Chandler, who endeavoured throughout his career, like Lethem, to imbue generic narrative conventions with stylistic innovation and literary aspiration.

Playback nonetheless seems a curious choice on first inspection. Not only does its title refer obliquely to the fact that the novel was reworked from a rejected screenplay, and thus is itself a kind of re-playing or faulty transmission, it also tacitly admits to its own tiredness, the way the novel regurgitates tough-guy clichés within a far more simplistic narrative than its predecessors, particularly *The Long Goodbye* (1953). As its title suggests, *The Long Goodbye* played out a protracted, sentimental farewell to a detective fiction genre no longer able to sustain a romantic humanistic myth of the good man in the midst of a postwar society unrelentingly fixated on commodities, surfaces, fakes and simulations. In this sense, it postulated a proto-Jamesonian critique of the depthlessness of late capitalist American society. *Playback* does none of this, and the reintroduction of Marlowe's old flame, Linda Loring, at the conclusion should be seen less as an example of postmodern *retour de personnages* than as a nostalgic attachment to the earlier, superior work and an affirmation of Roger Wade's cynical assertion that a writer is 'washed up' when he starts trawling through his own writing for inspiration (Chandler, 2005: 285).

Lethem's epigraphic citation, then, intervenes at the point of playback, of empty repetition, and makes that one of the themes of his text. Partly this is jokingly revealed by the tinny music emerging from inanimate objects (including guns, hence the title) toward the end of the novel, a hollow playback which attempts to distance people further from the material reality of their oppression. But most significantly it is revealed in the way he takes a rhetorical figure of resemblance, the simile 'as easy to spot as a kangaroo in dinner jacket', and turns it into another specific kind of metaphor; that is, a literary character. To some extent this is an extension of the author's penchant for taking idiomatic metaphors and concretising them, seen in short stories such as 'The Hardened Criminals'. Yet in this context it proclaims much more. By taking a typically Chandleresque hardboiled wisecrack and prematurely evolving it (in the manner of many of *Gun*'s characters) into a walking, talking embodiment of all that is skewed and ethically dubious about the futuristic environment of *Gun, With Occasional Music*, Lethem manages to tie together the ideas crucial to the argument of this chapter – chiefly genre mappings and evolution – while signalling his awareness that literary influence is an 'example of evolutionary change' in itself (Hopkins, 2004: 35). The kangaroo in the dinner jacket pays homage to its literary ancestor, then, while circumscribing it and recognising the possible limitations of his ancestor's vision in the contemporary world. Moreover, the quantum leap from one form of metaphor to another suggests that any playback, transmission or citation in a new context is necessarily a misrepresentation, whether wilful or otherwise, and hence a kind of misremembering or amnesia.

Lethem's openness about influence – an openness taken to entertaining extremes in his now-notorious 'The Ecstasy of Influence:
A Plagiarism' (2007b), which extols the virtues of creative stealing
from other artists and is composed almost entirely from a series of
cunningly assembled plagiarisms – allows us insight into the self-
conscious manner in which he conceives and constructs his earliest
novels in particular:

> I sometimes use the word 'exoskeleton' of plot or concept. With the
> first couple books, there was always an exoskeleton of concept, which I
> then filled with all sorts of ephemera, emotions, autobiographical feel-
> ing, jokes, and so forth. But there was always that exoskeleton of plot or
> concept: *Let's put Philip K. Dick and Raymond Chandler together*, or *Let's
> put Don DeLillo and Italo Calvino together.* (Weich, 2003)

The stylistic and conceptual influences of Chandler have already
been outlined; *Gun*'s debt to Philip K. Dick, briefly, is disclosed in
the pervasive dystopian atmosphere which serves partly as critique of
hegemonic power structures, and in the minutely imagined details
of that dystopian world: the use of cryogenic incarceration (derived
from *Ubik* (1969)) and the centrality of animals, whether real or ge-
netically altered (derived in part from *Do Androids Dream of Electric
Sheep?* (1968)).

This uncovering of the exoskeleton is amusing enough. Yet what is,
arguably, more interesting about Lethem's idiosyncratic treatment of
genre, notably in *Gun, With Occasional Music* and later in *Motherless
Brooklyn*, is that the author's evident self-consciousness is frequently
shared by the characters. Specifically, this means that genre functions
for protagonist (and, of course, reader) as a form of cognitive mapping, to employ an evolutionary term returned to presently. In providing templates or simulation models for human behaviour, genre
becomes a means of orienting oneself in geographical, ethical and
literary space. Quite simply, one knows roughly how to behave when
the generic boundaries, allowing for the original elements that indi-
vidualise a text, are clear. The problem for character and reader is that
in Lethem the boundaries are almost never clear.

As a result, hints of self-consciousness about generic conventions
(and the disruption of those conventions) can be found throughout
Lethem's work. It is as if, in fact, the characters know full well they are
participating in genre narratives and feel genuine anxiety when expected conventions are rudely overturned. For example, at one point

during *Gun, With Occasional Music*, the narrator reflects on 'the actuality of the violence' which erupts through the smart-aleck dialogue: '[v]iolence isn't part of the ping-pong game of wisecrack and snappy comeback', he says; 'it puts an end to all that and leaves you wishing you'd stayed in or under the bed that morning' (Lethem, 1994: 57). The disorientation the reader may feel at Lethem's generic mixing therefore mirrors the characters' experiences as their personal schemata become obsolete in what one might call 'postmodern' environments. (These are environments which are, for the sake of argument, media-saturated, driven by technology and the market, commodifying, heterogeneous and fragmentary.) As Joseph Carroll argues, '[t]he desire to construct reliable cognitive maps assumes unmistakable prominence in a period of serious cultural disorientation' (Carroll, 1995: 387). But as I shall argue, Lethem is much more afraid of scientific, taxonomic impulses such as those exemplified by the literary critic and rabid anti-poststructuralist Carroll, than he is the potential chaos of dismantled categories.

Secondly, and relatedly, there is a close connection between genre stylistics and the narrative preoccupations of Lethem's first two novels. In this chapter and the next, it is argued that the way genres intermingle and evolve in his work, ultimately achieving a kind of unstable hybridity, is consistent with the author's interest in evolution itself as a scientific, ethical and political standpoint. These chapters focus on three key interlinked themes: evolution, amnesia and, in Chapter 2's discussion of *Amnesia Moon* (1995), regionalism, demonstrating that Lethem tends to approach evolution as an adaptive process ironically, and that evolution is therefore not viewed as progressive, but frequently as a retreat into deliberate amnesia or denial of history, coupled with an increasingly atomised and parochial world view.

In both *Gun* and *Amnesia Moon*, it is the ascendance of science fiction tropes that heralds the radical forgetfulness and narrowing of perspectives suffered by the characters. Therefore, science fiction occupies a contradictory position: it is the common endpoint of an evolutionary trajectory of genre that simultaneously reveals its own ethical and literary inadequacies. It should be stressed once again that Lethem's attitude toward genre is in no way rigid or hierarchical: his concern is precisely that when hierarchies are constructed for political ends, when for example a sci-fi obsession with advanced technologies and scientific progress begins to take precedence within society, seemingly old-fashioned concepts like 'community' and 'freedom' are fatally compromised.

Ostensibly, Lethem might appear to set up a classic (and naive) opposition between the literary – that which is ambiguous, contested, questioning – and the scientific – that which delimits, avoids equivocality, seeks answers. However, even these categories eventually become destabilised, especially, as Chapter 3 demonstrates, in his third novel *As She Climbed Across the Table* (1997). In fact, Lethem is at pains to present the complex relationship between science and literature in a far more nuanced way than a theorist such as Joseph Carroll in his mammoth polemic *Evolution and Literary Theory* (1995). Carroll's book belongs to a venerable critical tradition, a pivotal contributor being Ferdinand Brunetière with his *L'Evolution des Genres* (1890–94), which draws on Linnaean and Darwinian classificatory models to label and fix the boundaries of genre. As Rick Altman says, such work aims to prove that genres 'operate systematically, that their internal functioning can be observed and systematically described, and that they evolve according to a fixed and identifiable trajectory' (Altman, 1999: 6). It also represents an attempt to make a historically determined scientific viewpoint seem universal and timeless. Moreover, such work maintains a naive distinction between the scientific and the literary precisely by its need to circumvent ambiguity and its faith in science's ability to do so.

For Lethem, science and literature are not mutually exclusive discourses. Evolution is a story unfolding in unpredictable ways; science creates space for literary interpretation or storytelling and is itself a form of literature. Therefore, it cannot pretend to objective 'truth'. Joseph Carroll, impatient with rhetoricians who 'insist that the laws of discourse take precedence over the laws of science', at least recognises that literature itself constitutes, just as science does, a form of knowledge (Carroll, 1995: 31). However, he fails to acknowledge that the reverse is also true: science deals in narrative speculation as well as knowledge. More damagingly, he chooses to ignore the ideological undercurrents of evolutionary theory and its more nefarious ramifications (notably eugenics)[1], and then proceeds to incorporate all literature into an evolutionary paradigm that reduces literary knowledge to a series of taxonomies. For instance:

> Protagonists can be motivated by any combination of the following purposes: the need (1) to define, develop, or integrate the self (psychodrama, *Bildungsroman*); (2) to find or fulfill sexual romance (love stories; quantitatively by far the largest category); (3) to protect or nurture a family

or to establish a right relation of family functions (domestic dramas, for which *Oedipus Rex* is a classic prototype); (4) to found or reform a society or to protect or establish the protagonist's position within a given social structure (political drama, novel of society); (5) to define some peculiarly human ideal (heroic quests, cultural romance); (6) to live and thrive, to survive or come to terms with death (naturalist fiction; any work in which the author concentrates on man's animal nature); and (7) to achieve a religious vision or sense of cosmic order (religious and philosophical dramas). (Carroll, 1995: 250–1)

To rehearse the ideas discussed in the introduction: if Lethem's work illustrates anything, it is that human life is not readily amenable to the imposition of generic boundaries, and that even if genres do indeed offer a form of cognitive mapping, the vicissitudes of experience will eventually, and necessarily, re-draft those maps. Although Carroll acknowledges the complex interrelations between the genres listed above, there is surely the risk of placing even more emphasis on forms of discourse than those critics he savages for denying a reality beyond the text. Literature does indeed reflect human experience, but such categorising risks an inadvertent inversion: human experience can best be described through textual species. Carroll merits close attention, if only for his unblushing adherence to what he calls the 'truth' of science (Carroll, 1995: 5); for his bludgeoning collective dismissal of thinkers as diverse as Fredric Jameson, Richard Rorty, Terry Eagleton and Jacques Derrida; and for his remarkable equation of queer theory with a postmodernist conspiracy to rob the world of material reality and replace it with autogenous text (Carroll, 1995: 166). In the words of Philip Engstrand, the narrator of *As She Climbed Across the Table*, he truly has '[p]aradigm eyes' (Lethem, 1997: 80). The following analysis demonstrates that Lethem's texts at least approach evolution, as a scientific, ethical and literary concept and as a way of reflecting on Lethem's own development as an artist, with somewhat more maturity and inclusiveness than this.

A brief synopsis of *Gun, With Occasional Music*, appears to bear out, at least in diegetic terms, the blurb's assertion that the novel is a scintillating marriage of Philip K. Dick's dystopian visions and Raymond Chandler's literary detective fiction. The protagonist, Conrad Metcalf, is unmistakably a gumshoe wisecracker in the Marlowe mould:

> By this time we'd gotten the attention of Mr. Suit. He put down his magazine and stood up, rubbing his jaw with his big beefy hand as if

considering the possible juxtaposition of jaw and hand; mine and his, specifically. (Lethem, 1994: 14)

In a fictionalised Bay Area in the early twenty-first century, Metcalf is investigating the death of a former client, a doctor called Maynard Stanhunt, on behalf of the chief suspect Orton Angwine. Angwine, whose karma has reached zero and is merely hours from his time in 'the freeze', believes he is being framed. The maelstrom of corruption, violence and sexual intrigue which ensues involves a deeply unpleasant crimelord called Danny Phoneblum as well as the 'Inquisitors', a futuristic police force intent on controlling the state. Ironically, given their collective name, one of the ways they seek control is through restrictions on the asking of questions. Metcalf has a brief affair with one of the inquisitors, Catherine Teleprompter, whose name and ascension to power at the close of the novel imply the irresistible force of technology.

There is nothing especially unconventional in this outline, apart from the names. Yet right from the beginning, generic expectations are challenged. Our hardboiled narrator, traditionally the epitome of masculinity, admits 'I wasn't a man anymore' (Lethem, 1994: 15). After 'one of those theoretically temporary operations where they switch your nerve endings around with someone else, so you can see what it feels like to be a man if you're a woman, a woman if you're a man' (Lethem, 1994: 15), his girlfriend Delia Limetree disappeared without trace, leaving Metcalf emasculated and angry. In one sense, Metcalf's stated desire to recover his 'personalized nerve endings' (Lethem, 1994: 15) and thus to reinstate his masculine feelings serves to reinforce normative heterosexual roles, and it also necessitates the isolationism that has traditionally characterised detectives from Auguste Dupin to John Rebus. Yet the sex role-reversal element, popularised in science fiction stories such as A. M. Lightner's *Day of the Drones* (1969) at least proffers the possibility of destabilised and defamiliarised genders and sexualities, even as it warns of the dangers of empathy in a society increasingly antipathetic toward it.

In addition to this radical modification of the protagonist, the narrative throws up characters one would not normally expect to find in a detective narrative. Chief amongst these are Joey Castle, the talking, gun-wielding kangaroo assassin, and Barry the 'babyhead', whose paternity is one of Metcalf's main avenues of investigation. How these two outlandish individuals have come to be, and how they might disrupt the trajectory of the detective narrative, are central to understanding the text's ethical orientation. With another nod to generic self-consciousness, Conrad reveals Barry and Joey's provenance:

> The streets were a bit too quiet for my taste; I would have liked it better to see kids playing in front, running, shouting, even asking each other innocent questions and giving innocent answers back. That's the way it was before the babyheads, before the scientists decided it took too long to grow a kid and started working on ways to speed up the process. Dr. Twostrand's evolution therapy was the solution they hit on; the same process they'd used to make all the animals stand upright and talk. They turned it on the kids, and the babyheads were the happy result. Another triumph for modern science, and nice quiet streets in the bargain.
> (Lethem, 1994: 18)

One consequence of the mysterious Dr Twostrand's therapy is that for the detective, the streets no longer seem mean enough; they have, in fact, ceased to feel alive at all. His natural environment has been stripped of the idle talk that so often provides him with answers.

If any one character has stayed mean, it is Joey the kangaroo. It is illuminating to treat Metcalf and Joey's relationship as the central agon of the text. Not only does the kangaroo's participation in several murderous episodes drive the narrative forward, leading to the eventual showdown between detective and marsupial baddie, but it is also made clear that these antagonists embody two contrasting epistemological standpoints that are crucial to Lethem's ethical concerns. The following exchange, taken from the first meeting between Metcalf and Joey, illustrates the key differences:

> 'Don't play human with me, Joey. I've got the same privilege with you as anybody has with a kangaroo. Who sent you?'
> In case I forgot about the gun, he stuck it in my gut. Like so many of the evolved, he didn't like being reminded of his lineage. (Lethem, 1994: 56)

Initially, it should be noted that Joey's attempts to 'play human' reveal a tenacious misconception about evolution itself. As Chris Colby contends, '[o]ne common mistake is believing that species can be arranged on an evolutionary ladder from bacteria through "lower" animals, "higher" animals and, finally, up to man' (Colby, 2006). As Darwin's extended 'tree of life' metaphor illustrates (Darwin, 2003: 484), fitness is connected to changing environments, not to innate perfectibility in species; it is contextual rather than inherently progressive. (This is true for genres just as much as for the natural world, of course, as the work of Rick Altman forcefully demonstrates.) In fact, there are significant passages in *On the Origin of Species*, notably one in which he alludes to 'our ignorance of the precise cause of the slight analogous difference between species', where Darwin is happy to compare 'differences between the races of man' with, for example, the propensity of certain colour cattle to be pestered by flies (Darwin, 2003: 219). In *The Descent of Man* he is famously more explicit: 'there is no fundamental difference between man and the higher mammals in their mental faculties' (Darwin, 1981: I.35).

Lethem/Metcalf's tendency to employ animal similes – at one point Orton Angwine has 'the look of a rabbit frightened into fierceness' (Lethem, 1994: 46) – is designed to highlight this proximity. Likewise premature evolution results in a closeness between man and animal which supports Darwin's thinking and threatens certain comforting perceived hierarchies that reinforce man's superiority. For Dulcie the sheep, tragically, this leads to her brutal murder (Lethem, 1994: 96) precisely because (and here is a typical Lethemite joke with a serious intent) she 'knew things that could have broken the case open' (Lethem, 1994: 236).

Apart from wrongly privileging man in essence, rather than simply as an organism adept at adapting to and imposing upon its environment, the belief in the 'evolutionary ladder' is implicated in the melancholic tendencies Joey in particular exemplifies. Attendant upon his aspiration to be human is the desire, which Metcalf recognises, to deny lineage, to erase history. When Metcalf discovers that the kangaroo has promoted himself from thuggish hit-marsupial to kingpin toward the close of the narrative (Lethem, 1994: 257), the evolution in status he has undergone is laden with irony. His ascent to the top of the ladder, as it were, shows him to be perfectly suited to survival in this twisted, inhumane environment but therefore, rather than proving him 'more human', it further distances him from human(e) behaviour and societal connections.

Evolution here is a form of willed forgetting, combined with a desire to bring the future forward more quickly, and it is epitomised by the sci-fi ingredients of the story. It betrays a melancholic fixation on the futuristic present, despite the ghostly physical evidence of the 'past' animal body. Another example would be the babyheads Metcalf encounters in the bar later in the novel, drinking themselves to death 'to counteract the unpleasant side effects of the evolution therapy'

(Lethem, 1994: 145), trying to forget themselves even as they are dressed absurdly in toddlers' clothes and smoking cigarettes. Most importantly, this forgetting stands in direct contrast to the avowed aim of the detective. Throughout the narrative, Metcalf is referred to, seldom admiringly, as '[a] question asker' (Lethem, 1994: 147). Questions have of course always been the primary weapon in the detective's armoury, but in this increasingly sci-fi-inflected environment, conducive to individual and collective forgetting, the need to uncover past connections through interrogation, to re-establish a sense of community in the face of increasing isolationism, becomes essential.

Then again, Metcalf's own attitude toward questions is marked by the same suspicion and ambiguity common to others involved in the Stanhunt case: 'I'm willing to break the taboo against asking questions – in fact it's my job – but I'm pretty much like the next guy when it comes to answering them. I don't like it. That's just how it is' (Lethem, 1994: 4). Embedded in this cynicism are issues of philosophical import. At the simplest level, one can state that a question demands a response, and thus some form of human interaction. Even in Metcalf's increasingly atomised and divisive world, this need not constitute a significant threat so long as one regards an answer merely as the dissolution of a question, as a problem thereby solved. If, however, one postulates a dialectical relationship between questions and answers, such that a question initiates an ongoing dialogue which does not inevitably lead to any definitive answer, then more power must necessarily be imputed to the question. In this Socratic model of interrogation, assumed power is challenged through the asking of questions, and thus the question assumes a problematising function within society. As Michel Meyer says in *Of Problematology*: 'Socrates asks questions. He calls his interlocutors to account to show them that they do not know what they claim to know. As Socrates knows that he knows nothing, the question that begins a dialogue will remain unresolved at its end. It is in these aporetic dialogues that we can most clearly see his antiestablishment attitude' (Meyer, 1995: 67–8). It was partly the antiestablishment drive of the dialectical question that saw it relegated, so Meyer argues, to the realms of rhetoric rather than science, which in turn became, post-Socrates, the province of the philosophical proposition and syllogism (Meyer, 1995: 66).

Metcalf is no Socrates, but he does understand the problematic power of the question. And in a neat inversion of Joey's anthropomorphism, Metcalf's honest appraisal of himself as 'the creature who asked questions, the lowest creature of them all' (Lethem, 1994: 130), reveals the dread and antipathy the population has developed towards the problematising detective. The detective, as someone who carries 'the weight of the past like ballast, something only [he is] stupid enough to keep carrying' (Lethem, 1994: 234), strives for a sense of connection, ethical responsibility and collective narrative in the face of atomisation. Appalled by the 'disconnected creatures pass[ing] through the blackness, towards solitary destinations', Metcalf is 'stupid enough to think there was something wrong with the silence that had fallen like a gloved hand onto the bare throat of the city' (Lethem, 1994: 130).[2] His addiction to question-asking speaks of his need to break the silence.

Obviously, it is not at all unusual for science fiction to offer dystopian visions. What is interesting here is that the detective tries to maintain, through the asking of questions, classic, romantic hard-boiled genre values in the face of the sci-fi elements which resist his efforts – artificially evolved animals, anti-gravity pens, the state-sanctioned accounting and docking of citizens' 'karma' (Lethem, 1994: 33). Ultimately, the unravelling of the case hinges on another such element – the drug called (making the point explicitly) Forgettol. The novel's twist hinges on the discovery that the victim, Maynard Stanhunt, actually 'hired his own hit' (Lethem, 1994: 251). His excessive consumption of Forgettol, an attempt 'to carve his life up like a Thanksgiving turkey' (Lethem, 1994: 5), has caused a radical bifurcation of his personality, such that his professional self cannot even remember that his private self is enjoying an illicit affair with his estranged wife Celeste in a seedy motel. Tragically, the professional self takes out a successful contract on the private self, with Joey the kangaroo as hitman.

Not only does this scenario represent a narcotically enhanced update of the Calvinist split self, it also points to an underlying paradox operative both narratively and meta-narratively; namely, that despite the detective's old-fashioned craving for the recollection of facts and thus for communal culpability for past events, it is the radical act of forgetting which creates the very narrative in which Conrad Metcalf is involved. Indeed, Forgettol, if the chemist's analysis is to be believed, can potentially be used as a narrative drug:

> 'Anytime you try to regulate Forgettol, it's a delicate balancing act. Someday they'll work it out, but they haven't yet.' He smiled a funny smile. 'If he's doing it right, he can eradicate whole portions of his experience

with the make, then sew up the gap for a sense of continuity'. (Lethem, 1994: 106)

As he says, 'a sense of continuity' can be achieved if the correct balance between amnesia and memory is found. Discomfiting elements can be strategically rejected in favour of the comforts of concatenation. It appears, then, that narrative is a combination of remembering and forgetting, and that the assumed purity of the detective's drive for recollection is no more palatable than the denial practised by the artificially evolved.

Though this occupies a short scene in the novel, it raises potentially crucial questions about Lethem's treatments of amnesia throughout his career. Clearly, widespread amnesia is an insidious phenomenon, and the extreme consequences of it are symbolised by another illicit drug favoured by some of the characters – 'Blanketrol', a substance that almost completely empties the user of consciousness and humanity. Equally clearly, however, a preoccupation with and an insistence on total recollection, as well as being impossible, has ethical implications of its own. To a certain extent, amnesia has a function, in that gaps in memory require contributions from others to fill them in. Continuous narrative is a combination of remembering and forgetting, and there are implications for Lethem's own prose practice, notably in *Motherless Brooklyn* and *The Fortress of Solitude*, of obsessive remembering. Immersion in tiny memorial details can trigger a kind of blindness, excessive localism or amnesia. Metcalf's desire to return to 'the case', *his* case, even after six years of enforced respite in the freeze, is symptomatic of such blindness and pays less attention than it should to indicators of the more generalised destruction of civil liberties occurring all around him.

Yet the biggest problem in *Gun, with Occasional Music*, as the chemist at least recognises, is that forgetting cannot and should not be externally controlled. Moreover, Lethem has created a fictional world where it is the state that increasingly attempts to control it through manipulation of technology, in order effectively to relax society's critical faculties and disable resistance or free thinking. Evolution therapy is one aspect of this. Mass-produced Forgettol is another. Undoubtedly the most egregious examples are 'the slave boxes', devices implanted in the heads of girls taken out of the freeze, giving them a semblance of consciousness and activity so that Phoneblum, with the help of the inquisitors, can use them for prostitution (Lethem, 1994: 175).

These innovations are just the tip of the iceberg. Leaving the freeze after six years (Lethem, 1994: 211), Metcalf finds a world more saturated with the qualities of science fiction than ever before. The drug 'makery' has become completely mechanised (Lethem, 1994: 239) and the time-release version of the drug, which completely obliterates memory, is now the most commonly used (Lethem, 1994: 216). Most telling of all are the little boxes everyone seems to own which have supplanted recollection. Metcalf attempts to interview again several of the people involved in the case, only to find them stripped of integral memory, obliged instead to consult the electronic box for their 'memories'. Memory itself has become abstracted, 'externalized, and rigorously edited' (Lethem, 1994: 224). Thus the population is condemned to the numbing drudgery of an eternal present, free to listen to the muzak 'which was sure to be coming out of the nearest water fountain or cigarette machine' (Lethem, 1994: 224) and divested of the potentially unsettling cognitive maps memory might supply in order to inspire resistance. The ending of the novel is resigned and pessimistic: once the case has been 'cracked', Metcalf, who has effectively been 'cut loose, so to speak' by his repeated zero karma status (Lethem, 1994: 262) finds himself in a kind of atemporal limbo even without the aid of the drug he steadfastly refuses to take – time-release Forgettol. The freeze is no longer much of a punishment, he admits: instead it enables his own temporal discontinuity; it frees him from history and produces a profound, carefree isolation and amnesia in a series of perpetual presents.

Gun, With Occasional Music begins as a noir detective novel with elements of science fiction, and rapidly evolves into a dystopian sci-fi text, which has rendered the ethical and literary aspirations of the detective obsolete. Consequently, the narrative trajectory describes a retreat into atemporality and solipsism. Evolution is depicted not as a process whereby living organisms adapt their physical and cognitive faculties to suit their environments, but as one of many techniques, along with the administration of drugs and the seductions of consumerism, for detaching the individual completely from his or her environment and a sense of collective responsibility. An overly enthusiastic acceptance of Darwin's optimistic evolutionary prediction, that 'all corporeal and mental endowments will tend to progress towards perfection' (Darwin, 2003: 397) results in its antithesis – social breakdown and withdrawal into a numb individualism. In Lethem's terms, the individual's drive to perfectibility, based largely on 'technological opportunities', suggests 'a search for zipless transcendence which [is] usually a mistake' (Kelleghan, 1998: 228).

It is time to return to the questions posed at the beginning of this chapter in light of the novel's supposed postmodernism. What has been summarised in the last few paragraphs is a fictional scenario that can accurately be described as 'Jamesonian', given that so many of its characteristics correspond with Fredric Jameson's concerns over the cultural and political manifestations of late capitalism in an era commonly labelled 'postmodern'. Metcalf's world is distinctly schizophrenic, in Jameson's (previously Jacques Lacan's) specific sense of 'a breakdown in the signifying chain' (Jameson, 1991: 25) which Jameson makes homologous with the breakdown in temporality so destructive in *Gun*:

> The connection between this kind of linguistic malfunction and the psyche of the schizophrenic may then be grasped by way of a twofold proposition: first, that personal identity is itself the effect of a certain temporal unification of past and future with one's present: and, second, that such active temporal unification is itself a function of language, or better still of the sentence, as it moves along its hermeneutic circle through time. If we are unable to unify the past, present, and future of the sentence, then we are similarly unable to unify the past, present, and future of our own biographical experience or psychic life. With the breakdown of the signifying chain, therefore, the schizophrenic is reduced to an experience of pure material signifiers, or, in other words, a series of pure and unrelated presents in time. (Jameson, 1991: 25–6)

Schizophrenia is a loss of reference, and it is powerfully symbolised in Lethem's novel by the memory boxes mentioned earlier. Jameson famously extrapolates from this state of schizophrenia, symptomatic of a pervasive crisis in historicity, modes of cultural production that privilege 'the randomly heterogeneous and fragmentary and the aleatory' (Jameson, 1991: 25).

An example of such cultural production from Lethem's debut would be 'the musical interpretation of the news' (Lethem, 1994: 3) that has replaced the spoken-word news in order to anaesthetise the populace and relax their capacity to engage with historical events; what people receive instead are vague, abstracted and unrelated fragments. Elsewhere, the 'anti-grav' pen (Lethem, 1994: 33) epitomises a drive for technological and stylistic innovation at odds with functionality. As Metcalf observes: 'It seems like the biggest innovations always announce themselves in the tackiest ways ... It's never a very good pen, either. You use it for a week, and it runs dry' (Lethem, 1994: 33). Therefore its breaking free from gravity also symbolises its breaking free from time by virtue of its built-in obsolescence and its negligible use-value. By the time Metcalf emerges from the freeze for the first time, it has already become a kind of pastiche, a quaint antique 'collector's item' for which one of the Inquisitors is prepared to pay Metcalf good money (Lethem, 1994: 211). What unites these examples, and other dystopian marvels such as Forgettol and evolution therapy, is their reliance on a technology which is 'mesmerizing and fascinating not so much in its own right but because it seems to offer some privileged representational shorthand for grasping a network of power and control even more difficult for our minds and imaginations to grasp: the whole new de-centered global network of the third stage of capital itself' (Jameson, 1991: 37). And that power is revealed most eloquently and most frighteningly in mass amnesia, the severing of connections between past, present and future.

In the light of this analysis of *Gun, With Occasional Music* one might wish to modify Jameson's contention that sci-fi exists in a dialectical relationship with the historical novel (Jameson, 1991: 284). It is clear that it corresponds to the 'waning or the blockage of that historicity' (Jameson, 1991: 284) but here the second term of the dialectic is surely the detective novel, a genre that Lethem sees as concerning itself with the past, with history, with collective culpability, with the potential for change through recognition of that culpability. As I have suggested, it is the dialectical interplay between the two genres that produces the narrative and serves as critique of both: it is not the case that detection stands alone as a model of ethical responsibility. As it too becomes dislocated in time and fades into a kind of empty playback or pastiche, detection's own limitations, notably the very temptations to nostalgia it affords, are disclosed.

Recent work on the 'dystopian turn' in Anglo-American cultures at the close of the twentieth century has identified 'critical dystopia' as a genre which, among other things, blends genres the way Lethem does in *Gun*. Indeed, critical dystopia 'is the ideal site for generic blends' because in any case '[t]he borders of utopia and dystopia are not rigid, but permeable' (Donawerth, 2003: 29). Thus so-called 'conservative' forms 'are transformed by merging with dystopia, a merge that forces political reconsideration, and traditionally conservative forms can progressively transform the dystopian genre so that its pessimism shifts from being resigned to being militant' (Donawerth, 2003: 29).

Both utopian, in the sense of possessing an emancipatory drive, and
dystopian, in the sense of revealing pessimism about 'the dystopian
elements of postmodern culture' (Miller, 1998: 337), critical dystopias
differ from traditional utopias by virtue of particular formal strategies.
They open 'in media res within the nightmarish society' (Baccolini and
Moylan, 2003: 5) rather than bringing a travelling protagonist to a
new world; they place, in a manner consistent with postmodernism's
emphasis on textuality and signification, a heavy emphasis on the role
of language in facilitating resistance to an oppressive society (Metcalf's insistence on asking questions would be one example); and they
display a tendency to leave endings open so that, whether or not hope
is evident within the texts' narratives, hope may be available 'outside
their pages ... if we consider dystopia as a warning that we as readers can hope to escape its pessimistic future' (Baccolini and Moylan,
2003: 7).[3]

   Clearly, Gun, With Occasional Music (and its successor, Amnesia
Moon) appears to fit quite comfortably within what is itself a hybrid
genre – the critical dystopia. Equally clearly, it employs genre blending dialectically in order to paint a bleak, Jamesonian picture of a contemporary society in thrall to technology, intent on depthlessness and
increasingly ahistorical. But do these factors make it postmodern?
And, to call on Ralph Cohen once more, do postmodern genres exist? Are these questions ultimately even worth asking? If texts have
always mixed, satirised and undermined genres (Cohen's primary example is Tristram Shandy, but one could go further back and cite Don
Quixote or any number of other examples), then the critical dystopia
does nothing new but merely reinvigorates genre blending in order to
comment on the social and cultural realities of its time. Once again,
genre texts have long done this, and such observations return us to
the points made in the introduction about the role of the historically
situated reader and the various constellated communities in which he
or she participates at any given moment.

   If Brian McHale can state that there is no cultural dominant, only
multiple dominants emerging from a text 'depending upon which
questions we ask' of it (McHale, 1987: 6), then he is surely not arguing for unchanging genres perceived in different ways, but for genres
transformed in the very process of perception. In other words, to re-
visit a term which links the evolutionary theory this chapter has drawn
upon and Fredric Jameson's thinking on postmodernism, genres in
any era help us cognitively map ourselves within social and cultural

space but are themselves changed in that mapping. If that mapping proves especially difficult, as it does in *Gun, With Occasional Music*, it does not mean that the genres involved are 'postmodern' or absolutely, radically new, only that they reflect by means of reality effects and reader interpretation the disorienting times from which they have emerged. (This is a point Jameson's dismissal of contemporary fiction's ability to portray reality overlooks; reflecting a reality out of touch with history is itself an important political move (Cohen, 2009: 21).) Even McHale's belief that postmodern texts impose an ontological conflict between the text as object and the world the text projects (McHale, 1987: 70) – an argument for metafictional reflexivity, basically – flounders if one accepts the view of genre as reality effects or games played with real-world materials. By provoking a 'split subjectivity' in the reader through the contrasting pulls of generic norms and cultural norms (Altman, 1999: 146), genre texts have always been about ontological conflict and this is part of their capacity for both entertainment and transformation.

Nonetheless, critics who, as Altman's work reminds us, have a vested interest in cementing labels and maintaining at least some boundaries, continue to tie themselves in knots over the postmodernness or otherwise of Lethem's writing. (I must confess to almost doing the same in the conclusion to this book.) Umberto Rossi, one of the few critics to have written on the novel which is the subject of the proceeding chapter, *Amnesia Moon*, employs the term 'avant-pop' to describe Lethem's writing in this novel, specifically the way it refers to popular genres and to the detritus of Americana (Rossi, 2002: 20). 'Avant-pop', as its staunchest advocate Larry McCaffery conceives it, is distinct from reflexive high postmodernism in its eschewal of 'metafictions, or antifiction, or irrealism, and so on' (McCaffery, 1995: xxi) and its return to a kind of realism. This realism, however, is the realism of the age of global hyperconsumerism and hypertext in which popular culture (as Fredric Jameson suggested it would) has saturated all aspects of life and now provides the 'key images, character and narrative archetypes, metaphors, and points of reference and allusion' in postindustrial societies (McCaffery, 1995: xviii). Combining 'the avant-garde's spirit of subversion and emphasis on radical formal innovation' with 'Pop Art's focus on consumer goods and mass media' (McCaffery, 1995: xvii–xviii), avant-pop is, according to its supporters, the literary movement best equipped to portray and critique the cacophony of sounds and the maelstrom of popular cultural images emerging from the 'global hive mind' of the twenty-first century (McCaffery, 1995: xxix). Maybe. But despite the best efforts of McCaffery, as well as Mark Amerika and Lance Olsen, the term 'avant-pop' has never really caught on in a significant way. This is partly because it casts its net so wide as to render itself meaningless – McCaffery's list of avant-pop texts includes *Slaughterhouse-Five* and Donald Barthelme's *Snow White*; Talking Heads and Tom Waits, Robert Altman's *Popeye* and Quentin Tarantino's *Pulp Fiction* – and partly because it cannot sufficiently distinguish itself from the 'postmodernism' dismissed as a meaningless term. Most of all, I would stress, it tends to privilege the artist as the one uniquely able to weld together avant-garde experimentation and popular cultural references, and tends to ignore the role of constellated communities of historically situated readers for whom the distinction between avant-garde and popular might never have been meaningful or useful. The coinage of 'avant-pop', in the end, may just be another means of prolonging a critical career and provides little help in analysing Lethem's aims in a novel like *Amnesia Moon*.

Notes

1   See, for example, Lois A. Cuddy and Claire M. Roche (eds), *Evolution and Eugenics in American Literature and Culture, 1880–1940: Essays on Ideological Conflict and Complicity*. Lewisburg, PA: Bucknell University Press (2003).

2   This scene, in which Metcalf imagines the lives outside his office window, pays homage to a similar scene in *The Long Goodbye* in which Marlowe gazes from the open window in his living room at '[a] city no worse than others, a city rich and vigorous and full of pride, a city lost and beaten and full of emptiness' (Chandler, 2005: 322).

3   In Lethem's short story 'The Dystopianist, Thinking of His Rival, is Interrupted by a Knock on the Door' (2004), the work of the rival, much less contrived and much more disturbing than that of the protagonist, has a critical dystopian feel: 'This was the Dire One's pitiless art: *his utopias wrote reality itself into the most persuasive dystopia imaginable*' (Lethem, 2004: 110, original emphasis).

2

The nightmare of the local: apocalypse on the road in *Amnesia Moon*

Amnesia is a kind of immobility. To obliterate connections between past and present is to preclude the possibility of movement or change in the future, to condemn oneself to the anaesthetised drudgery of the endless present. It is appropriate, then, that Jonathan Lethem so often employs spatial metaphors in his interrogations of the condition of American amnesia. In *Amnesia Moon* (1995), which collides the road narrative with dystopian science fiction, the road performs this metaphorical function. Mikhail Bakhtin cites the road as an example of a literary chronotope, something he defines as 'the primary means for materializing time in space ... providing the ground essential for the showing forth, the representability of events' (Bakhtin, 2004: 250). On the road, he insists, 'the unity of time and space markers is exhibited with exceptional precision and clarity' (Bakhtin, 2004: 98). Having ancestry in Greek 'adventure time' – ahistorical, unchanging, undifferentiated, dictated therefore by chance – the chronotope of the road articulates the spatio-temporal logic of the 'encounter'. As Bakhtin explains: 'the chronotope of the road is both a point of new departures and a place for events to find their denouement. Time, as it were, fuses together with space and flows in it (forming the road)' (Bakhtin, 2004: 243–4). Rick Altman also stresses the importance of the encounter in his analysis of the road movie genre, and for him the repetition integral to genre recognition 'tends to diminish the importance' of endings. Far more important, he argues, 'are the repeated and similar encounters that make up the middle of the film' and 'the cumulative effect' of these meetings (Altman, 1999: 25).

It is important to remember the historicising disposition of Bakhtin's thesis. The chronotope does not merely describe how literary texts represent space–time relations; rather it discloses how these relations are historically, culturally and politically constituted. So if the museum expresses, say, the spatio-temporal dynamics of evolution and acquisitive empire, and the airport the 'time-space compression' (Harvey, 1989: 283), centrifugal propulsion and dislocation of contemporary globalisation, then the road can be seen in the late twentieth and early twenty-first centuries as modifying a traditional romantic conception of individual freedom.

It becomes a model of disengagement from surroundings, or, in Margaret Morse's terms, of 'distraction', 'fiction effect' and 'mobile privatisation' which segments activities and effectively isolates the individual in time and space (Morse, 1998: 99, 100). Lethem would, of course, employ his catch-all term – amnesia. Seen in this way, the frequent intersections Bakhtin identifies between the chronotope of chance and the chronotope of the road (Bakhtin, 2004: 92) participate in what Fredric Jameson argues is the ascendancy of the random in late capitalist culture.

The road chronotope is also another example of a characteristic literary trope in Lethem's writing – the metaphor concretised or, in Bakhtin's words, 'made real'. He continues: 'Time, as it were, thickens, takes on flesh, becomes artistically visible; likewise, space becomes charged and responsive to the movements of time, plot, and history' (Bakhtin, 2004: 84). In *Amnesia Moon*, as well as allowing the road metaphor to take on flesh and embody pressing questions about regional identity, the relationship between present and past, and American frontier mythology, Lethem extrapolates from and exaggerates the very notion of 'fleshing out' an idea, making it an integral part of his dystopian vision and a theme of the novel. In a US roughly composed of Finite Subjective Realities (FSR), environments literally dreamed up by individuals (Lethem, 1995: 200), grotesque obesity functions as a metaphor for the power to put flesh on one's dreams and impose them on others. This is seen in 'the gigantic body' of Kellogg (Lethem, 1995: 8), the man who oneirically controls Hatfork and Little America, and later in the protagonist's sudden endomorphic transformation at the hands of Lucky, the former inmate of a local mental hospital who shapes the dream-world of Vacaville, California (Lethem, 1995: 229). To have the power to create and put flesh on metaphors that everyone then recognises is to create a powerful hegemony indeed. Evidently, and this is something explored in more detail later in this chapter and in the next, Lethem is also commenting on the author's role as a fashioner of dreams.

These ideas are not unique to *Amnesia Moon*, even if they are powerfully distilled there. Before beginning an extended discussion of that novel, it is worth taking a look at another narrative which draws on the chronotope of the road in a science fiction setting. 'Access Fantasy' was first published in the short story collection *The Wall of the Sky, the Wall of the Eye* (1996). The dystopian city it imagines is one which, at least on the wrong side of the 'One-Way Permeable Barrier' separating the haves from the have-nots (Lethem, 1996: 56), is in a state of perpetual gridlock. When the story begins, we are told that the unnamed protagonist 'couldn't remember seeing a car move recently' (Lethem, 1996: 55). So crippling has the citywide traffic jam become that citizens are now living in their vehicles, resigned to inertia, but occasionally dreaming of a 'start-up' (Lethem, 1996: 55). As a substitute for real accommodation, residents of the traffic jam can experience the virtual pleasures of the black market 'Apartment on Tape', footage of luxury apartments located on the other side of the One-Way Permeable Barrier (Lethem, 1996: 56). While watching one of these tapes the protagonist notices what he thinks is a murder and decides to play detective. With this ambition, he gets himself fitted with one of the 'Advertising Patches' (Lethem, 1996: 63) which allows him to penetrate the barrier by being turned into a walking, talking advertisement on behalf of 'some vast, faceless corporation' (Lethem, 1996: 56), and sets out with his attractive young 'neighbour' Margaret (from the car in front) to investigate.

'Access Fantasy' is precisely that: a fantasy of access to some dimly perceived real beyond the barrier, and its anxieties about the very possibility of an available reality resurface in Lethem texts from *As She Climbed Across the Table* to *Chronic City*. What it shares with *Amnesia Moon* in particular is its ironic citation of the road genre. The road has become a place of stasis rather than movement and the promise of fortuitous encounters is denied because each individual is tied to his or her own tiny fragment of space. So space and time do fuse, to recall Bakhtin's words, but only in the sense that they have been simultaneously negated and cease to exert much authority. Time, in the sense of narrative or history, has succumbed to an endless, routinised present while space, as something traversable, something reproducing social relations in flux, has been atomised and reimagined merely as an imprisoning form of place. Thus the road in 'Access Fantasy' serves as a perfect example of what one might dub 'the chronotope of amnesia' in Lethem's writing, the spatio-temporal embodiment of excessive localisation and willed forgetting. Typically, it operates metagenerically, too: the road genre itself, so long a participant in the American myth

of the frontier hero, so long associated with freedom, is shown to be
tired, enervated and in need of a 'start-up'.

At first glance, *Amnesia Moon* reads like a revivification of the genre,
opening as it does with a classic image of self-reliance and autonomy
on the road:

> Edge had the highway to himself. It was his trinket, all this paint and
> asphalt, thanks to Kellogg's new law about ownership. *You merely have
> to decide it's yours.* Edge had a knack for recalling Kellogg's exact words.
> *What you see is what you get, Edge.* Adrenaline pumping, Edge leaned on
> the accelerator. The landscape sped past.
>   He drove through the left lane and crashed over the dead grass of the
> divider, into the lanes heading west. I'm my own man, he thought. I
> drive on the wrong side of the highway. My highway. (Lethem, 1995: 1)

A brief synopsis of the opening episodes would appear to support a
claim for the novel as celebration of independence on the road. Our
hero is a man named Chaos (Lethem is seldom shy about using heav-
ily allegorical names, and the true significance of this one emerges in
due course) who, at the start, is living in a disused multiplex cinema
in Wyoming after the unspecified apocalyptic event. After an alterca-
tion with the local self-appointed tribal leader Kellogg, Chaos hits the
road in a stolen car and heads out west to California with a young girl
named Melinda (who might be his daughter), in a bid to discover his
forgotten pre-apocalyptic identity as a man called Everett Moon that
continues to haunt him analeptically in his dreams.

This westward journey, as well as reproducing the one Lethem un-
dertook after dropping out of Bennington College, is an archetypically
American one. Characteristically, it suffers from what Edwin Fussell
calls 'double vision' (Fussell, 1965: 14) in that it symbolises a new
beginning, the Turnerian transition from 'Old World to New, reality to beatitude' and hence the future (Fussell, 1965: 14), but also a
mythological retracing of steps and in Chaos's case an obsessive mining of the past. So if the westward expansion at the heart of Frederick
Jackson Turner's frontier thesis has an evolutionary thrust, with the
creation of a kind of national species characterised by 'dominant individualism, working for good and for evil' as its most devout wish
(Turner, 1999: 40), then in a novel which, like its predecessor, subverts the idea of evolution, Chaos's road trip west should be seen as
ironic evolution, resembling, depending on where he finds himself,
mutation or regression. For in a world in which, as Chaos observes,

'[t]he animal kingdom is dead' as a probable result of the catastrophe (Lethem, 1995: 5), the almost logical outcome is the diversification of human physical forms (and genres) into different sub-species. Melinda, for example, is covered in smooth brown fur and resembles a seal (Lethem, 1995: 30); she is at least aesthetically more pleasing than the other mutants of Hatfork, Wyoming. So in a similar way to *Gun, With Occasional Music*, Lethem's second novel invalidates a weak evolutionary concept of man as the pinnacle of biological adaptation, just as it subverts the mythology of the progressive journey west.[1]

In recent years New Western Historians such as Patricia Nelson Limerick and Brian W. Dippie have challenged the linearity and evolutionary triumphalism of Turner's frontier thesis, sought to reappraise frontier mythology and promote 'a more balanced view of the western past' (Limerick *et al.*, 1991: xi). Proceeding from the assumption that each generation interprets history in new ways, these historians re-visualise and re-map the frontier to include 'defeat as well as victory ... women as well as men; varied ethnic groups and their differing perspectives as well as white Anglo-Saxon Protestants; an environment that is limiting, interactive, and sometimes ruined as well as mastered ... and, finally, a regional identity as well as a frontier ethic' (Limerick *et al.*, 1991: xi). 'The West', envisaged in this way, becomes a series of diverse regions, races, and cultures interacting in complex ways.

Lethem takes this notion of a nation comprised of regions with distinct identities to extremes. Thus the novel rather gives the lie to Istvan Csicsery-Ronay's view that science fiction has long been uninterested in national identity (Csicsery-Ronay, 2002: 218). It is expressly concerned with what happens to a sense of national identity when an obsession with the local begins to gain the ascendancy. For in *Amnesia Moon*'s landscapes of fear and confusion, regionalism becomes a parochialism so narrow that the citizens of one region, town or even street are barely even aware of the existence of other areas, let alone these other areas' distinct and idiosyncratic interpretations of and reactions to the cataclysmic event. (Various theories are propounded – alien attack and nuclear accident, to mention but two – but the true cause is never known.) This is not a classic American regionalism balancing, as Tom Lutz expresses it, 'local and larger perspectives' (Lutz, 2004: 192), it is a deliberate form of atomisation. Retreat into blinkered localism is, ironically, what connects people post-catastrophe and, as Umberto Rossi suggests, the precise nature of the event therefore becomes irrelevant: 'It is obvious that amnesia *is* the catastrophe, while at the same time it *hides* the catastrophe' (Rossi, 2002: 16). Ethically there are strong links between this extreme regionalism and the theme of evolution. These are most lucidly revealed through the paranoid fantasies of one of the incidental characters, a soldier called Vance with a particularly outlandish cataclysmic theory:

> Vance waved his hand impatiently. 'Listen: why do you think the world got broken up? *Because the aliens landed.* It was a defensive response, an evolutionary step. Reality shattered to isolate the hives'. (Lethem, 1995: 181)

Even if the alien theory is false, the defensive reaction it postulates is significant. Evolution is, as in *Gun*, a form of retreat into blinkered perspectives even as the idea of progress it promulgates represents a return to grand narratives. It is certainly evidence of adaptive facility in the face of fear and a destabilised cultural, political and generic environment. But its outcomes are a regionalism which remains unaware of the exquisite tension between differing regional and cultural identities necessary to sustain a sense of identity in the first place, and thus division and control.

The primary means of control takes the form of the FSRs, the projections of worlds from the minds of individuals of varying degrees of psychological derangement. Kellogg euphemistically calls it the process of creating 'a little area of control' (Lethem, 1995: 200). Each location visited on Chaos's/Moon's odyssey is an FSR. Hatfork and Little America, where he starts out, are dreamed by Kellogg; White Walnut, the exclusive school where privileged pupils can find respite from the '*Biochemical trauma*' nicknamed 'the green' (Lethem, 1995: 44), is projected by an old woman named Elaine; Vacaville is dreamed by Lucky from inside his maze; West Marin results from a mental tug-of-war between two men called Tree and Hoppington (Lethem, 1995: 157); and, most oppressively, the superficially rather more hospitable enclave of San Francisco is controlled by the malevolent megalomaniac Ilford Hotchkiss. It is Ilford who chillingly sums up the dystopia of the FSR when he casually remarks to Chaos, 'I'm sure you've noticed how local things can get nowadays' (Lethem, 1995: 139).

The remainder of this chapter explores the multifarious ways in which the FSR, the single most resonant and important idea in *Amnesia Moon* and one reconfigured, as the next chapter shows, in the bespoke universes of 'The Happy Man' and *As She Climbed Across the*

Table, might be read. Clearly it functions on one level as a familiar satire on the widely perceived provincialism of much of Middle America. Equally clearly, it highlights the inherent absurdity in mythical American notions of newness, the forgetting of the Old World as one moves out west to forge a new identity. But the FSR also expresses in a surreal and exaggerated manner the paradox at the heart of American democracy: that we are most like each other when we are utterly individual and self-reliant. As well as expressing these concerns, the FSR articulates Lethem's anxiety about the power of authorship – the possibility that if an author wishes to articulate concerns about the tendency of human beings to fashion mini-utopias, to break off into generic hives of activity, he or she can do this only by creating his or her own discrete, miniature universes – novels and short stories and essays.

Seen from within the framework of the FSR, then, the evocations of the road genre that begin the novel cease to be in any way a celebration or affirmation. Edge is a marginal character, virtually a slave to Kellogg, and his employment of clichés such as '[a]drenaline pumping' and '[t]he landscape sped past' betray the borrowed, generic texture of his emotions as he first hits the road, heading to Chaos's multiplex home in Hatfork. Failing to appreciate the internal contradiction at work – that his exhilarating sense of freedom derives from an arbitrary law projected by another dominant individual – Edge at least realises that he is only 'a messenger' for Kellogg (Lethem, 1995: 2). His thoughts, including his romantic dreams of the road, are 'his ... and Kellogg's all mixed together, and often Kellogg's thoughts seemed stronger. They didn't leak away as fast' (Lethem, 1995: 2). Edge can only read the road, in other words, the way Kellogg wants it read; Kellogg's metaphors hold sway in this territory. Thus when Edge observes that '[t]he road to Hatfork was littered with abandoned cars' (Lethem, 1995: 2), his response can only adhere to Kellogg's ideology of individual property and ownership: 'The Hatforkers, Edge thought, didn't know how to take care of their stuff' (Lethem, 1995: 2).

If we as readers are fortunate enough to step outside Kellogg's thoughts, then we are permitted to read the abandoned vehicles in a different way, again metagenerically. They are symbols of a road mythology based in 'universal' ideas of freedom and self-transcendence that has been itself abandoned and superseded by a road colonised by individual imagining, one that is wholly dependent, and merely a product of local effects. Once again a familiar enough idea – that

'universal' concepts and imaginaries are always to some extent he-
gemonically constructed by the dominant ideology – is concretised
and taken to its logical extreme. Weak-minded individuals like Edge
succumb quite willingly to the ideology because in lieu of any hard
facts about the event, they have, in Lethem's words, 'made a tradeoff.
They've exchanged freedom and awareness for some kind of organ-
izing principle or explanation' (Kelleghan, 1998: 233). *Amnesia Moon*
is therefore, in part, about the political capital to be gained from fear
and ignorance, and, as in *Gun*, the politics are revealed through genre
decisions.

So *Amnesia Moon* can be called a road narrative, and the road has an
important structuring and diegetic function for readers as the means
by which we follow Chaos from one FSR to the next. These functions
fail to mask its internal inconsistencies, however. In assuming the
character of each FSR it enters, the road genre is divided into discrete
idiosyncratic subgenres which are intended, in the minds of those
responsible for the projections, to have little or no relation to each
other. Rather than serving as a superordinate genre for the novel,
then, the road risks disintegrating into miniature critical dystopias
and becoming a chronotope of amnesia, a symptom of mass retreat
into parochialism.

An apt image of this occurs soon after Chaos has rejected Kellogg's
invitation (which gives a clue to Chaos's true significance, fully revealed much later in the novel) to claim his 'share of things' and 'take
over the reins' (Lethem, 1995: 24). Escaping in Kellogg's car, Chaos
and Melinda drive until they arrive at a mountain range where as they
climb, a green fog descends and rapidly thickens, 'masking the road,
lacing the sky with green banners that admitted less and less blue'
(Lethem, 1995: 37). Eventually they are forced to abandon their own
little enclave, the car, and walk. They find themselves at White Walnut
school, the FSR of the elderly woman known as Elaine. The fog – 'the
blinding green' (Lethem, 1995: 38) – serves as literal and metaphorical blindness, the closing off of perception, and White Walnut as a
psychological retreat which tautologically creates an external danger
in order to maintain hierarchies of power and a sense of exclusivity. In
this context the road, as something at least with the potential to connect, has to be rendered completely defunct. And in a statement that
can be read as a metaphor for Lethem's attitude toward FSRs, Chaos
suggests another interpretation of the green. As it begins to drift into
the car, he says: 'A car's not really airtight, even with the windows up'

(Lethem, 1995: 38). So the fog, even as it impedes vision and sustains the paranoia displayed by Elaine and her employees, reminds us of the impossibility of total disengagement from the outside world, of total seclusion in mini-utopias such as the car and White Walnut. It is an important paradox: if one views the FSRs as genres of behaviour, then the green fog performs the 'principle of contamination' (Derrida, 1980: 57) at the heart of all genre distinctions. Although in his argument with White Walnut's psychiatrist Chaos denies bringing himself and Kellogg into Elaine's dreams, which are only an extension of her created metaphor, being nothing but green (Lethem, 1995: 53–5), subsequent events lead him to understand his own contaminating, and therefore emancipating, effect.

After their eviction from White Walnut, Chaos and Melinda walk out of 'the green' and fall asleep by the side of 'the empty highway' (Lethem, 1995: 58). They are awoken by a marginal character, 'the hippie in the pickup, like the beginning of a joke' (Lethem, 1995: 58), whose appearance nonetheless heralds a narrative episode which, for all its comic levity, represents the novel's bleakest critique of the contemporary moment. Boyd the hippie offers a slightly revised interpretation of the post-event reactions, one delivered in his quaint 1960s idiom but which explicitly connects the dreamworlds of the FSRs with the exigencies of contemporary late capitalism:

> 'You know, the weirdness just came out, that's all. It's not like it wasn't always there. Things got all broken up, *localized*. And there's the dreamstuff, you know. The Man got into everybody's head, so I guess everybody suddenly got a look at how severely neurotic The Man actually was'. (Lethem, 1995: 60)

'The Man' is a characteristically vague denotation; Boyd intends it to refer, of course, to those in control, the unseen hegemonic powers who dictate the forms and habits of society. (It becomes clear, when Chaos and Melinda are introduced to the McDonaldonians, that 'The Man' is an expression which implicates giant corporations under global capitalism.) In the fictional landscape of *Amnesia Moon* the appellation specifically refers to whichever individual's FSR exerts the most force in a particular locale.

However, Boyd is distinguished by his immunity to the coercive power of the FSR: 'I got a problem with The Man – all that dreamstuff doesn't work on me. I'm immune, got a built-in bullshit detector' (Lethem, 1995: 59). He is therefore in the luxurious position of choosing to leave California and later to avoid Elaine's psychological territory simply because he feels like it and desires '[m]aximum headroom' (Lethem, 1995: 59). When Chaos and Melinda meet him, he is living on 'the Strip' with 'the McDonaldonians' (Lethem, 1995: 65), McDonald's employees who, after the mass exodus from their town, 'just stuck, because they didn't know anything else' (Lethem, 1995: 64). With all romantic associations excised in this version of the road known as 'the Strip', the chronotope of the road here assumes the form of an isolated and moribund fragment of ribbon development, emblematic of economic disparities and the waste attendant on consumerist excess: 'The Strip began with dingy trailer parks and sprawling, concrete-block motels, all abandoned. Then came gas stations and gift-shops and fast-food restaurants and auto dealerships and topless bars, all with their neon signs lit up and glowing in the sun, all completely vacant and still. The Strip went on for miles, mindboggling in its repetitiveness' (Lethem, 1995: 61–2). Utterly generic and anonymous, it occupies something of a paradoxical position: it is distinct from the FSRs largely because it embodies in miniature a USA where 'large portions ... from Tucson to Milwaukee and from Seattle to Tampa Bay, look and feel largely identical' (Kowalewski, 2003: 12).

But the global brand lives on and, as Chaos and Melinda discover, the burgers still get made. This is the real tragedy of the McDonaldonians – they do *not* inhabit a dreamworld, a projected FSR. The 'pocket of weirdness' they inhabit, though it is analogous to existence within an FSR, with Ronald McDonald performing the same demiurgic function as Kellogg or Elaine (Lethem, 1995: 65), is merely a continuation of their everyday existence pre-catastrophe, in a world of pasty faces and slavish monotony all too familiar from our present and from other Lethem tales such as 'Procedure in Plain Air'. In fact, their unquestioning adherence to the 'company rulebook' (Lethem, 1995: 64), when considered in conjunction with Boyd's views on events, calls into question the reality of the catastrophe in the first place, or at least starkly exposes the political investment certain individuals with an interest in power have made in the idea of a catastrophe.

In fact, some manner of apocalypse is convenient in many ways: it enables a particular kind of historicity, a rough division into 'before' and 'after' which reinforces a conception of the future, whether utopian or dystopian. (Critics make use of such divisions, as this study has been keen to show: they have a vested interest in the perceived catastrophic breaks between modernism, post-modernism and, as we shall see, post-postmodernism, and in the supposed generic breaks between detection and anti-detection, or popular and 'literary' science fiction. The unspecified event in *Amnesia Moon* is partly a critical catastrophe, one which allows individuals to critique the world in distinct ways.) Far more disturbing and egregious than even a dystopian future is mute submission to an endless drudging present, because it suppresses any will or capacity to change. Looked at from this perspective, the McDonaldonians are the embodiment of Slavoj Žižek's recent observation that it is easier to imagine the complete destruction of the world than to conceive of an alternative to liberal capitalism (Žižek, 2006a: 301).

Although it does not obviously privilege technology in the way Adam Roberts suggests is a primary characteristic of the sci-fi subgenre known as 'cyberpunk' (Roberts, 2006: 124), there is a definite cyberpunk sensibility about the McDonaldonian sequence. Not only is it revealed in the setting, in the 'abandoned buildings, decaying factories, and the waste products and "throwaway" populations of twentieth-century capitalist culture' (Wegner, 2003: 174), but also in the subtle questioning of what constitutes humanity. The McDonaldonians are not cyborgs, but so thoroughly assimilated are they into the mechanistic processes of burger production that they have effectively merged with the technology. Whether or not the notion of being 'part of the machine' is familiar enough to have become cliché, the complete reification of the McDonaldonians' collective consciousness and their unthinking incorporation into the processes of consumer capital lends weight to Fredric Jameson's concerns about the fate of cyberpunk as a subgenre. For him, the schizophrenia of postmodern culture (as discussed in Chapter 1) provokes the possibility of 'an ultimate historicist breakdown in which we can no longer imagine the future at all, under any form – Utopian or catastrophic' (Jameson, 1991: 286). Such thinking predicts Žižek's observations on the impossibility of imagining anything other than capitalism, but it has for Jameson specific generic effects. 'A formerly futurological science fiction (such as so-called cyberpunk today)', he argues, 'turns into mere "realism" and an outright representation of the present' (Jameson, 1991: 286).

'The Strip', then, really is a road that goes nowhere, a chronotope of total amnesia: the very possibility of a future is cast into doubt in the McDonaldonians' repetitive production. It is this nightmarish

vision of the present, not itself an FSR, that highlights the irony of
the FSRs: though they are also based on power and control, and are
also divisive, they at least involve thought and imagination. They are
nothing if not creative. Even if they require mass amnesia about the
precise nature of the catastrophe, their imaginative reliance on the
idea of a catastrophic break, as has been suggested, implies a historical sense of past and present and, therefore, of a possible future. The
impossibility of this for the McDonaldonians, and thus their tragedy,
is summed up baldly by the hippie: 'They don't think, man. That's the
point' (Lethem, 1995: 64).

   After Chaos and Melinda leave the Strip, they find their way to
Vacaville, California. The Vacaville episodes, apart from occupying
more pages than any of the others (approximately one-third of the
novel), have an ethical importance based in the bizarre family unit –
Chaos, Melinda, Edie and her two sons Ray and Dave – which evolves
by the end of the novel. Despite the collective amnesia imposed upon
the city by its dominant dreamer, Lucky, there is hope to be found
here in concrete social and familial relations. This is in turn despite,
or in fact because of, the unconventionality of these relations. Clues
to Vacaville's significance are offered even before Chaos meets Edie
and they begin a romantic relationship. First is the fact that Chaos
and Melinda's car breaks down just outside Vacaville, 'on a quiet strip
of highway between exits' (Lethem, 1995: 72). Clearly these exits are
symbolic of choices, but perhaps more relevant is the fact that the two
travellers are forced to abandon the non-space of the car and enter the
city on foot. We are told that the other highway drivers 'ignored them'
(Lethem, 1995: 72), so the opposition between driving and walking is
here deliberately framed as a choice between isolationism and some
kind of active involvement in the world. As Melinda expresses it: 'We
can't skip every town. Gotta go in sometime' (Lethem, 1995: 72).

   The second clue to Vacaville's centrality is a formal one. Most of the
novel's chapters employ a form of Free Indirect Discourse, a third-
person narration which nonetheless privileges Chaos's consciousness. Having entered Edie's new house at the end of Chapter 6 in the
company of Chaos and Melinda, however, we start Chapter 7 in her
old house and much closer to Edie's point of view. More than simply
highlighting Edie's importance as a character, this perspectival shift
makes a conceptual point about the need to recognise difference and
escape the narrow confines of one's viewpoint which is consistent
with Lethem's broader use of genre. One can never fully enter another

person's consciousness, the narrative voice suggests – indeed to do so would be as invasive and unethical as the FSRs – but one must at least acknowledge the diversity of experience.

When Edie is introduced to the reader, loading her belongings into the trunk of the car, her reflections reveal both her family situation and some of the key idiosyncrasies of the Vacaville FSR: 'It was Wednesday. Moving Day again. Every Wednesday and Saturday, but Saturdays were simpler, because the boys were with their father. That was how she thought of him now, not Gerald, not my ex, but *their father*' (Lethem, 1995: 75). The Vacaville government, comprised of exaggeratedly charismatic individuals who double as the stars of magazines, soaps and reality TV shows (Lethem, 1995: 88–9), forces citizens to move house and to change jobs twice a week. In a society factitiously structured on the principle of fluctuating luck, with government 'Luck Investigators' like the unctuous Ian Cooley, would-be boyfriend of Edie, charged with checking up on those whose luck appears to be dangerously diminishing, it is appropriate that new occupations and houses (they can surely not be called 'homes') are randomly generated. Cooley, however, demonstrates how those in power are actually able to manipulate 'luck' when he appears to assign Edie a remote house on the outskirts of the city very close to his (Lethem, 1995: 79). Thus 'luck' is exposed as a tool for robbing citizens of their autonomy.

If amnesia does indeed correspond to immobility, the government, conversely, exercises power by enforcing excessive mobility to bring about amnesia. Mobility in this form is the opposite of freedom; the road is reduced to a local function of the authorities' desire to suppress a sense of identity rooted in an individual and shared sense of belonging and of community. In effect, it operates like Forgettol and the remote memory boxes in *Gun, With Occasional Music* by attempting to make memory itself the victim. Quite simply, there is not enough time for the people of Vacaville to accumulate meaningful memories and a sense of belonging in a place before they are required to move on again. Moreover, citizens are asked to fulfil a quota of 'citations' against each other for minor infractions such as vacating a house late or taking items with them from one house to another (Lethem, 1995: 76). These pernicious versions of citizen's arrest contribute to the decline in an individual's luck. Suspicion, retreat and paranoia are thus positively encouraged so that the desire to establish communities is stifled along with memory.

So when Edie moves into her latest residence and finds Chaos and Melinda in her kitchen, her first instinct is to issue them with a citation (Lethem, 1995: 80). Yet it is the very fact that they hail from somewhere outside Vacaville which intrigues her and prevents her from following her initial instincts. In a stultifying environment where 'everything you see and hear tells you that it's the same everywhere' (Lethem, 1995: 92), Chaos and Melinda represent the possibility of expanded knowledge and of difference: 'what did she know about the man downstairs, or the place they'd come from? She knew things were weird in other places right now, and these two were definitely weird' (Lethem, 1995: 83). Chaos becomes, for Edie, 'an antidote, a glimmer of something, a refutation, however small, of Cooley's seamless, terrible version of the world' (Lethem, 1995: 92).

For his part, Chaos gains two things through his relationship with Edie. First, it awakens in him a previously dormant desire for close human attachment, desire which has a temporal aspect in that it implies a need for an alternative mode of living in the future. Even though Edie becomes embroiled in Chaos's frequent dreams about his ex-lover Gwen (a further clue to his influence), Chaos insists to himself that he is not 'getting Edie and Gwen mixed up ... But maybe the dreams about Gwen had helped him to want Edie, to recall what it was to be with a woman' (Lethem, 1995: 96). He begins to associate Edie, rightly or wrongly, with a sense of reality and substance all too difficult to attain in a world subject to the caprices of the FSR. In fact, the second consequence of Chaos's spell in Vacaville is his increased questioning of the relationship between appearance and reality, of the predominant structure of local effects, and crucially of his role within or beyond it.

Despite looking less dilapidated, less generically post-apocalyptic than Hatfork or Little America, Vacaville is potentially a far more dangerous place than either precisely because the government stars exploit the confusion between reality and representation in more subtle and pervasive ways. As Umberto Rossi observes, in Vacaville, where the glamourised lives of the political elite are the only popular entertainment available, '[m]ediation is abolished' in the 'suffocating enclosure' achieved through 'the perfect superimposition of mass-media on political representation' (Rossi, 2002: 24). This becomes clear to Chaos as he browses through the magazines in the local mall; he notices that '[t]he cover stories were all about the television and the government, even when they were versions of magazines like *Time* and *Rolling Stone* and *Playboy*, which Chaos knew from before. Nothing referred to anything outside Vacaville' (Lethem, 1995: 98). Such a hermetic environment, which Rossi notes has a lot in common with Fredric Jameson's famous description of the Westin Bonaventure in Los Angeles (Rossi, 2002: 25), relies on a series of highly effective paradoxes and contradictions, chief amongst which is the idea of a meritocracy based on 'luck'. If citizens can be made to believe that Cooley, President Kentman and the other government celebrities are simply luckier than they are and that this fact justifies the disparities in social and economic status, then all capacity for resistance is destroyed. One may resent the situation, as Edie apparently does when she scoffs at the television 'it's nothing but luck' (Lethem, 1995: 89), but to accept its fundamental premise is to remain paralysed by it.

Chaos, though he is aware of its power, refuses to be paralysed by it. Confronted by Cooley, who claims, in a bid to get Chaos out of the picture so that he can continue his pursuit of Edie, that Chaos and Edie have 'nothing to offer each other but trouble' (Lethem, 1995: 107), Chaos thinks to himself, 'I'm not surrendering to the local crap this easy' (Lethem, 1995: 106). Part of his confidence in stating that he refuses even to believe in luck (Lethem, 1995: 107) is his ability to retain a sense of his past, of a narrative that is not apparently random:

> Here in Vacaville he had managed to hold onto his previous identity, his memories of Hatfork and his trip west. He felt a certain pride in that. He wanted to believe he was getting stronger, building up an immunity to local effects, and Vacaville obviously had its share of changes. Chaos didn't remember much, but he knew people shouldn't have to move twice a week and work a different job every day. Or have their luck tested.
>
> On the other hand, the effect was milder here. The Vacaville equivalents to Kellogg and Elaine – the government stars – lived in the media instead of invading dreams. And you could always turn the television off. So maybe his ability to hold onto his old self was just a part of local conditions. (Lethem, 1995: 99–100)

Though it is tempered toward the end by uncertainty (uncertainty mirrored in the very last image of the novel), Chaos's provisional optimism here predicts the discoveries he will make in his confrontation with Ilford Hotchkiss in San Francisco and his decision to reject atavistic dreams of the past and opt for some kind of material future.

For the trip to San Francisco, as well as marking 'the end of his journey west' (Lethem, 1995: 149), is essentially a trip into Chaos's dimly perceived and subjective past, one that in the end turns out to be little more than another constructed element of the FSRs created by Cale Hotchkiss and his father Ilford. When Billy Fault arrives in Vacaville to take him away, Chaos believes initially that 'his life and his dreams were finally coming together' (Lethem, 1995: 116). Inspired by a cliché, romantic notion of breezing into the city on a motorbike to find his woman, he feels momentarily invigorated by the traditional tropes of the road narrative Fault appears to represent: 'He also wanted to ride on the motorcycle again, wanted to feel the wind' (Lethem, 1995: 117). His final decision to leave Edie and head to the city in search of Gwen is precipitated by the videotape of his childhood friend, Cale, given to him by Fault. It is this short VCR clip that provides clues not only to what Chaos will discover in San Francisco, but to many of the dilemmas encountered by future Lethem protagonists such as Lionel Essrog and Dylan Ebdus and by Jonathan Lethem himself. 'All the stuff you used to say about what mattered, you were right', Cale says to Chaos (now Everett): 'Everything else is just what you have to work through to get back to what you know matters when you're twelve or thirteen' (Lethem, 1995: 128). Chaos is being lured into a trap: he is being offered the chance to escape the arrested present of Vacaville for an arrested past in San Francisco where he will, very much like Dylan Ebdus, find himself stuck in adolescent affiliations and patterns of behaviour.

Whereas in *Gun, With Occasional Music* drugs are taken to ensure that memory is obliterated, in *Amnesia Moon* the past endures in the form of intravenously administered drugs. In Fault's squalid basement apartment, Chaos feels that his destination has been 'condensed to a pinprick point' as he rolls up his sleeves and literally injects Cale and Gwen into his bloodstream (Lethem, 1995: 143). He narrates the story of his post-break existence to Cale, who in turn tells him that he deserves 'more credit' for the things he experienced (Lethem, 1995: 146). Cale is suggesting that Chaos is as responsible for shaping worlds as Kellogg, Elaine or Lucky. This is a refrain picked up more explicitly by Ilford later on, when he tells Chaos: 'You're receiving, but you're also sending. Warping the local concept ... You've been unaware of your ability. That's the only limitation' (Lethem, 1995: 151). While under the influence of the drug, Chaos also meets Gwen and has an elliptical conversation with her as they attempt to describe the nature of their forgetting, in words that move 'in circles, unmoored in reality' (Lethem, 1995: 147).

This phrase is the key to the revelations Chaos experiences in San Francisco. Literally disembodied and immaterial, Gwen has nothing to do with reality. The idyllic house about which he has dreamt throughout the story does not precisely correspond to his and Gwen's home pre-catastrophe; rather it has been approximately constructed by Cale, another creator of FSRs, using fragments of Chaos's memories (Lethem, 1995: 174). When Chaos mentally transports Gwen to Hatfork and she rejects this part of his life, 'the worst part' (Lethem, 1995: 194), he responds by observing first that she is 'one of the fake things that define [him]' (Lethem, 1995: 195) and secondly, more vehemently, that she is 'a simulation' modelled by Cale: 'He made you from a few scraps, a few memories. He built you around the idea of me, of us together. That's why that's all there is of you. He was counting on me to finish the job, to flesh you out and make you real' (Lethem, 1995: 196).

There is a fundamental truth here, one which both determines and ultimately transcends the paradoxes of the FSR. Memory is not coterminous with past events; it is a representation of events, mutable over time in light of circumstances in the present. Ironically, it is Ilford, the closest thing we have to a villain, who appears to understand this best, when he accuses Chaos of being 'too fixated on the past'. He continues: 'You can't go back. Especially when you're changing things as you go along. You can't reclaim a thing that changes as you touch it' (Lethem, 1995: 152). Regardless of his perspicacity in this regard, Ilford's desire to enlist Chaos in his project to create, as his colleague Harriman puts it, 'a broader coherence, a sort of viral coherence that would roll outward from here, reclaiming other territories, other realities' (Lethem, 1995: 161–2), is nefarious, a bid to establish a truly totalitarian or imperial FSR. However, Chaos comes to realise that Cale's request that he dream Gwen into reality is just as unethical: both schemes provide opportunities to put flesh onto Chaos's preoccupations and metaphors but both dictate that he become like Kellogg, Elaine or Ilford (Lethem, 1995: 153), and that is something he refuses to do.

If one views FSRs as analogous to genres, then it becomes evident that Chaos, as his name implies, functions as the 'principle of contamination' (Derrida, 1980: 57) which defeats any attempts to keep genres distinct from each other and which, in fact, is a necessary element of genre definition. Even his 'past' name – Everett Moon – suggests lunacy, the madness that is inherent, according to Derrida, in the law of genre. In this, he stands absolutely opposed to the totalitarian impulses of Ilford Hotchkiss, who, we discover in the climactic scenes of the San Francisco section, reacted to the break by turning people into objects trapped in a room 'like a museum' in his house (Lethem, 1995: 137). Ilford's room is another chronotope of amnesia, the embodiment of his attempt to arrest time, and it is appropriate that he should try and trap Chaos in the clock whose metallic clacking has resonated throughout this section of the novel: Chaos's smashing of the clock (Lethem, 1995: 213) represents the final escape from Ilford-time, which is, of course, atemporal, an entrapment in the present. With these ideas in mind, the following exchange between Chaos and Ilford, just before Chaos's return to Vacaville, is highly significant:

> 'You can't run forever.'
> 'Well, I'd rather try. Than turn into you.' Everett suddenly saw his running as a talent, one more distinctive than the dreaming, even. It was what he'd had to offer Melinda back in Hatfork. It would be what he offered Edie now. (Lethem, 1995: 216)

'Running' here does not only refer back to the chronotope of the road and the rather tired tropes of freedom and movement it triggers; the word also connotes the seepage between categories Chaos performs, as well as the re-entry into chronology and historicity enabled by his decision to reject Cale's and Ilford's proposals.

The bizarre family unit which escapes from Vacaville at the end of the novel encapsulates this osmosis between categories in its extremes of physical type. Upon his return to Vacaville, Chaos discovers that the government stars (who appear at this stage to be overriding even Lucky's dreaming power) have exaggerated the physical deficiencies of the population in order to make themselves impossibly heroic and attractive. Now, 'everyone [is] taller or shorter or wider than they should be, or else they [are] missing a limb or two' (Lethem, 1995: 220). Edie has been transformed into a midget, Ray is hugely fat and Dave has acquired a tail (Lethem, 1995: 222); Chaos eventually goes the same way as Ray (Lethem, 1995: 229). After a final, rather farcical confrontation with Cooley, it is this band of grotesques, together with Melinda, that hits the road in Chaos's car. Together they form a constellated community of disparate individuals retaining characteristics foisted upon them by the FSRs from which they have escaped, and thus they become a familial model of generic mixing. In fact, when Chaos manages to dream Melinda's fur and Dave's tail away, they demand them back (Lethem, 1995: 246). Though the sight of a 'flying thing, a propless helicopter, like the one Vance flew' (Lethem, 1995: 247), reminds us that the threat of totalitarianism still looms, the family Chaos has acquired acts as a makeshift defence against isolationism and dreams of control. As Edie says: 'You'll never create some monster world, or seal yourself off in some fantasy. Because we're here ... We're in there with you. Inside your dreams. You let people in' (Lethem, 1995: 247). In effect, the family is another version of the Lethemite mini-utopia, but it is one 'that has a little more historical consciousness, perhaps, and is a little more capable of encompassing imperfection or paradox' (Personal Interview, 2009).

L. Timmel Duchamp argues that the ending of *Amnesia Moon* represents the rejection of the ideological structures and the naturalised authority of the FSRs and the embrace of 'the material concreteness of the other' (Duchamp, 1998: 15). Chaos's apparent decision not to dream himself thin again is for Duchamp evidence that he 'accepts his fleshliness' (Duchamp, 1998: 17); now he is not some special dreamer, destined for world-shaping power, but 'just a fat slob getting out of town' (Lethem, 1995: 238). It is interesting, when one looks back to the McDonaldonians, that Duchamp sees this 'learning to live in the flesh and love it' as standing in opposition to 'the carnephobia that most male-authored cyberpunk, for instance, so notably celebrates' (Duchamp, 1998: 15). The most cyberpunk of the novel's many encounters on the road, the McDonaldonians episode uses the processed beef patties that make the burgers as the fleshly symbol of naturalised authority and dehumanisation. The more meat gets consumed, the less material and substantial the workers become.

Another of Duchamp's observations, that 'Everett Moon represents the artist, struggling against the naturalized rationalization of authority while at the same time unwittingly serving it' (Duchamp, 1998: 17), deserves attention. Clearly there is a tension between the ethical need to escape discrete imaginative worlds of one's own devising, to recognise the different experiences of others, and the author's need to create imaginative, self-contained worlds. Regardless of whether it manipulates genre conventions in radical ways in a bid to highlight the importance of embracing difference, a novel or a short story is yet another FSR. So it would seem that the very process of writing has the potential to stand at odds with the ethical concerns the writer wishes to explore.

Just as they do in *Gun, With Occasional Music*, these concerns become embroiled in questions of literary influence. Although there is evidence of other influences – 'the green' has echoes of the 'airborne toxic event' in Don DeLillo's *White Noise*, for example (DeLillo, 1985: 107) – the review on the back cover of the 2005 Harvest edition is right to describe *Amnesia Moon* as 'the Philip K. Dickiest of Lethem's novels', an appraisal borne out by Umberto Rossi's meticulous tracing of the Dickian elements (Rossi, 2002). Rossi notes, for example, that the disappearance of animals in *Amnesia Moon* is an idea borrowed from *Do Androids Dream of Electric Sheep?* (1968), in which, after a nuclear war, the very few remaining real animals have become fashionable accessories for the affluent and connected, most people having to make do with cyborg versions. There are also distinct similarities between Vacaville's luck-based society and the imagined worlds of Dick's *Solar Lottery* (1955) and *The Game Players of Titan* (1963). Even the geographical specificities of Lethem's novel enforce the links between its author and his hero: West Marin, the FSR fought over by Tree and Hoppington, is a version of Marin County, north of San Francisco, where Dick lived for many years.

The reader should refer to Umberto Rossi's article if he or she wishes to find more examples of the Dickian influence on *Amnesia Moon*, but for now there are significant things to observe about the relationship itself. While it is ironic that Lethem chooses to *remember* Dick, as it were, by means of tropes of amnesia and fake subjective realities partly borrowed from novels such as *Eye in the Sky* (1957), *The Man in the High Castle* (1962) and *The Three Stigmata of Palmer Eldritch* (1965), it is also the case that Dick's influence offers a way of circumventing the problem of authorial FSR-creation. Although, as Rossi is keen to stress, Lethem's work is 'fresh, not imitative' (Rossi, 2002: 19), the playful and often overt citations from Dick constitute Lethem's acknowledgement that past and present are interlinked and dialectically related, that his writing is, in a profound sense, not entirely his own, and thus that the very relationship of influence recognises difference, mutual dependence and a need to resist inertia, pastiche and amnesia. Just as Chaos lets people into his dreams, so too does the author 'let in' other writers, particularly Dick, to ensure that the work is both individual and collective. As Lethem says: 'it seems to me there's a constant dialogue between sources and originality, to such an extent that you couldn't possibly talk about your impulse to write something honestly unless you also did a lot of acknowledging of sources and references and echoes and things you, at different levels of conscious realisation, appropriated' (Sussler, 2008).

In an idea taken further in *Girl in Landscape* (an homage to *The Searchers*), and taken to extremes in Lethem's article 'The Ecstasy of Influence: A Plagiarism' and his 'Promiscuous Materials' project, one can therefore regard complex literary relationships of influence and affiliation as forming another constellated community of writers within the work. Writing therefore avoids amnesia by explicitly remembering and acknowledging what came before; in this way it achieves a kind of mobility.

Notes

1   In this, Lethem's novel displays distinct similarities with the novels of the British cyberpunk writer Jeff Noon, especially his *Vurt* trilogy. The hero of *Pollen* (1995), for example, is an impossibly cool black cab driver called Coyote – half man, half Dalmatian.

3

Alice in the academy: *As She Climbed Across the Table*

As these words are written, Humanities scholars across the United Kingdom are engaged in urgent dialogues about the forthcoming Research Excellence Framework, or REF. Chief amongst their concerns is the increased emphasis on 'impact' outside the academy. According to the Higher Education Funding Council for England, 'significant additional recognition will be given where researchers build on excellent research to deliver demonstrable benefits to the economy, society, public policy, culture and quality of life' (2009).[1] While it is easy to conceive of the impact medical research or stem cell research or structural engineering research might have, it is perhaps harder to imagine the demonstrable benefits to the economy of research, no matter how original or rigorous, into, say, an obscure American poet of the 1930s or the bee symbolism in eighteenth-century Scottish political tracts. For Humanities scholars in particular, then, the REF reanimates that most troubling of questions: 'what if my work means nothing in the outside world'?

This question has always been central to the campus novel genre; indeed, one of the common criticisms is that campus novels themselves tend not to engage with the outside world at all. As Gore Vidal puts it: 'they tell us what they know about, too, which is next to nothing about the way the rest of the population of the Republic lives ... What tends to be left out of these works is the world' (Vidal, 1988: 180). Other critics more readily recognise the utopian seductions of the university and the university novel. J. P. Kenyon, an academic himself, says: 'The theme of a closed community, outside the mainstream of modern life, has always had obvious attractions. It explains the appeal of much science fiction, which is concerned with closed communities, whether on a space ship or on an alien planet' (Kenyon, 1980: 83). Though his characterisation of science fiction might be rather stereotyped, the link Kenyon draws between it and the campus novel is a revealing one, partly because it opens the door for an experimental writer like Lethem deliberately to bring the two genres into commune. Most importantly, it reminds us that the enjoyment of genre texts in general, as the work of Rick Altman shows, dramatises the vexed relationship between textual norms and real-world norms. To debate whether the university novel is an 'arcadian remove, the land of lost content' (Moseley, 2007: 16) or 'a kind of microcosm of society at large' (Lodge, 1986: 169) is missing the point; the very impulse toward removal from society reveals, ironically, an inherent truth about the way groups operate within wider society.

In what is widely perceived as a distressingly 'dumbed-down' contemporary society, the relationship between the inner academy and the outside world has become even more vexed. As Sally Dalton-Brown states, the lecturer today is 'unsure of his role in a world in which he is no longer the cloistered scholar, or a figure in the ivory tower of academe, but is rather a deeply troubled member of a contemporary cultural landscape permeated by an equally ambiguous attitude toward the role, and status of, the life of the mind in an increasingly reified world' (Dalton-Brown, 2008: 592). If the general public is suspicious of academic activities, the campus novel frequently gives it plenty of ammunition for its suspicion and derives much comedy from the self-regarding futility of research projects. 'There seems remarkably little point to most of the work undertaken by many academic protagonists' observes Dalton-Brown. Jack Gladney, non-German-speaking Professor of Hitler Studies in Don DeLillo's *White Noise* (1985) is just one example of a scholar 'enmeshed in [his] own driveling discourse' (Dalton-Brown, 2008: 595).

Philip Engstrand, first-person narrator of *As She Climbed Across the Table* (1997),[2] which follows the debut novel's homage to Lewis Carroll in the form of talking animals with a fabulist revisiting of Alice and her looking-glass, is an anthropologist at a campus university in northern California who makes no attempt to hide his discomfort at applying 'the social sciences, those fun-house mirrors, to real people engaged in real pursuits' (Lethem, 1997: 6). The geography of his lifestyle reflects this difficulty: 'there were days when I never crossed out of the benign square mile that included the buildings where I taught, ate dining-hall food, and read faculty notices' (Lethem, 1997: 7). After a 'severe departmental review' he has a revelation about how to turn this weakness to his advantage: 'I would study academic environments, the departmental politics and territorial squabbles, the places where disciplines overlapped, fed back, and interfered' (Lethem, 1997: 6). Dedicated to 'the phantom curricula that wavered into existence in the void between actual ones', he earns the nickname 'Interdean' and evidently takes perverse pride in the fact that his work is 'irrelevant and strong' (Lethem, 1997: 6). The text that we read called *As She Climbed Across the Table* is effectively one of Engstrand's studies, then: one of its main aims is to detail the jostling for supremacy among the various disciplines as they try to promulgate the theory which best explains what comes to be known as 'Lack', a hole in the fabric of the world formed in the physics lab after an attempt to create a universe.

Yet it is also, of course, a novel and a love story narrating Engstrand's doomed attempts to win back the heart of his physicist girlfriend Alice Coombs, who has fallen in love with Lack. The parallel jostling for supremacy between the novel's scientific and literary attributes reveals Engstrand's vital importance, despite his status as an increasingly desperate and haggard figure of fun. No matter how resolutely self-circuiting and meta- his work is, and no matter how keen Lethem appears to be to satirise critical positions that are entirely reflexive and carved out merely to keep people in tenure, the narrator's 'inter' prefix marks him out as someone who straddles and thus problematises boundaries between disciplines and fields of endeavour. In this sense he performs a similar vital function to Chaos in *Amnesia Moon*. Moreover, his desire to find phantom curricula in the void foreshadows the arrival of Lack, an entity which, precisely because it is nothingness, can assimilate, violate and mix any number of disciplinary approaches. While other academics such as Carmo Braxia intransigently insist that Lack is 'a physics text. From physics comes physics' (Lethem, 1997: 97), Engstrand is at least sagacious (or maybe just bewildered) enough to recognise that 'lack was obviously an explosion of metaphor into a literal world' (Lethem, 1997: 26). With this statement, he sets the scene for a cerebral comedy of manners with the historic Two Cultures debate, which has sometimes raged, sometimes simmered since C. P. Snow's Rede Lecture in 1959, at its heart.

So in this chapter the initial contention is that in *As She Climbed Across the Table* one should read 'disciplines' for 'genres'. Underpinning the tragi-farcical action of the story is the same interrogation of boundaries between mini-utopias, and the same need to analyse why humans are obsessed with maintaining these boundaries and looking at the world through 'paradigm eyes' (Lethem, 1997: 1), that is so central to its predecessors but is this time played out in the airless environment of campus politics. However, it is also my contention that the fusion of literary genres – the campus comedy, the romance, science fiction and fantasy – with the actual practice of science is achieved in a more integrated and more efficacious fashion in this novel precisely because it is preoccupied, above all, with the inter-penetrative relationship between 'literature' and 'science' not just as terms denoting large fields of academic endeavour, but as terms implying epistemological, philosophical and ethical standpoints. Continuing from observations in Chapter 2, this chapter also examines the ways in which *As She Climbed Across the Table* is another novel about writing. Lack's absolute nothingness makes it absolutely writable-upon; it is therefore the perfect vehicle for the writer's (and indeed all the main characters') 'frantic compensation' for loss (Lethem, 2005: 148). Less explicitly autobiographical than *Girl in Landscape* and *The Fortress of Solitude*, Lethem's third novel nonetheless begins to put traumatic loss or absence at the centre of events in ways which clearly prefigure those later novels and which are more obviously personal and less abstracted than in *Amnesia Moon*.

One might insist that 'frantic compensation' has long been a vital ingredient of the campus novel, and that again it has to do with the dichotomy of inside and outside. The generic stereotypes, certainly of the male lecturer, are either of the 'befuddled, chalk-covered, impotent half-man' (Lyons, 1962: 14) or of the fragile egotist unable to cope with the pressures of life outside the academy, emboldened within his protected sanctuary to ever more dubious acts of hubris, petty competitiveness and sexual inappropriacy until he either quits in despair or is sacked in shame. Either way, he feels himself traduced by life in the real world of families and everyday commerce; it shatters his confidence and saps his will. In his office, in the staffroom, in the lecture theatre and in his mind he can (over)compensate for his fears and inadequacies.

A recent example would be Chip Lambert in Jonathan Franzen's *The Corrections* (2001) (which is not a campus novel as such but voluminous enough to subsume various genres). Chip's lavish entertaining, his self-regarding deconstructions of popular texts for undergraduate critical theory classes and his disastrous affair with one of his undergraduates, Melissa Paquette, all serve to compensate for his loneliness and the distance between his self-perception and his parents' perception of him. 'As he entertained his sympathetic colleagues', we are informed, 'Chip felt secure in the knowledge that his parents could not have been more wrong about who he was and what kind of career he was suited to pursue' (Franzen, 2001: 35). Other examples would include Grady Tripp in Michael Chabon's *Wonder Boys* (1995), a frustrated novelist and creative writing tutor who is unable to finish his mammoth new manuscript, sees his marriage collapse, and becomes embroiled in an absurd crime with one of his students. Tripp's misadventures remind us how closely the writing and teaching of literature are linked in the campus genre. Sansford Pinsker expresses the popular view that English lecturers tend to be frustrated novelists, and that the campus novel seduces with its easy self-referentiality: 'After all, the formula seems simple enough: plant a sensitive young professor in a garden of academic vipers, add a fetching student here and a soused administrator there, and *voila*, yet another novel about higher education on the ropes' (Pinsker, 1999: 440). Following Pinsker, and taking the reflexivity to (surely unfair) extremes, one might suggest that the campus novel, so concerned with the compensations of the academy, is itself a form of compensation for writers unable to craft anything more substantial.

As *She Climbed Across the Table* has its fair share of over-compensating academics – Engstrand himself; Georges De Tooth with his 'feigned poly-European accent' and his 'slim, unreadable volumes' of post-structuralist critique (Lethem, 1997: 109); and Cynthia Jalter, whose research into '[o]bsessive coupling ... the delusory or subjective worlds that exist in the space between two halves of any dual cognitive system' (Lethem, 1997: 79) not only implicates Engstrand, Alice and Lack but her own lack of a stable relationship. (She tries, rather farcically, to lure Engstrand into an affair, but he is too obsessed with reclaiming Alice to succumb to her approaches.) But with Lack as a central symbol for all the characters of 'what both binds them together and what lies between them' (Bredehoft, 1998: 9), Lethem's novel takes the notion of compensation far beyond professional rivalry or sexual insecurity and into much bigger questions of meaning and existence. Essentially, it all comes down to language as the ultimate compensation for lack and desire. Whether it is the physicist Professor Soft with his talk of 'anti-trapped surfaces, in an asymptotically Minkowskian background' (Lethem, 1997: 4) or De Tooth with his astute but equally self-serving pronouncement that Lack is 'a verb both active and passive; an object and space at once' (Lethem, 1997: 111), these thinkers, in the face of Lack's absolute silence and otherness, are doomed forever to go on throwing language at it in a desperate bid to explain, to rationalise and therefore in a sense to possess. For example, when Engstrand dismisses Lack as 'Soft's thing', Alice retorts, '[i]f I describe it it's my thing' (Lethem, 1997: 17). Similarly, when Engstrand defuses a student protest against the physics department's decision to feed Lack a live cat by proclaiming to the assembly, 'Lack is here to help you take science less seriously' (Lethem, 1997: 54), Alice surprises him with her anger: 'You think if you describe him he'll suddenly belong to you. Just like everything else ... But this time you're wrong ... lack is mine' (Lethem, 1997: 54). The fact that in one sense she turns out to be right does not alter the fact that the desire to describe barely masks the desire to possess, and that the desire to possess stems from the fear of not understanding.

This is a novel, then, about 'the impossibility of escaping from language' (Bredehoft, 1998: 10), about the excessive verbalisation that comes from never being able to say what you really mean to say, and what is crucial about these issues is that scientists are afflicted just as much as social scientists and humanities scholars. Thus Lethem is at pains to overturn a classic (and naive) opposition between the ambiguity of the literary and the cold rationality of the scientific. The discourses might be different according to the discipline, but the scientists' creation of narrative frameworks to describe phenonema they can never completely understand ends up analogous to the work of the novelist working in a medium cacophonous with words and akin, as Lethem puts it, to the 'buzzing of insects' (Peacock, 2009). In response to Engstrand's weary assertion that '[w]e were all physicists now, thanks to Lack' (Lethem, 1997: 43), one might retort that more accurately Lack turns everyone into novelists.

Lack is 'like the metaphor as lens that can be used everywhere' (Personal Interview, 2009), a multivalent symbol or metaphor for all the losses and lacks – the death of the author's mother, Engstrand's loss of Alice, Professor Soft's loss of scientific certainty, the reader's sense of disorientation – that need to be described or narrated but can never be to any satisfying degree. It is – and forgive this author if momentarily he sounds like Georges De Tooth – simultaneously the absence of signification and the excess of signification and metaphor which, Chapter 4 argues in relation to *Girl in Landscape*, lies at the heart of science fiction as a genre.

Genres in general invest deeply in, and derive much of their power from, a sense of lack. Scott McCracken evokes Ernst Bloch and

Theodor Adorno when he suggests that the consumption of popular genres provokes the feeling that 'something is missing' from the real world (McCracken, 1998: 13). Like Rick Altman, he emphasises the frequent disparity between real-world norms and generic norms: 'The pleasures and transgressions involved in the experience of popular fiction are a constant reminder that a better, more fulfilled life is a possibility' (McCracken, 1998: 14). Although it is ultimately Alice to whom Lack, in her words 'the idea of perfection' (Lethem, 1997: 83), appears to be most closely affiliated, it is nonetheless evident that it comes to function as a kind of utopian possibility, 'a better, more fulfilled life', for many of the characters who attempt to offer themselves mentally and bodily to the void – Alice, De Tooth, Soft, Braxia and ultimately Engstrand. It is utopian first because it represents the luminal space where all disciplinary and generic boundaries dissolve, where physics, sociology, literature, science fiction, romance and campus comedy meet and coalesce and cease to have any particular relevance on their own terms.

Secondly, and relatedly, it is utopian because the defeat of disciplinary and generic discourses brings the inevitable defeat of language as an over-compensatory strategy for trying to explain and contain absence. As her obsession grows, Alice adopts a deliberate strategy of silence out of respect for Lack, whom another female professor describes as 'the Other ... the mysterious, the silent, the withdrawn and enigmatic' (Lethem, 1997: 165). Whether or not this same professor, who is succumbing like others to the need to theorise, to describe, is right to assert that Alice's silence is also a 'refusal' of language 'constructed by males' as an instrument of oppression (Lethem, 1997: 164), it is true that Alice has realised the futility of language in the face of the irreducibly different. The paradox, of course, consists in the novel itself, which sets out to narrate Alice's silence in yet more compensatory words.

Nowhere is the idea of language as compensation made more explicit than in the novel's depiction of the two blind men, Evan Robart and Garth Poys. They arrive at Engstrand's apartment as early as Chapter 4 looking for Alice, and are a persistent presence and, to Engstrand, annoyance around the campus and in the apartment until they successfully achieve what every other character bar Engstrand does not – disappearance into, or more accurately acceptance by, Lack (Lethem, 1997: 181). The following dialogue between Engstrand and

Alice (the former speaking first), summarises the key characteristics and implications of Evan and Garth's meticulous verbalising:

> 'They're incredible.'
> 'They can't help it.'
> 'The talk. It's obsessive.'
> 'Compensation. They can't see. They map their environment verbally.'
> 'It requires a lot of confirmation, the map.'
> 'Listen to them. It's poetic.' (Lethem, 1997: 16)

As previous chapters have suggested, the concept of mapping is fundamental to understanding the behaviour of Lethem and his creations. By means of genre, subculture, race, musical tastes and artificially constructed realities, characters produce cognitive maps in order to locate themselves in a world which has become increasingly strange and alienating. In Evan and Garth's case the process is laughably pedantic and scientific, exemplified by the endless synchronising of their 'bulky Braille watches' (Lethem, 1997: 19), but, as Alice's final comment suggests, poetry may occasionally emerge from the stream of discourse. It is a hope all of Lethem's obsessive mapmakers share.

In a sense, Evan and Garth's condition distils the problem of mapping to its essence, and it is in this sense that their blindness is used emblematically, as a means by which the universally applicable 'observer problem' might be explored. What the novel proposes is that we are all blind, essentially, first because we cannot really know or understand anything, or at least can only ever arrive at 'extremely local certainties' before passing on 'to uncertainty again' (Lethem, 'Hypergraphia', 2007), and secondly because even those local certainties founder on the fact that all apparently impassive observation is coloured by subjective judgement. As Garth puts it: 'Observing is like thinking' (Lethem, 1997: 19). In a moment of bitterness, soon before he and Evan enter Lack in order to try and escape their blindness and, presumably, their garrulousness (Lethem, 1997: 183), he goes further in his thoughts on the subjective nature of blindness as a concept: 'See is a movie. But when something goes wrong in their movie, when something is odd, they don't question themselves. They don't say, gee, things are disappearing in this laboratory, something must be wrong with my eyes or my brain, I must be blind. They put it outside of themselves, they say, gee, something is wrong with the *world*. There must be a Lack' (Lethem, 1997: 121). One of the many profound ironies of the novel is that the greatest Lack is in fact a presence – the omnipresence of the self in all negotiations with the world, that which makes the existence of real-world phenomena ultimately unverifiable. What this all means – and the conclusion of the novel makes this abundantly clear – is that observation, 'be it scientific or novelistic, is at heart narcissistic. Rather than seeing the world, one sees the world through the distorting prism of selfhood. Alice therefore places such faith in Garth's 'blindsight', his apparent ability to see 'without consciousness' and without subjective judgement (Lethem, 1997: 20) because she envisages a way to bypass the observer problem in her experiments with Lack. Garth's subsequent failure to do successful physics, however, pushes Alice toward a new mode of experimentation and a new attitude to Lack. When Engstrand echoes Soft's concerns that Alice's work is becoming too personal, she responds: 'Lack doesn't require detachment. That's Soft's error. Lack requires engagement, a relationship' (Lethem, 1997: 67). After this, Alice begins to offer Lack things in a bid to establish a reciprocal relationship: her paintings, her hair, parts of her body, her whole body. Her need is to be recognised, to feel her own attraction, to be sure that she is loved.

And this reciprocity is crucial to the observer problem and to the nature of Lack. Logically, the subjectivity of observation dictates that objects only come into existence through observation. For Engstrand, this resonates purely at a romantic frequency: as he tells Alice, 'I'm not sure I really exist, except under your observation' (Lethem, 1997: 21). For Lack, whom Alice views as a phenomenon of pure discernment, pure preference (Lethem, 1997: 32), it becomes absolutely constitutive, a fundamental question of physics which nonetheless is entwined with romantic concerns. It is Carmo Braxia who most persuasively articulates Lack's engagement with Alice. Starting with the Cartesian declaration that '[c]onsciousness writes reality, in any direction it looks' (Lethem, 1997: 153), he explains to a desperate Engstrand that the creation of a new reality requires a sophisticated intelligence to observe it; without such it 'collapses into unreality' (Lethem, 1997: 154). Lack, rather than waiting for an adequate observing consciousness 'to evolve' (Lethem, 1997: 154), latches onto the most powerful proximal consciousness in order to confirm its existence and reality. Yearning for this confirmation, and with limited options, Lack cannot be 'impartially hungry' (Lethem, 1997: 155), but instead borrows its 'personality' from Alice and her likes, dislikes and prejudices (Lethem, 1997: 155). One of these prejudices, Braxia maintains, is against science itself, and this is why he now regards the experiment as useless, and Lack merely 'a pothole malformed by subjectivity' (Lethem, 1997: 156). Astute though his theory turns out to be, he still lacks the necessary open-mindedness to appreciate how inextricably linked the discourses of science, romance and the arts are. Lack's bias is not against science as such, only a conception of physics as generically distinct from all other disciplines.

Drunk, lovelorn, disappointed, Engstrand attends the Christmas party (an essential part of what Lethem calls 'the machine of the academic novel' (Personal Interview, 2009)) and, sinking to the floor amidst a mass of sweaty and leering faculty bodies, muses: 'How easy it was to disappear. Nothing to be afraid of' (Lethem, 1997: 168). These words form the prelude to his final romantic act, his final bid for love requited. Under cover of darkness, Engstrand enters the physics lab and enters Lack. What he finds is a surreal, imperfectly reproduced campus, a wry comment not only on the comedy of science (of which more presently) but also on the weaknesses of representation. The objects which Lack accepted, including 'a fountain pen, an eight ball, and an argyle sock' as well as, appropriately, given that Lack is so obviously Alice's looking-glass, '[a] boxed edition of Carroll's *The Hunting of the Snark*' (Lethem, 1997: 176), are all here, randomly scattered around a bizarre facsimile of Alice's world. Philip muses:

> Braxia was right. The new universe was clinging to its parent reality. The results were poor. Lack was trying to make a world, but he couldn't get the parts. He'd manufactured a version of campus made only of the elements Alice found charming or harmless. Another example of rotten collaborative scholarship. (Lethem, 1997: 177)

Pleased to know that he can be listed among the 'charming or harmless', Engstrand heads back to the lab to re-enter the real world and, one assumes, tell Alice what he has learned. Unfortunately, he discovers that Lack has reproduced itself in a never-ending series of worlds: he tumbles through into blindness (and meets Evan and Garth) and then, entering Lack once more, finds himself, literally, dissolved into nothingness. He has become Lack and, surprisingly, seems fairly happy with the situation, especially when Alice appears, strips off and prepares to enter him.

As She Climbed has a bittersweet ending: as she climbs across the table, her eyes 'full of love' (Lethem, 1997: 192), the strong suggestion is that Alice's desire to enter Lack will finally be sated, and that Philip's desire to regain her love will also find fulfilment. Philip/Lack also claims to have solved the observer problem by dissolving both observer and observed (Lethem, 1997: 186). Yet all these things are enabled only because Philip has become the void, albeit one which is no longer mute and enigmatic (at least not to the reader) but is now a disembodied, considering consciousness intent on articulating its own absence: 'I hummed to myself. Nothing, by Philip Nothing and the Nothings. Sung to the tune of Nothing. Nothing with a bullet. Ten weeks at the top of the nothing charts./Nothing's greatest hits./Supernothing. Hypernothing. Cryptonothing. Nothing ventured, nothing gained./Goo goo ga joob' (Lethem, 1997: 187).

As well as wryly acknowledging Lethem's cultural antecedents (Lewis Carroll's 'The Walrus and the Carpenter' in *Through the Looking Glass* filtered through John Lennon's nonsense lyric in 'I am the Walrus'), such entertaining ramblings serve as reaffirmation of two of the novel's constitutive ideas. First, that the lack at the heart of events – whether it stands for trauma, loss, truth, knowledge, the proof of the universe's love for humanity or all of the above – is impossible adequately to verbalise. Even if you give the void itself a voice, it can only produce words, approximations of itself, in a vain attempt to describe, know and possess its own being, to become identical with itself. Philip's/Lack's nonsense in these concluding pages is thus a precursor to Lionel Essrog's Tourette's in *Motherless Brooklyn*, which is depicted as an over-enthusiastic attempt to smooth the world's imperfections, absences and mysteries, an attempt to rationalise leading inevitably to chaos and comedy. Tourette's, one might argue counterintuitively, functions in the first instance not as a kind of poetry, but as a kind of science.

This brings us to the second reaffirmation: Philip's/Lack's words of nothingness demonstrate once again how science cannot be taken too seriously. All the way through the novel, scientists have done laughable things: the graduate students' probe, 'a cube of compacted garbage, or an assignment by an eccentric art teacher' (Lethem, 1997: 123), which fails to penetrate Lack's secrets and instead falls bathetically off the table, is but one example. But the exhortation to recognise science's absurdity goes much further than merely mocking misguided experiments. It evokes the courageous, ludic spirit, the defiance of gravity, which invigorates Friedrich Nietzsche's *The Gay Science* (1882).

Although space does not permit a detailed reading of this work, it is worth outlining particular aspects of Nietzsche's thought which are germane to Lethem's novel. First, as Bernard Williams' introduction to the Cambridge edition notes, the German term for 'science' – 'Wissenschaft' – denotes not only the natural and biological sciences, but also any systemic body of knowledge, including history and the humanities in general (Nietzsche, 2004: x). Additionally, the title refers to 'gai saber', the medieval troubadours' love songs which evoke a tradition of courtly love going back to Ovid (Nietzsche, 2004: x). Thus Nietzsche's work quite deliberately merges disciplines and genres, just as Lethem latterly produces a narrative of physics, social science and amorous adventure.

In section 108 of *The Gay Science* Nietzsche makes his famous declaration that 'God is dead' (Nietzsche, 2004: section 108). For Nietzsche, the consequences of this loss for twentieth-century civilization may well be catastrophic, but this is partly because 'The Christian resolution to find the world ugly and bad has made the world ugly and bad' (Nietzsche, 2004: section 130) and partly because attempts to supersede Christian metaphysics such as liberalism and socialism have merely aped the structures of Christianity in, for example, its facile opposition of good and evil.

If, in contrast, one adopts a nihilistic approach and denies any defining metaphysical structure whatsoever, then one becomes disinclined '[t]o find everything profound', something Nietzsche dismisses as 'an inconvenient trait' which 'makes one strain one's eyes all the time' (Nietzsche, 2004: section 158), and more inclined toward the 'gaiety' of the title. This denotes not simply contentment, and certainly not a relaxed or uncritical attitude to the horrors of existence, but a 'hyper-sensitivity to suffering' (Williams, 2004: xiv), an absolute refusal to ignore those horrors which is nonetheless coupled with a refusal to be weighed down by them. To be 'gay' is to be free-spirited, daring, bloody-minded and creative in the face of a universe that may not love you, and it is the only serious way to be. As he says: 'the secret for harvesting from existence the greatest fruitfulness and greatest enjoyment is – to live dangerously' (Nietzsche, 2004: section 283). One crucial aspect of 'living dangerously', tied in with the loss of a monolithic metaphysics, is the acceptance of the fact that 'we cannot reject the possibility that it [the world] includes infinite interpretations' (Nietzsche, 2004: section 374). Yet – and this is an idea rehearsed in Lethem's ongoing analysis of FSRs, genres, mini-utopias, subcultures – it is extremely difficult to see other people's interpretations beyond the abstract: 'we cannot look round our corner' (Nietzsche, 2004: section 374).

Alice's bespoke campus universe is thus a tragicomic model of how we *all* see the universe, according to Nietzsche: as partial, idiosyncratic and incomplete. Philip's entering of Lack is a lover's frenzied attempt to confirm that he is loved, to be 'the first lover in history to receive an absolute answer, a *yes* or *no* notarized as cosmic fact' (Lethem, 1997: 174) and finally to fulfil the romantic tryst that has been delayed since the very beginning of the novel. Yet it is also a sincere attempt to 'look round the corner' at another individual's version of the universe (though a paradoxically self-interested attempt). In one sense it is a success. Philip does indeed get to see the world Lack has created in its symbiotic relationship with Alice.

What makes his expedition tragic, ultimately, is his decision to re-enter Lack within Alice's world, which brings him first into Evan and Garth's blindness and eventually into the nothingness. The tragedy lies specifically in its recursivity. Philip realises that: 'Along with making a facsimile of our world, Lack had reproduced himself. His chamber, his table, and his hunger for reality. Like a Persian carpet maker, every world Lack made would have a flaw, a Lack of its own. And every Lack would want to make a world. Soft's experiment would never end' (Lethem, 1997: 182). Any effort to familiarise oneself with a subjective world uncovers yet more worlds within, the pursuit of which results in potentially endless movement inward into ever more obscure psychic landscapes. The nothingness might appear a solution to the problem, in that it obliterates all worlds, and in becoming the void, Philip appears to have transcended the distinction between inside and outside which troubles the entire narrative. His inner landscape and the world beyond have become absolutely coterminous.

However, the true nightmare of the ending, despite the lightness of the writing and the mock sentimentality of the last line, is that Philip's status as Lack represents the ultimate act of recursion, and of incorporation. His narration of the text as the void suggests that he holds within himself, in infinite regress, all the worlds that have been depicted. *As She Climbed Across the Table* has its last rancorous laugh when Philip becomes this disembodied voice, containing all and nothing. When language is all there is, then one can be gay in the face of life's mysteries and tragedies by using language as creatively and as boldly as possible. As the novel makes apparent, we all become novelists. But as the whole narrative folds into itself, language and the novel itself are revealed as literally nothing. As Alice is also (presumably) incorporated into the void, the nihilistic erotic fantasy of *As*

She Climbed Across the Table is ironically consummated; to paraphrase Philip's/Lack's words – in the end, nothing has been ventured, nothing gained. It may be comic in tone, but it is profoundly disheartening in effect. It seems the ultimate compensation is annihilation.

There is clearly an element of poking fun at work here. Lethem carefully constructs a series of worlds-within-worlds like a Russian doll: the world, the States, the campus, the physics lab, Lack, and the infinite worlds within. Such layering is reminiscent of much stereotypically postmodern practice in works by, for example, John Barth and Paul Auster, and the fact that Lethem has it all collapse into nothingness implies his suspicion of metafictional writing that tends to disappear, to allude once again to Alice, up its own rabbit hole. However, it does have its tragic side, and elsewhere the author employs recursive narratives in less satiric, more obviously horrific ways. The short story 'The Happy Man' provides a dystopian counterpart to the utopian bespoke universes of *As She Climbed*. If one considers the novel as having a non-specific, amorphous, and therefore helplessly over-determined trauma at its heart in the form of Lack, the short story veers into more specific, explicitly psychoanalytical territory where *mise-en-abyme* mirrors the endless mining and repetition of defined traumatic incidents. It is useful to examine 'The Happy Man' alongside *As She Climbed* because they represent the two contrasting sides of Lethem's approach to childhood trauma in subsequent texts such as *Girl in Landscape*, *Fortress* and *The Disappointment Artist*: the tendency to 'hide in plain sight' behind playful uses of genre and language even as painful experience is apparently laid bare.

'The Happy Man' uses a familiar science fiction premise: technology has accelerated to the extent that it is now possible for the dead to be resurrected. In the words of the narrator, Tom: 'they warmed me up and put me together' (Lethem, 1996: 11). There is one severe side-effect, however. Those who have undergone the procedure are doomed to 'cross over' at irregular intervals from the real world to the afterlife, which takes the form of a personalised hell (Lethem, 1996: 12). In a wry comment on the zombie-like drudgery of public life (a satirical strain the story shares, indeed, with most zombie movies), the doctor tells Tom that when he crosses over '[m]ost people won't know the difference'. He continues: 'You'll be able to carry on most conversations in a perfunctory way. You just won't seem very interested in personal questions. Your mind will appear to be wandering. And you won't be very affectionate. Your co-workers won't notice, but

your wife will' (Lethem, 1996: 12). This is all too true. Lethem's narrative mimes this crossing over as it frequently switches between the
'real world' and its vivid descriptions of Tom's hell. Before the true
symbolic significance of hell is revealed, life on the other side rapidly deteriorates as Tom's wife Maureen, frustrated by the unpredict-
ability of her husband's absences, starts an affair (Lethem, 1996: 32),
the mysterious Uncle Frank comes to stay, and Tom's son Peter becomes more and more immersed in his computer reproduction of his
father's hell (Lethem, 1996: 9). On one level, then, Tom's crossing
over into hell is an obvious metaphor for the emotional distance that
inevitably develops between family members under the pressures of
everyday life.

But it is much more than that, and the clues are there from the
beginning. From the declaration – 'In Hell I'm a small boy' (Lethem,
1996: 6) – through the macabre fairytale descriptions of the 'damned
garden' adjacent to the witch's house which acts as antechamber to
the landscape of Tom's hell (Lethem, 1996: 6), to the abuse Tom suffers at the hands of Colonel Eagery, The Happy Man (Lethem, 1996:
24), hell is a landscape of childhood trauma endlessly revisited and
repeated. Whatever variations occur within each visit, Tom at some
point encounters The Happy Man: as his counsellor says, the horrific
abuse can be considered the 'reentry episode', the symbolic situation
which constitutes 'the key to Hell, the source of the unresolved tension' (Lethem, 1996: 22). The counsellor encourages Tom to 'identify the corresponding episode in your own past' (Lethem, 1996: 22),
to consider hell, like the universes created within Lack, as a 'psychic
landscape', a symbolic representation of real-world events and figures (Lethem, 1996: 13). Tom initially dismisses such a reading: 'Hell
doesn't *mean* anything ... And it's not symbolic. It's very, very real'
(Lethem, 1996: 13). Furthermore, he stresses that '[t]here's nothing in
my life to correspond to Eagery' (Lethem, 1996: 22).

Uncle Frank arrives immediately after the narration of the first abuse
scene, and for the reader it becomes evident that Tom is doomed to
relive these traumatic scenes forever unless he acknowledges precisely the symbolic correspondences suggested by the counsellor. 'Frank'
thus connotes the necessity for frank admission of past trauma. It is
only when Tom, acting on 'Hell-reflexes', enters Peter's room to find
his son 'spread-eagled on the bed, bound with neckties' and with Uncle Frank standing naked over him (Lethem, 1996: 52), that he finally
accepts the truth embodied in this hellish tableau of repetition: 'Yes,

Uncle Frank was Colonel Eagery, aka The Happy Man. He'd molested me as a boy, right in our house, while my father was away, and with my mother in the kitchen making breakfast. I remember it all now' (Lethem, 1996: 53). Suddenly, the whole of Tom's personal hell is revealed as symbolic significances: the witch, whom he describes as '[t]he most beautiful woman I've ever seen' (Lethem, 1996: 8), stands for his mother, and the children in the garden are all, in effect, Tom, waiting for the breakfast endlessly deferred by acts of abuse.

Clearly, Tom's hell has been a psychic, symbolic landscape all along, and while one might reject this exposition as almost parodically Freudian, it nonetheless has important implications in terms of the relationship between reality and representation. Given that it represents in symbolic form the trauma of his childhood, Tom achieves a fuller understanding only when he comes to accept the literary qualities of his hell, the very fact that it does function as a mode of representation. If the story ended with the rape scene and Tom's beating of Uncle Frank with the computer keyboard (Lethem, 1996: 53), then Lethem might perhaps be accused of too convenient a resolution and too neat a reification of the symbolic elements of his hell. However, when one considers that the beating is itself a partial re-enactment of a scene earlier in the tale, then issues are further complicated. It is when Peter describes Uncle Frank as 'some kind of cartoon character, or somebody you'd tell me about in a story ... somebody from Hell, like the robot maker' (Lethem, 1996: 45) that Tom strikes his son. Partly this is because Peter's observation begins to trigger, at an unconscious level, Tom's memories of Frank's abuse, but also because Tom starts to understand the power Peter's computer representation of hell holds over him.

And this is the twist in the tale: having confronted and overcome one version of hell by acknowledging fully the constitutive trauma, Tom is only able to replace it with another form of representation with even less likelihood of escape. His new hell finds him in the house with Maureen and Peter, but 'unable to speak, or reach out to them', reduced permanently to the state of an adult zombie (Lethem, 1996: 54). Eventually, he ends up 'standing in the doorway' of Peter's room, 'looking over his shoulder at the computer screen./Watching him play my Hell' (Lethem, 1996: 54). It is as if the act of representation itself has become hellish and the symbols real; the trauma victim resigns himself to repetition in the form of a metafictional recursion similar to that enacted inside Lack, both endlessly representing and

endlessly watching himself represent his own suffering. Once again
the spirit of Nietzsche's *Gay Science* is evoked: in the final horrific
tableau of 'The Happy Man' is posed the question underlying Nietzsche's hypothesis of Eternal Recurrence: 'Do you want this again
and innumerable times again?' (Nietzsche, 2004: section 341).

Both *As She Climbed Across the Table* and 'The Happy Man' address
traumatic loss or suffering. If the latter appears to do so more directly and with more obvious cathexis of symbolic events, it eventually
reaches a similar conclusion to the novel: that representation itself (as
language, as symbolic text) is traumatic and inescapable. Both texts
fold into recursive psychic landscapes while urging the reader and
the writer to accept correspondences between fictional worlds and
real experience. The question they pose – is it better to deal with loss
through playful generic experimentation, 'hiding in plain sight', or
through direct, specific confrontation with events – is peculiarly relevant to the novel in which Lethem first dares himself to 'open that
box and really let it come' (Zeitchik, 2003: 37); that is, to write about
the loss of his mother. The extent to which *Girl in Landscape*, a novel
bringing together science fiction, the Western and the bildungsroman, is able to 'open that box', is the subject of the next chapter.

Notes

1   From the HEFCE website, www.hefce.ac.uk/research/ref/impact/, ac-
    cessed 13 November 2009.
2   Philip's surname connotes enclosed spaces and boundaries; it brings
    together corruptions of the Swedish words meaning 'meadow' and
    'beach'.

4

Far away, so close: Brooklyn goes to space in *Girl in Landscape*

So far it has been argued that there is a high degree of correspondence between form and content in Lethem's work, and that the genre decisions he makes are integral to his view of the world as a series of semi-imagined subcultural groupings or, to reprise Rick Altman's term, *'constellated communities'* (Altman, 1999: 161). In the eccentric family unit formed at the end of *Amnesia Moon* and in Alice Coombs' parallel campus world, one sees a yearning for workable mini-utopias congruent with the implicit (and sometimes explicit) ties formed between readers of genre fiction. Genres reflect, initiate and are complex and developing communities. They are particularly complex in Lethem's universe because protagonists and readers are constantly forced to re-imagine and redefine generic boundaries when confronted by alterity; and they are developing precisely because of the communal need for constant redefinition.

It is at least curious, then, that Lethem's fourth novel *Girl in Land-scape* (1998a), while signalling a sincere and deepening engagement with the idea of community-formation, as well as introducing the author's first explicit fictional foray into his Brooklyn childhood, failed to reach as large a reading community as its predecessors. Lethem regards it as his 'first flop' and attributes its relative lack of popular and critical success to its direct emotional content, which contrasted with the arch playfulness of the previous novels and was 'uncomfortable for a certain constituency' (Personal Interview, 2009). Such a claim is, in the end, unverifiable, which is not to deny that *Girl in Landscape* is a much more obviously heartfelt autobiographical work, but is to suggest that the specifically generic reasons Lethem offers for its status as 'a sort of secret book' (Personal Interview, 2009) are potentially more illuminating. Quite simply, he feels he pushed the sci-fi too far: 'on the whole people, even literary readers who have made some accommodation to the idea that there's some things that science fiction writers do that might be *okay*, another planet is the line they won't cross, and so no one wants to read a book set on another planet' (Personal Interview, 2009).

It is true that *Girl in Landscape* 'crosses the line', but this argument proceeds from a desire to unpack Lethem's statements with the aim of complicating them and demonstrating that, on the contrary, the novel has to be set on another planet. Certainly, the author crosses the line into avowedly autobiographical territory and into outer space for the first time, but the text poses difficulties not simply because it is emotionally demanding or because the relocation to the Planet of the Archbuilders is liable to excite literary snobbery, but because it dramatises symbolically the hermeneutic and ethical challenges posed by reading generally, and by genre texts specifically. In Lethem's fourth novel, the mix of generic elements – science fiction, coming-of-age, the Western frontier narrative, regionalism – are so acutely attuned to the subject matter of loss that the text cannot help but be about its own inadequacy in dealing with loss. This is revealed as a problem both of writing about the world and, in the case of the teenage protagonist Pella Marsh, of reading the world after traumatic loss. In *Girl in Landscape* this problem is analogous to the difficulties (and potentially intensified pleasures) inherent in reading novels and genre texts. Brooklyn, as it is presented and generically transformed in this novel, becomes another complex novelistic text, one which must be interpreted and negotiated in order to reconcile the protagonist to loss and to bring about a modified and more sophisticated conception of community as a reading process in itself.

If, as Frank Kermode stated, literary texts 'interpret, or deceive, their interpreters, who should know they do so, and make allowances for it' (Kermode, 1979: 13), it is partly because, in the case of the novel, there is simply 'too much stuff' in them for 'a kind of persuasive internal architecture' to emerge (Lethem, in 'Hypergraphia': 28). Lethem continues: 'they're a journal of impressions with the kind of electricity, in a Frankenstein sense, shot through them of causality or thematic unity that seems to make the pile stand up and wobble around and do a wonderful performance. But the truth of them is that there's too much matter there. There are too many individual moments, too many connections between words in sentences, sentences in paragraphs, paragraphs in chapters, and also too many different possible realms of activity' (Lethem, in 'Hypergraphia': 28). Novels, in other words, are not just 'dialogic' in Mikhail Bakhtin's formulation (Bakhtin, 2004: 262), but excessive.

One sees this excess of realms and connections humorously enacted in *As She Climbed Across the Table*, where discourses and worlds are multiplied and compete for pre-eminence. Yet in this novel, as the previous chapter argued, the excess comes from the lack at its centre which remains, for all the characters' theorising and proselytising, utterly opaque, endlessly different, always unfathomable. Thus Lack demands to be read like a novel itself, as the negative embodiment of the novel's tendency to hide in plain sight: it is excessively productive of language, character, situation and apparent meaning, while always holding back that *something* which might permit the unlocking of the 'true' meaning. Call it 'opacity' or 'wilful narrative deafness' (Kermode, 1979: 25, 13), a salient feature of the novel is the thoroughly misleading opportunity it appears to afford for interpretive efficacy through sheer abundance.

If the novel is broadly viewed as a play of openness and concealment, the genre narrative for Lethem represents a condensed version of this play which he feels, in ways germane to *Girl in Landscape*, has an autobiographical impetus. In 'The Beards', he confesses that writing became 'a beard on loss' (Lethem, 2005: 149) and that his immersion in genre writing was in the first instance a self-conscious attempt to disappoint the highbrow expectations of his father, the expressionist artist Richard Lethem, while simultaneously acting as 'a beard' for his own ambitions to create higher art than might be expected from someone using popular cultural forms (Lethem, 2005: 145). Science fiction in particular, he contends in the same essay, enables the writer to hide in plain sight. Although in the subsequent analysis of the novel there is further detail on why science fiction is peculiarly amenable to this desire, it is worth prefacing that discussion with some preliminary observations.

Lethem's manipulations of genre, no matter how ludic they sometimes are, have an ethical impulse in that they mirror the necessity in real life of allowing the fantastic and the unexpected into one's narrow realms of activity. Science fiction, even if it is put to primarily dystopian uses as in Lethem's first two novels, has a privileged role to play in this never-ending ethical process because it is above all about encounters with difference, with 'the meeting of self with other ... the most fearful, most exciting and most erotic encounter of all' (McCracken, 1998: 102). Darko Suvin's concept of the 'novum', referring to the point of difference between the imagined world and our world, retains much of its currency in contemporary critical discussions of sci-fi because it succinctly expresses the importance of this encounter for characters and readers alike. Any science fiction text is likely to have several nova: in *Gun, With Occasional Music*, for example, there are prematurely evolved animals, Babyheads, Forgettol and remote memory boxes. No matter which choices of nova the reader makes, what makes these narrative elements ideal means of hiding in plain sight is that they simultaneously embody difference *and* similarity through their symbolic qualities, in much the same way that genre recognition relies on a paradoxical play of resemblance, repetition and differences (Rosmarin, 1985: 24). As Adam Roberts states: 'the novum acts as a symbolic manifestation of something that connects it specifically with the world we live in' (Roberts, 2006: 14). Indeed, its appeal derives not only from its alien elements, but from readers' recognition of its critical, satirical or political qualities in relation to their constellated communities and the wider world. A memory box, for instance, might be strange, but it nonetheless speaks of the amnesia impelled by the distracting effects of contemporary mass media and hypertechnology.

In deference to the need for a convincing connection with the reader's world, and in order to avoid the confusion of sci-fi with the much-maligned fantasy genre, Suvin insists on coherence within the imagined world. Science fiction, he says, is a 'symbolic system' that is 'centred on a novum which is to be cognitively validated within the narrative reality of the tale' (Suvin, 1979: 80). This is the essence of what Suvin calls 'cognitive estrangement': individual elements of the world may be strange, but brought together they obey a certain internal logic and intelligibility. One of the ways science fiction achieves this is through the proliferation of material detail, allowing for cognitive validation: stereotypically this includes aliens, spaceships, time machines and other advanced technologies. Without reproducing our world mimetically, the sci-fi world urges us to believe in its symbolic system just as willingly as we might believe in a more straightforwardly 'realist' text by Zola or Bennett, and it does this by multiplying what Adam Roberts calls 'material symbols' (Roberts, 2006: 14).

This brief outline shows that the relationship in science fiction between the metaphorical and literal, symbolic and real, sublimated and overt, is notoriously complicated and therefore very alive. It is why science fiction becomes so expedient to Lethem as he both confronts and disguises the mourning of his mother in his fourth novel. Science fiction exploits the dialectical or, as Paul Ricoeur has it, paradoxical relationship between metaphor and the literal: 'there is no other way to do justice to the metaphorical notion of truth than to include the critical inclusion of the (literal) "is not" within the ontological vehemence of the (metaphorical) "is"' (Ricoeur, 2003: 302). And always, as Karl Simms stresses, readers suspend disbelief in the consumption of such texts (Simms, 2003: 75): they accept a created world that is and is not simultaneously, in the same way that genre consumers temporarily balance transgressive generic expectations with real-world proprieties.

Yet, as Samuel Delaney argues, sci-fi metaphors attain their power by means of a 'psychological surplus' comprised of poetic significances at the level of individual words and elements within (but also beyond) the overall semantics of the metaphorical scheme (Delaney, 1994: 174). Adam Roberts' expansion of Delaney's idea returns once again to the notion of excess: 'it is the infusoria of detail, the minutiae of starship-design, characters, imagined backstories, ... social structures, alien biology, timelines, religions, languages and so on that give *Star Trek* or *Dune* their heft, their purchase upon the minds of fans, and not any supposedly core "metaphorical" meaning' (Roberts, 2006: 139). When one considers in conjunction with this 'infusoria of detail' the symbolic aspects of science fiction – and symbols are by their very nature pluralistic and elusive – then it becomes clear that science fiction allows a writer both to pursue a central metaphorical or even allegorical path while filling the text with vividly imagined details that have the potential to render meanings endlessly diffuse.

In the case of *Girl in Landscape*, Lethem is thus able to confront his mother's death quite directly and 'with documentary specificity' (Peacock, 2009), while hiding behind outlandish sci-fi elements. As the most symbolic of his novels, *Girl in Landscape* appears to offer up the alien landscape as a kind of objective correlative of the protagonist's mourning for her mother, but it is much more than that. With its alien landscape full of 'crumbled arches' (Lethem, 1998a: 48) reminiscent of Monument Valley, and its malevolent loner in the mould of John Wayne, the novel also functions as a kind of fan fiction, a homage to John Ford's *The Searchers* (1956). This is a movie Lethem claims to have spent most of his life defending against critics, one he describes as 'everywhere shrugging off categories, refusing the petitions of embarrassment and taste, defying explanation or defense as only great art or great abomination ever could' (Lethem, 2005: 14). *Girl in Landscape*, so deliberately modelled on and in defence of Ford's film, thereby provides a good example of the way Lethem's writing participates in its own constellated communities of genre consumers. Moreover, the decision to combine science fiction with the coming-of-age novel, equally characterised by alienation and estrangement, as well as the western frontier narrative and regionalist novel, themselves concerned with encounters with otherness, makes *Girl in Landscape,* though remarkably restrained and coherent in terms of prose, mood and length, the most excessive of Lethem's novels in terms of the specific ways it combines genres and symbols as a complex compensation for loss.

It shares with *As She Climbed Across the Table,* however, a fundamental concern with the inescapability of language as a symbolic system doomed to over-determination and imprecision. As Pella's mother informs her children from her hospital bed, the Archbuilders, each of whom speaks hundreds of languages, find English quaint and amusing precisely because its vocabulary is so narrow and each word therefore so hopelessly overburdened with potential meaning: 'Archbuilders describe English as a language of enchanting limitations. The English vocabulary is tens of thousands of words smaller than any language native to their planet. English words seem, to an Archbuilder, garishly overloaded with meaning. One Archbuilder describes speaking English as 'stringing poems into sentences', another compares it to 'speaking hieroglyphs' (Lethem, 1998a: 32). Lack was difficult enough to describe with these imperfect tools: for the teenage protagonist of *Girl in Landscape* and for its author, the inadequacy of language provokes a conscious desire to create visual symbols equal to the task of articulating loss and honouring the memory of those lost. That these also frequently fail is both the tragedy and the success of a novel dedicated to interrogating processes of reading and symbolisation.

The first three chapters are set in Brooklyn. For Lethem, these chapters represent a sort of homecoming and pave the way for his subsequent Brooklyn fictions: 'For years, I was overwhelmed by Brooklyn ... The richness of my own upbringing was too much for me to contend with, either in my life or my writing, and so I was in a kind of flirtation. When you see me going back in the first couple of chapters of *Girl in Landscape,* you're seeing me daring myself to open that box and really let it come' (Zeitchik, 2003: 37). Yet this is not a straightforward autobiographical Brooklyn. First, when one considers that the younger brothers, Raymond and Dave, share their names with Edie's sons in *Amnesia Moon*, it becomes apparent that this Brooklyn is to some extent intertextual. On the one hand, Lethem updates the idiosyncratic family unit which ends his second novel into something much more conventional in his fourth. On the other hand, the decision to allude so directly to his fiction keeps things partially within the realm of fictionality, and thus is another technique for hiding in plain sight.

Secondly, Lethem distances his Brooklyn from the real thing by making his a dystopian, sci-fi version of the borough.[1] As the Marsh family embark on one last outing to the beach before their emigration to the mysterious Planet of the Archbuilders, they travel on a computerised subway system that literally lifts them out of their basement and fastens them to the driverless train (Lethem, 1998a: 6). When they arrive at their destination, where 'the blackened armatures of the abandoned amusement park' introduce a dystopian, futuristic Coney Island (Lethem, 1998a: 9), they don protective 'cones' and 'headpieces' to protect them from the sun's rays on the beach (Lethem, 1998a: 8). This is the horror of Pella's Brooklyn: global warming has reached its logical conclusion and the sun is now 'the enemy: horrible, impossible, unseeable' (Lethem, 1998a: 9). And at the beach Pella becomes fixated by the three scars on her mother's arm 'where cancers had been taken off' (Lethem, 1998a: 13). These scars are material signifiers of the sun's power to harm which serve both as reminders of the past and as premonitions of future traumas.

Environmental catastrophe provides a familiar backdrop to science fiction narratives, but here the blasted skies and the 'unseeable' sun also presage the horror Pella feels at having to witness the rapid deterioration of her mother, Caitlin, after she collapses suddenly in the shower and is diagnosed with a brain tumour (Lethem, 1998a: 22). From the moment she first sees Caitlin lying unconscious in the water, it is evident that in a novel full of powerful symbols Pella is the character most predisposed to read her world symbolically and in ways which multiply figurative connections between things. In an image that conflates Caitlin's importance to her daughter, the loss of the sun as a warming and protecting entity, and Pella's anxieties about their imminent emigration, the mother's naked body is described as 'terribly big, a kind of world itself, a thing with horizons, places where Pella's gaze could founder, be lost' (Lethem, 1998a: 23). The link between the maternal body and the landscape is made manifest, as we shall see, in the melancholic topography of the Archbuilders' planet.

Pella's tendency to employ metaphor and symbol is first revealed at the end of the Coney Island visit, just after her brother Raymond discovers the body of a suicide victim lying on the rocks (Lethem, 1998a: 18). Her reflections on the incident again telegraph the fall of her mother and the haunting description of the alien planet's architectural ruins: 'Pella felt only she knew it was a warning: dare to go out under the sky, dare to enter the sky, and trouble will touch you. Your tunnels will collapse. A body will fall' (Lethem, 1998a: 20). But the image of the fallen man also evokes Pella's father, Clement, who remains significantly absent from the action until after Caitlin's collapse. One of the reasons for the Marsh's emigration is Clement's recent election defeat, a loss of political status attributed first to civilian deaths in subway tunnel collapses (Lethem, 1998a: 13) and secondly to the 'lemming thing' (Lethem, 1998a: 15), mass suicides brought about by the environmental disasters. Thus the body on the rocks inspires for Pella (and for the reader) a symbolic cathexis: materially connected to the failings of Clement's political party, it is also a material symbol of the father himself as he falls from grace as a public figure and, in Pella's eyes, as an authority figure within the family. In both contexts he has lost his constituency – his public and his children – and it is telling that after taking Caitlin to the hospital he seems 'to grasp for the first time their presence in this episode in his life' (Lethem, 1998a: 29). In fact, Pella feels a perverse 'satisfaction' at Clement's shock when he eventually comes home. She thinks: 'You carry her. You be here in the first place' (Lethem, 1998a: 26).

The fact that the fallen body also predicts the mother's death confirms the excessive nature of symbolic identification and, by association, the complex negotiations of parental identification so central to the coming-of-age process. Providing a surplus of meaning and connections, as well as remaining irreducibly other, the body hints at the lessons Pella and the reader will have to learn when confronted by the alterity of the Archbuilders.[2] When Caitlin dies after unsuccessful cancer surgery, Pella explicitly ties the symbolic identifications of the first three chapters together: 'It would forever be linked for Pella to the collapse of the subway. The tunneling devices that had hollowed out too much of the city's bedrock, the failed surgical incision that had destroyed Caitlin, taken too much of her with her tumor,

left her half-paralyzed and inarticulate and dying anyway. Hollowed'
(Lethem, 1998a: 37–8). The hollowing of the maternal body is echoed
in the emptiness of loss experienced by Pella and her family and it, in
turn, is made into symbol in the final lines of part one as they travel
through space in suspended animation: 'It was as though Clement
had replaced Caitlin with the ship. As though they had tunneled inside her departing body for comfort and escape. Then hurtled with it
into the void' (Lethem, 1998a: 39).

There is a layered complexity to this image to match anything found
in *As She Climbed Across the Table*. A meaningful confusion of inside
and outside (something else this novel shares with its predecessor)
originates from an attempt to externalise a mourning process which
nonetheless also remains stubbornly in the internal psychological
realm. The occupants of the spacecraft are simultaneously inside and
outside Caitlin's body. Clement's replacement of his wife's body with
the ship heralds the start of his attempts to reassert authority within
the family, but it is by no means an unambiguous process. For if the
ship assumes a symbolic status as the hollowed-out maternal body, so
surely does the void into which they fly. Any 'escape' enabled by their
emigration founders on this doubling: they are escaping the material, somatic reality of loss into various symbolic re-imaginings of the
body.

So clearly, the evacuation of Caitlin's body betokens loss but simultaneously clears a space within which symbol and metaphor can be
planted in order to begin the mourning process in the second part
of the novel. To the extent that Part 2 can be regarded as a power
struggle between competing elements at a new frontier, it is useful
to consider Eric Cheyfitz's notion of 'power in terms of eloquence'
(Cheyfitz, 1991: 23) – that is, the ability to plant metaphors and symbols so that they take root and become dominant – as a description of
what takes place on the Planet of the Archbuilders (like the FSRs of
Amnesia Moon). Pella, her father and Efram Nugent vie, in the face of
the unutterable strangeness of the alien landscape and its organisms,
to express, and in some cases impose, their symbolic readings of the
new world in relation to worlds left behind.

With this in mind, one might argue that rather than simply moving there, Pella produces the Planet of the Archbuilders as the symbolic manifestation of her loss. There are numerous candidates for
the novum here: the planet itself, with its melancholic yet elegant ruins; its native viruses (exposure to which allows settlers to inhabit the

household deer that roam almost unnoticed across the landscape); and
the Archbuilders themselves, the remaining, unambitious members
of a once impressively sophisticated race, with their strange, frond-
like hair and their penchant for curiously poetic names like 'Hiding
Kneel' (Lethem, 1998a: 61). Yet the most disorienting novum of all
is Caitlin's death, and all the other outlandish science fiction compo-
nents are in the service of that loss, there to be read as symbolic correspondences. Central to Pella's coming-of-age process, as we shall see,
are her increasingly sophisticated readings of this landscape, readings
which refuse to dissolve into personalised myth-symbol complexes
but are able to entertain and acknowledge the ineluctable difference
embodied by the aliens.

So strong are the correspondences between the Brooklyn of part
one and the landscape of Part 2 that it is tempting to see a kind of
biblical typography at work. In part one, Pella comes to understand
the personal, elegiac quality of their trip to the coast: 'This trip was
on Clement's behalf. Caitlin was saying goodbye to her own Coney
Island' (Lethem, 1998a: 14). Part 2 is equally concerned with place
and memory: Pella here says goodbye, though she is millions of miles
away, to her own Brooklyn. For Lethem, as for Pella, Brooklyn is inextricably connected to the loss of the mother. However, Lethem's
technique here – part of his bid to hide in plain sight – is to relocate
and re-imagine the maternal Brooklyn in the Planet of the Archbuilders, a surreal landscape littered with ancient ruins from former Archbuilder civilizations. As fragmented as the Brooklyn left behind, this
is a 'landscape of remembrance' (Lethem, 1998a: 49) not just because
the ruins are testimony to the ambitious creativity of previous gen-
erations, but also because Pella envisages it as a maternal landscape:
'Her voice hung over this landscape ... Caitlin had left but was still
here' (Lethem, 1998a: 48–9). The proceeding analysis of Part 2, 'The
Planet of the Archbuilders', in which Pella, her brothers, and the children of the Grant and Kincaid families attempt to carve out a new life
away from Earth, links the transposed, fragmented Brooklyn of Pella's mourning consciousness to the ethics of reading alluded to at the
start of the chapter. This link is most apparent in the novel's status as
a highly unusual kind of regionalist text.

As Carl Abbott (2005) observes, *Girl in Landscape* is a homesteading novel which uses archetypal frontier narratives and generic conventions – the inhospitable wilderness landscape 'on the edge of
nothing' (Lethem, 1998a: 63); the charismatic and malevolent loner,

here called Efram in homage to John Ford's Ethan in *The Searchers*; the trading post, here the pitifully stocked shop owned by E. G. Wa (Lethem, 1998a: 53) – to dramatise concerns about a society's future. More specifically, it deals with the evolution of community through the settlement of disparate individuals. What distinguishes it from more traditional frontier narratives, however, is not simply the sci-fi inflection, but the way in which the alien landscape speaks simultaneously of the mourned past and of the optative future, as well as linking personal and collective concerns.

For Pella, the development of the new community is co-terminous with the traditional elements of the coming-of-age narrative (in particular rebellion against paternal authority), and with her personal project to externalise the mourning of her mother in the landscape. These symbolic connections are confirmed by her culminating verbal rejection:

> 'He's nothing without my mother.' The words snuck out of her like a thread between her lips, a betraying filament that stretched back to Brooklyn. (Lethem, 1998a: 240)

Here the symbolic linking of her former home and the alien landscape is explicitly acknowledged. Pella's aim is evidently to become 'a feature of the landscape' she associates with Caitlin (Lethem, 1998a: 173), but this does not imply a method of retreat from the reality of her suffering. Rather, it signals her awareness of what the landscape represents: a chance to reassemble the scattered fragments of memory in the establishment of a new community. The town of 'Caitlin' founded at the novel's close is her maternal Brooklyn re-imagined, the culmination of the mourning process (Lethem, 1998a: 279).

After Benedict Anderson, of course, it is impossible to forget that any community grouping is to a significant extent always involved in a process of re-imagining, and the imagined 'constellated community' of genre consumers has been central to this study. Though Pella's re-invention of Brooklyn in space is a radical one, she is by no means the only protagonist of contemporary Brooklyn novels actively to engage in such re-invention. What characterises many of these fictions, however, is a tendency to go too far. As Elizabeth Gumport has persuasively argued, there is a desire in recent fictions to romanticise Brooklyn as a pocket of small-town community values and bohemian tastefulness while eliding the issues of politics and economics underlying these depictions. Though there are more extensive comments on this theme in Chapters 5 and 6, where it is particularly relevant to *Motherless Brooklyn* and *The Fortress of Solitude*, it is nonetheless worth noting at this stage that in novels such as Kitty Burns Florey's *Solos* (2004) there are two related approaches to Brooklyn's romanticisation, both of which have some relevance to the translocation of the borough in Lethem's first Brooklyn novel. One is the fetishisation of what Gumport calls 'the only legitimate past' (Gumport, 2009), a personal history marked in, say, *Fortress* by an obsession with making the 'right' cultural decisions, with authenticity, and with a rejection of the acquisitive values associated with gentrification, and in *Girl in Landscape* by the elevation of the mother's memory. All elements outside the idealised vision of one's childhood are jettisoned. In Gumport's words, which summon yet again the problem of amnesia: 'we forget the past when it suits us; we obliterate whatever it is that most tarnishes our vision of our selves' (Gumport, 2009). The other, concomitant approach is the fetishisation of signs and symbols – in *Solos'* case the shop signs in Polish connoting Williamsburg's diversity, so prized by its middle-class, arty settlers, and in the case of *Girl in Landscape* the broken land which comes to symbolise rupture, memory and grief.

In thus reading the alien landscape symbolically as her maternal Brooklyn, Pella might appear to romanticise the place and fabricate a myth-symbol complex every bit as incorporative and solipsistic as the protagonists' in sentimental Brooklyn novels such as *Solos* and Paul Auster's *The Brooklyn Follies* (2005), yet there is a fundamental, redeeming difference. Whereas the nostalgia for the present that characterises many contemporary Brooklyn fictions requires, in fact, a denial of difference and of what came before (thus locating it in a mythic tradition which includes Thomas Cole's 'Essay on American Scenery' and Frederick Jackson Turner's frontier thesis), Pella recognises the importance of the indigenous inhabitants, the Archbuilders, in the development of the new community. In an obvious allegory of the encounter with Native Americans in *The Searchers*, *Girl in Landscape* envisages the new Brooklyn as a process of continual meetings with absolute otherness. Lethem visualises this as a transgression of the boundaries of the self, and employs one of his science fiction nova – the household deer, into which Pella is transported as a result of her family's refusal to take the anti-viral drugs (Lethem, 1998a: 77) – as a concretised metaphor for this transgression. Although Pella eventually stops having these out-of-body experiences, the opportunity they afford for her to 'cross the line' is essential to her coming-of-age: not only do they allow her to witness several key clandestine events, they also force her to experience and accept the otherness which is integral to true community. Entering the household deer, changing form in this manner, should therefore be seen as analogous to the blurring of boundaries between genres and subcultures enacted throughout Lethem's work.

When Pella first meets an Archbuilder, she feels shock and fascination both emotionally and somatically, much as she experiences being a household deer: 'The girl felt the sight of the Archbuilder move through her, a physical thing' (Lethem, 1998a: 62). Despite the fact that in one sense the alien is 'nothing, a joke, a tatter, too absurd to glance at twice', it nonetheless 'burn[s] a hole in the world, change[s] it utterly' (Lethem, 1998a: 62). This is partly because Pella, unlike many other settlers on the planet, feels her look reciprocated by the other creature (as revealed in the ambiguity of the phrase 'the sight of the Archbuilder'). In this meeting of gazes she realises something crucial: the Archbuilders are not merely curiosities or inconveniences for the settlers, and neither are they the planet's past, to be supplanted by the arrival of humankind; they are an essential part of the planet's living history: 'The place wasn't rubble everywhere. Somewhere there were more Archbuilders. The rubble and what grew in the rubble belonged to them. The girl felt her body understand' (Lethem, 1998a: 62). Again, symbolic resonances from Part 1 are felt in this encounter: the sight of the Archbuilder moves through Pella, as if the teenager's body, like her mother's, is being hollowed out to make room for new significances and new understandings. So for Pella to become a 'feature of the landscape' and thereby complete her mourning for Caitlin, she must embrace the Archbuilders' place in that landscape and accept them as part of the mourning process and, indeed, as a part of her that she can never hope fully to understand.

She faces stiff competition in the form of Efram Nugent. Spoken about before his first appearance with a mixture of awe and fear, and known initially to the Marsh children only as a set of rigid preferences (Lethem, 1998a: 72), Efram, as the original settler, already seems to have achieved integration with the landscape (just as Ethan is consistently framed against Monument Valley's outcrops in *The Searchers*). When Pella first spots him, 'a silhouette against the pink' of the sky, he is 'almost like another of the broken arches on the horizon' (Lethem, 1998a: 80): his crooked smile, when he flashes it, is described as 'carved in rock' (Lethem, 1998a: 81). And his farm, unlike the other settlements that '[cling] to the floor of the valley like shells on a beach', seems to have 'carved out a portion of the planet' (Lethem, 1998a: 98). Indeed, such are Efram's charisma and monumentality that Pella senses immediately that she might be inclined to attribute too much power and importance to him: 'It seemed mistakes of scale were possible in this alien landscape ... Efram Nugent could seem too big, out here. She wanted him adjusted, made smaller' (Lethem, 1998a: 81).

Efram's granite masculinity provides a foil to Clement's liberal, political, accommodating version, and Pella's denunciation of paternal authority is balanced with the necessity of also making Efram 'smaller'. This is not simply a question of overcoming her sexual attraction to him, but of coming to understand that his view of life on the planet is antiquated, too monolithic, too driven by frontier metaphors of separation and irreconcilable difference. ('Not everybody turns out to like breaking new ground', he observes (Lethem, 1998a: 106).) Although he speaks Archbuilder languages (Lethem, 1998a: 151) and has reconstructed an Archbuilder interior in his main room (Lethem, 1998a: 175), Efram's opinion of the remaining indigenous population is entirely negative. Regarding them as passive 'fools' (Lethem, 1998a: 106) who have let the glories of former civilizations collapse, and as 'sexual deviants' (Lethem, 1998a: 180) who fail to make distinctions between children and adults (Lethem, 1998a: 150), Efram advocates a separatist approach to community-building in the valley. As he explains to Clement: 'I think we ought to draw a line around this town we're starting here, Marsh. Make it a *human* settlement, a place where kids are safe' (Lethem, 1998a: 114). These opinions lead directly to the nightmare of accusation and retribution which ensues after Truth Renowned and the artist Hugh Merrow are discovered to be having a relationship (Lethem, 1998a: 122). First Efram kidnaps Truth Renowned (Lethem, 1998a: 141), then Merrow's house is burnt down (Lethem, 1998a: 208) and eventually Efram is shot dead by Doug Grant after Pella, in a desperate bid to nullify Efram's threat, forces Morris Grant to accuse him of raping her (Lethem, 1998a: 273).

At heart, Efram's sentiments imply an elevation and circumscription of the 'legitimate past' described by Elizabeth Gumport, a separation from the present that precludes progress in its denial of continuities. In glorifying the departed ancestors of the Archbuilders, Efram refuses to acknowledge the reality and the importance of those that remain; appropriately, it is the Archbuilder Hiding Kneel who is perspicacious enough to remind Pella just how close her hagiography of Caitlin comes to Efram's attitude:

> 'So you too are concerned with the superiority of your lost ancestors', said Hiding Kneel. ...
> 'Caitlin isn't my ancestor', said Pella. 'She's my mother.'
> 'Yet you speak of her as legendary, like my departed fore-cousins', said Hiding Kneel. (Lethem, 1998a: 240)

Efram is inclined to talk in tired tropes of legendary frontier heroism: while criticising the current Archbuilders for 'picking through their own memories of greatness' (Lethem, 1998a: 180), he succumbs to the same romanticisation of the past when he refers to 'the real frontier' of the stars to which the former Archbuilders emigrated (Lethem, 1998a: 180). His metaphors are all about division, exclusion and opposition, rather than community.

Most damaging of all is Efram's insistence on privileged knowledge, based on his status as the first human pioneer. In response to Clement's earnest ambitions to '[w]ork together with the Archbuilders', to 'come to a real understanding of their culture and biology' (Lethem, 1998a: 218), Efram disparagingly says, '[b]e more specific, Mr. Marsh ... Some of us have a good understanding of the Archbuilders' (Lethem, 1998a: 219). Precisely this misplaced confidence in his knowledge inspires Efram to impose his personal brand of frontier metaphor on the nascent community. Pella comes to realise, soon after Hiding Kneel has warned her of her fixation on the past, just what an impediment to the formation of a working society Efram's presence has been: 'There is no town, thought Pella. There never was one. There had always only been Efram and whatever he wanted. A frontier, a prison, a fire' (Lethem, 1998a: 257). His vision is here reduced to a list of generic elements, all of which connote separation and destruction.

In one sense, then, the founding of 'Caitlin' represents not only the culmination of Pella's mourning process, but also her victory over Efram in the battle to metaphorise the landscape. However, what distinguishes Pella's view from Efram's is her acceptance that nobody can know 'the whole truth' about Archbuilders (Lethem, 1998a: 66). Hers is a material metaphor of inclusion, one which recognises that which remains irreducibly different and aspires to meet with it as best it can. Rather than explaining, rationalising and thus dismissing the Archbuilders like Efram, Pella accepts that the new community is founded on negotiations, on alterity, compromises and uncertainties. It is only through this acceptance that the past and the present (and therefore a possible future) can be reconciled and the mourning process completed for her. Pella ultimately distinguishes herself ethically, and truly comes of age, when she realises how important perceptions of the Archbuilders are:

> None of what happened was really about Archbuilders, Pella decided ... It was still all about the humans, what they saw when they looked at the Archbuilders ... Maybe now they would meet them. Maybe the Archbuilders would buy the bread. (Lethem, 1998a: 279)

Breaking free of an essentially solipsistic gaze frees settlers from a colonial or parochial mentality and allows them literally to transcend worlds in pursuit of a viable regional community.

This is why *Girl in Landscape*, for Lethem's purposes, has to be set on another planet, whatever the gatekeepers of the literary establishment might think. Not only does the Archbuilders' landscape perfectly capture how the death of a loved one renders the entire world, and any other worlds that might exist, utterly strange, utterly fragmented, and forever incomplete, it is also the perfect location for the cultural, ethical and generic complexities of Lethem's distinctive regionalist vision (and arguably a more successful one than the 'real' Brooklyn of the next two novels).

Bracketing off Lethem's own assertion that when it comes to Brooklyn he is 'a regional writer, testifying about a place I'm helpless not to think of, to dream of' (Birnbaum, 2005), it is important to consider the respects in which one might legitimately call this a regionalist fiction. Generically, it shares many features with classic American regionalist texts which, according to critics such as Amy Kaplan (1988) and Richard Brodhead (1993), served a reconciliatory function after the Civil War through the portrayal of 'a certain story of contemporary cultures and of the relations among them' (Brodhead, 1993: 121). Rather than describing in meticulous detail the distinctive and exotic dialects, topography and customs of a specific region in order to annex that region from the changing realities of the contemporary world, regionalist narratives – as opposed to local colour stories, often more inclined to indulge in caricature, sentimentality and nostalgia – stage encounters between urban visitor-observers (like the Marsh family) and local inhabitants (Archbuilders) with a look to exploring possibilities for new understandings across regional boundaries and thus for new communities. For Tom Lutz, the reader is placed in a privileged position to observe and assess these encounters: 'Regionalist texts represent the arguments alive in the culture about city and country, nature and culture, center and periphery, tradition and modernity, high and low, masculinity and femininity, the costs and benefits of progress, and any number of other issues; but instead of resolving these debates, they oscillate between the sides, producing, finally, a complex symphony of cultural voices and positions whose only resolution lies in the reader-writer compact to survey the fullness of the scene' (Lutz, 2004: 31). Indeed, for a regionalist text even to be designated 'literary', according to Lutz, it must hold in precarious balance both 'local and larger perspectives'; for a text to come down emphatically on the side of local colour is simply 'to absolve its readers emotionally of accepting the very invitations to openness the form affords' (Lutz, 2004: 192). Thus '[r]egionalist literary texts represent both sides of the major cultural debates of their time' and 'dramatize the differences between and within classes, regions, sexes, and communities, but not with the intention of resolving them' (Lutz, 2004: 28). It is the reader who, in a position to assess 'the fullness of the scene', is expected to embrace the essentially dialectical nature of the genre.

Though he stops short of arguing that regionalist texts can function as allegories of reading practices, the importance Lutz ascribes to the reader frequently becomes a diegetic element of unsentimental Brooklyn regionalist texts such as Lynne Sharon Schwartz's *Leaving Brooklyn* (1990) and *Girl in Landscape*. The former employs the deep metaphor of the protagonist's dysfunctional right eye (one borrowed by *Chronic City*) to deconstruct the elisions and prejudices necessary to sustain an atavistic, down-home myth of Brooklyn as safe haven from the world's tragedies. In learning to balance the disparate views of her two eyes, the protagonist learns to read Brooklyn, as a real and an imagined place, in something like the dialectical way Lutz advocates.

Like *Leaving Brooklyn*, *Girl in Landscape* combines a regionalist sensibility with an intense self-consciousness about reading place as a model for how one reads texts. Yet entering the landscapes of *Girl in Landscape* as a reader is by no means a comforting experience. Indeed, Pella's isolation throughout the novel stems largely from the epistemological and ethical supplement she is afforded as the most perceptive reader of events. It is she who has the 'lonely knowledge' that the whole truth is never available (Lethem, 1998a: 66), but at the same time she witnesses, during her series of virus-induced out-of-body experiences, a number of secrets. These include her father's affair with the biologist, Diana Eastling (Lethem, 1998a: 166) and Hugh Merrow's sexual relationship with the Archbuilder (Lethem, 1998a: 121–3). In bearing witness to these events '[i]t was Pella who was most alone in the end, knowing all she knew' (Lethem, 1998a: 169). Yet her transition from adolescence to adulthood combines awareness that reading is partly the uncovering of secrets with an understanding that, in the end, the textual landscape will always retain a certain 'clandestinity' amenable to ethical reading (Newton, 1995: 246). That is, any attempt fully to 'know', or to take in 'the fullness of the scene', becomes an incorporative and willfully amnesiac strategy like Efram Nugent's.

Crucial to this understanding, yet again, are the Archbuilders: their irreducible difference refuses incorporation. The ethical challenge they issue is symbolided by the figure of the arch itself: reading is an individual or solitary act, but to enter the landscape of 'crumbled arches ... [f]allen bridges, incomplete towers, demolished pillars' (Lethem, 1998a: 48) constitutes an ethical conjunction to 'explore the boundaries' (Lethem, 1998a: 125), to become a member of a wider community founded on true difference, not superficial diversity. An arch, after all, is something with the potential to connect. The Archbuilders are the embodiment of 'hiding in plain sight', offering a bold and challenging reality, inviting interaction, but remaining secret and unknowable. They exemplify the excess, the surplus of meaning typical not just of science fiction but, ultimately, of all encounters with others. In the specific context of mourning and memory Lethem constructs in this novel, they demonstrate that hiding in plain sight is not simply avoidance of the issue by resorting to symbol, metaphor and the excessive exotic minutiae of science fiction, but is the necessary acceptance that incomprehensible elements will always pose challenges to one's narrow view of the world (or worlds).

As has been suggested, Pella's success, and the novel's, lies in taking the process of private mourning – for Caitlin, for the Brooklyn left behind, and for the author's own mother – and in forging a community from it in the foundation of 'Caitlin'. Distinct from the prelapsarian cravings of nostalgia, such mourning is the recognition of the inseparability of past experience from the communal present and future. Most importantly, it lies at the heart of all reading. Every reading experience combines remembrance of stories which have passed with a series of encounters, negotiations and inventions of new relationships. With this in mind, I would argue that in the end *Girl in Landscape* is an especially powerful novel because, contrary to Tom Lutz's assertion, it deliberately disallows protagonists and readers privileged access to 'the fullness of the scene'. If 'Caitlin' is a community which requires the Archbuilders in order to function successfully, then it provides a useful parallel to the constellated communities formed when readers encounter genre texts. As Adena Rosmarin explains, 'each critical reading interprets both the text read and ... its "interpretive history", the communal text composed of previous readings' (Rosmarin, 1985: 20). In other words, it is doubtful that the 'scene' will ever be complete, given that any text can theoretically be read an infinite number of times, but what is certain is that the individual needs others to at least try and complete it, and that the resultant community is an endless series of what Martin Buber calls 'relational incident[s]' (Buber, 2004: 46). This is as true for texts as it is for places.

Clearly, Lethem sees the real Brooklyn in similar terms to the Archbuilders' landscape, which is why he 'crosses the line' into territory both familiar and alien in this novel:

> It's a place where the renovations that are so characteristic of American life never quite work. It's a place where the past and memory are lying around in chunks even after they've been displaced. (Zeitchik, 2003: 37)

Viewed in this way, it is very much a 'broken land' of mourning.[3] But Lethem's decision to take Brooklyn into space is laudable because his 'hiding in plain sight' deliberately unpacks the ethical implications of the reading process – the inevitable and necessary incompleteness of the reader's vision, and the need to acknowledge others' help in navigating the strangeness and, perhaps, enjoying the temporary transgressions offered by the text. Pella's translocated maternal Brooklyn is not an atavistic utopia, but rather a regional space representative of what readers do: the bringing of internalised fragments of memory and experience to bear on the ethical encounter with the alien (yet strangely familiar) landscapes of the text. *Girl in Landscape* is a novel less about amnesia than remembering, but it is also able to achieve a balance between looking back and looking forward. The chapters that follow investigate whether Lethem's two most famous novels, both of which are more immersed in the minute details of his Brooklyn childhood and adolescence, manage to do the same.

Notes

1   In an essay on Philip K. Dick, Lethem explicitly links Brooklyn – a marginalised space in relation to Manhattan – with science fiction – a marginalised genre in relation to mainstream fiction: 'Science fiction was a literary Brooklyn for me' (Lethem, 2009c: 5). Both enable him to carry out his literary plans almost unnoticed.

2   The corpse, Julia Kristeva argues, is a category-defying object. As 'the utmost of abjection' it represents 'the breaking down of a world that has erased its borders'. It is that which 'disturbs identity, system, order. What does not respect borders, positions, rules. The in-between, the ambiguous, the composite' (Kristeva, 1982: 4).

3   Brooklyn's name derives from the original Dutch settlement Breukelen, meaning 'broken land'.

5

'We learned to tell our story walking': Tourette's and urban space in *Motherless Brooklyn*

In interview, Jonathan Lethem has repeatedly evoked the idea of 'dreaming his way back' to the borough of his birth. His tendency to divide his time between Brooklyn and other places such as Toronto or Maine he explains like this: 'Dreaming my way back to Brooklyn seems to be a necessary part of loving it for me – continuing to also love it from afar' (Birnbaum, 2004). Elsewhere, in 'Patchwork Planet: Notes for a Prehistory of the Gentrification of Gowanus', he remarks: 'In the neighborhood of Gowanus, Boerum Hill, I'm forever a child' (www.jonathanlethem.com). It is true that Lethem's three 'Brooklynite' novels – *Girl in Landscape*, *Motherless Brooklyn* and *The Fortress of Solitude* – are also the most obviously preoccupied with filial relationships and parental loss. Yet it is also true that the two novels planting themselves most firmly and insistently in the 'real' Brooklyn run a greater risk of succumbing to a melancholic denial of loss, a fossilisation and fetishisation of childhood experience than *Girl in Landscape*, which, by transplanting Brooklyn to the Planet of the Archbuilders and reconceiving it as 'Caitlin' is able, we have seen, more successfully to complete the mourning process, to 'work through' trauma (La Capra, 2001: 70). Thus Pella Marsh simultaneously 'dreams her way back' to Brooklyn and moves on. This chapter and the next explore the ways *Fortress* and its predecessor problematise and retard the process of moving on by continually 'acting out' the losses of childhood (LaCapra, 2001: 46).

Motherless Brooklyn (1999), winner of the National Book Critics Circle Award, the Macallan Gold Dagger and the Salon Book Award, has thus far attracted considerably more critical attention than Jonathan Lethem's other work except *Fortress*. It is a hard-boiled detective novel. This simple statement becomes remarkable when one considers the novels that preceded it, all of which brought multiple genres rudely into collision. Conrad Metcalf, first-person narrator of *Gun, With Occasional Music*, struggles to maintain the ethical imperatives of detective fiction while dystopian science fiction takes over his world. His everyday realities include talking animals, amnesia-inducing narcotics and smoking babies rather than the minutiae of 'real' neighbourhood life – street names, sandwich shops and burger joints – which lend *Motherless Brooklyn* an aura of authenticity.

On the one hand, the decision to adhere, at least diegetically, to the conventions of a popular genre traditionally associated with powerful evocations of place (one thinks of Chandler's Los Angeles, Rankin's Edinburgh, Montalban's Barcelona) is understandable in that it is sympathetic to Lethem's desire to unearth a Brooklyn with which he is familiar from his childhood. But if his fifth novel does not employ genre fantastically or excessively, in the specific sense glossed in Chapter 4, it nonetheless tends toward excess in one significant aspect: the idiolect of its narrator protagonist. Chief among the novel's attractions, according to critics and scholars, is a first-person narrative voice which can be described, at the very least, as distinctive. Only ostensibly a hard-boiled detective novel, *Motherless Brooklyn* is in fact a kaleidoscopic, picaresque journey into the 'dense thicket' of Tourette's Syndrome sufferer Lionel Essrog's mind, 'a place where words split and twine in an ever-deepening tangle' (Mobilio, 1999: 7). Adam Begley, writing in *The New York Observer*, borrows a term of affectionate abuse frequently directed at Lionel by other characters to describe him more succinctly: 'Lionel is a freakshow', he says (Begley, 1999: 15).

Linda Fleissner correctly argues that the reader's attention to generic narrative elements is overridden by the novel's linguistic joys: 'one tends to forget the supposed "main narrative" of *Motherless Brooklyn* in the intervals between rereading. Who killed Minna again? Why did they do it? These puzzles are generic ones; the text achieves its distinctiveness, by contrast, in its proliferation of Lionel's verbal tics' (Fleissner, 2009: 390). Certainly a plot synopsis offers scant indication of the novel's dazzling originality and ingenuity: Lionel Essrog is an orphan who at thirteen is rescued from St Vincent's Home for Boys, along with three other orphans, and taken on by Frank Minna, a small-time neighbourhood crook whom the boys come to idolise as a walking embodiment of old Brooklyn and as a surrogate father figure. At first, Minna urges them to regard their mysterious tasks euphemistically as 'moving work' (Lethem, 1999: 50); they are, of course, unloading stolen goods. By their thirties Lionel, Tony, Gilbert and Danny, collectively known as 'Minna Men', are running a detective agency disguised as a car service. The action begins when Lionel and Gilbert, trailing Minna in Manhattan, fail to prevent his murder and a devastated Lionel immediately sets out to find the killer. His investigations force him to engage with the wider world outside his familiar territory of Court Street, Brooklyn; they bring about confrontations with the other Minna Men, especially Tony Vermonte, as well as minatory encounters with Frank's brother Gerard Minna; two ageing Italian crime lords called Matricardi and Rockaforte; a Buddhist Zendo on the Upper East Side; and the unimaginably rich and malevolent Fujisaki corporation. Significantly, these disparate threads are pulled together not in Brooklyn, but on the Atlantic coast of Maine, where the local fishermen are employed by Fujisaki to catch sea urchins for Japanese dining tables (Lethem, 1999: 269). We later learn that Frank Minna was murdered by the Japanese businessmen's giant enforcer because he and his brother were siphoning money away from Fujisaki.

So tragic loss forces Lionel to become a proper detective, a situation he approaches with a mixture of excitement, fear and disbelief: 'It seemed possible I was a detective on a case' (Lethem, 1999: 132). And at first glance, the eruptive language and compulsive physical behaviours generated by his syndrome would seem to render Lionel laughably unsuited to undercover detective work, and thus render the novel more of a loving deconstruction of detective conventions than a traditional treatment of the genre. After all, it is difficult to perform a discreet stake-out in a parked car or to menace someone into giving up vital information when one is likely to blurt out *'ghostradish, pepperpony, kaiserphone'* at any moment (Lethem, 1999: 244) or to experience an uncontrollable urge to tap each of one's interlocutor's shoulders precisely six times. To some extent, this impression of Lionel's unsuitability for the job and the novel's deconstructive approach is justified and is confirmed by the interpolated passages of generic reflexivity in which Lionel considers what is permissible or expected in detective narratives: 'Have you ever felt, in the course of reading a detective novel, a guilty thrill of relief at having a character murdered before he can step onto the page and burden you with his actual existence?' (Lethem, 1999: 119). Such generalising moments, as becomes clear, participate in a debate central to the novel, between

generic representativeness and uniqueness, between wide-reaching
metaphorical applications of conditions such as Tourette's and individual lived experience of those conditions.

Yet one of the pleasures of the story is the revelation that Tourette's
is, in fact, perfectly suited to detective work. Lionel is actually very
useful during stakeouts, 'since my compulsiveness forced me to eye-
ball the site or mark in question every thirty seconds or so' (Lethem,
1999: 4). Similarly, the exigencies of his condition make him a dili-
gent and talented listener to wiretaps: 'give me a key list of trigger
words to listen for in a conversation and I'd think about nothing else,
nearly jumping out of my clothes at the slightest hint of one, while the
same task invariably drew anyone else toward blissful sleep' (Lethem,
1999: 4).

These are practical applications, but there are deeper reasons for Lionel's ability to work undercover. First, there is the plain fact that most
people are unaware of the condition and therefore routinely dismiss
the Tourette's sufferer as 'crazy' (Lethem, 1999: 107). Holding such a
view, it is impossible to credit the Touretter with shrewd intelligence
or guile or to consider him or her a genuine threat. As Lionel observes
when reflecting on his high school years: 'I wasn't tough, provocative,
stylish, self-destructive, sexy, wasn't babbling some secret countercultural tongue, wasn't testing authority ... I was merely crazy' (Lethem,
1999: 84). Secondly, and relatedly, there is the general public's unfail-
ing ability to dismiss and forget elements in its midst which are momentarily disruptive or simply different. Recalling another Touretter
with a massive 'belching tic' (Lethem, 1999: 43) sitting on a busy bus,
Lionel says: 'I knew that those other passengers would barely recall it
a few minutes after stepping off to their destinations ... Consensual
reality is both fragile and elastic, and it heals like the skin of a bubble.
The belching man ruptured it so quickly and completely that I could
watch the wound instantly heal'. For the aspiring Tourettic detective
this revelation presents abundant opportunities because '[a] Touretter
can also be The Invisible Man' (Lethem, 1999: 44).

Brooklyn is especially conducive to Lionel's invisibility. It has become, Lethem admits, one of his 'hoariest set-pieces' to claim that
Brooklyn is 'my Tourette's' (Personal Interview, 2009), that the provocative street talk, the humorous negotiations which allow resident
Brooklynites to 'play at hostility' and 'flirt with aggression' (Personal Interview, 2009) have become deeply inscribed on his character
and are reproduced in Frank Minna and Lionel Essrog. Despite his

reputation as a 'freakshow', Lionel is able to some extent to blend in to Brooklyn life because his Tourette's is an only marginally amplified version of the linguistic playfulness and experimentation all around him; it is, indeed, shaped by and dependent on it. As he remembers his long afternoons reading books in the St. Vincent's library and watching old television programmes like *Bewitched* and *I Love Lucy*, Lionel says that these texts 'weren't showing me what I needed to see, weren't helping me find the language' (Lethem, 1999: 37), the words 'trapped like a roiling ocean under a calm floe of ice' (Lethem, 1999: 45). Leaving behind the 'Nowhere' of St Vincent's (Lethem, 1999: 37) for the bustle and excitement of Court Street and meeting Frank Minna, a man who savours his own vaguely Tourettic insults such as 'You boiled cabbageheads' (Lethem, 1999: 24), finally releases this flow of words. As Lionel says: 'it was Minna who brought me the language, Minna and Court Street that let me speak' (Lethem, 1999: 37).

The second chapter (simply called 'Motherless Brooklyn'), thus incorporates within its ongoing detective narrative a residual coming-of-age story. Just as Pella Marsh, in order to complete her mourning, has to ground her chosen metaphors for loss in the new community and thus find a voice, so Lionel finds in Court Street a place to establish his identity and discover his own unique mode of expression. It is a deliberately perverse bildungsroman, however. Whereas a common trajectory of such narratives describes an emergence into maturity characterised by the sublimation of youthful, instinctive and dangerous impulses, Lionel's arrival into adulthood, synonymous with his arrival into 'the only Brooklyn' (Lethem, 1999: 56), represents the flowering of instinctive impulses that, in any other location, might be considered dangerously anti-social. On Court Street they become, if not entirely acceptable, at least a neighbourhood entertainment and a constant reminder of the network of 'casual insults' that underpins this part of Brooklyn (Lethem, 1999: 55).

For this reason the novel's very first sentence, which pertains partly to the paradoxical combination of involuntary compulsion and intentionality peculiar to Tourette's, attains an additional geographical significance: context is indeed everything (Lethem, 1999: 1) when the Touretter claims a special place for his neighbourhood in the development of his condition. It is no coincidence that the opening paragraphs bristle with spatial metaphors and images of vehicularity; Tourette's produces words that 'course over the surface of the world' (Lethem, 1999: 1) and 'break into the stores', and it excites the urge 'to shout in the church, the nursery, the crowded movie house' (Lethem, 1999: 2). What is also significant, as we shall see, is that the manifestations of Lionel's condition are altered when he leaves Brooklyn for Maine or Manhattan.

To equate Tourette's so explicitly with Brooklyn is to stretch a conceit, to 'take this observation and make the kind of exaggeration of it that fiction thrives on. If I decide that Brooklyn is Tourette's, it's *wrong*, it's a mistake, but fiction loves those mistakes' (Personal Interview, 2009). Lethem's frank admission of this 'mistake', however, does little to dispel the suspicion that such an avowedly metaphorical use of the syndrome risks diminishing understanding of the unique, everyday lived experience of the Tourette's sufferer. What results is a situation one might call the 'everyman' syndrome: the tendency, with which *Motherless Brooklyn* implicitly and sometimes deliberately flirts, to deploy the neurological disorder in order to make general statements about humanity such as 'everyone's a little ticcish that way sometimes' (Lethem, 1999: 160). These are not in themselves new ideas, of course: Susan Sontag's landmark study *Illness as Metaphor* (1978), which examines Romantic associations of tuberculosis with passion and heightened aesthetic sensibility and contemporary portrayals of cancer as a disease of repressed emotion, argues that '[t]he most truthful way of regarding illness – and the healthiest way of being ill – is one most purified of, most resistant to, metaphoric thinking' (Sontag, 1978: 1). The companion essay, *AIDS and its Metaphors* (1989) examines the dangerous, prejudicial view of AIDS as a consequence of decadence, and therefore as a judgement on certain ways of life.

Since the 1990s, the illnesses and disorders co-opted by literature for metaphorical purposes have frequently been neurological ones. What Marco Roth calls 'the neurological novel, wherein the mind becomes the brain' (Roth, 2009) is a contemporary phenomenon resulting partly from 'a cultural ... shift away from environmental and relational theories of personality back to the study of brains themselves, as the source of who we are' (Roth, 2009) and partly from what Roth sees as 'the exhaustion of "the linguistic turn" in the humanities' (Roth, 2009). Accompanying these trends, as both Roth and Jennifer Fleissner identify, is the widespread discrediting of Freudian psychoanalysis as a totalising explanation for human behaviour. Fleissner, agreeing with Lethem that neurology has become 'the latest contender for the novel's crown' (Fleissner, 2009: 387), suggests that the shift from psychoanalysis to neurology dictates a change in interpretive strategies from an over-emphasis on the submerged meanings of symptoms and their first, probably traumatic causes, to an explanation of symptoms as manifestations of malfunctions in the brain's wiring, and thus as considerably less *meaningful* (Fleissner, 2009: 388).

This idea has important implications for a reading of Lionel Essrog's tics and compulsions, but what demands emphasis at this point is just how frequently writers and literary critics ascribe metaphorical meanings to neurological conditions. Chuck Palahniuk's *Fight Club* (1996), for instance, with its depiction of processes broken down into minute tasks carried out by drones with no awareness of the overall effects of their work, bears out psychologist Steven N. Gold's contention that 'ubiquitous features of modern society – advanced technology, rampant consumerism, and rapid mobility – induce, to a greater or lesser extent, a pervasive form of dissociation in its members' (Gold, 2004: 14). Dissociative identity disorder (DID) thus stands as metaphor for the effects of late capitalism and postmodern society. Working from a similar premise to Gold, Bent Sørensen makes a more general point about neurological syndromes in recent literature: '[t]he latest trend in disorders ... fits the glove of postmodernism so well, rife as it is with a celebration of fragmentation, loss of faith, history, *telos*, God etc.' (Sørensen, 2004). Bennett Kravitz, drawing on Sontag's work, argues that 'in the postmodern world, we can take the relationship between culture and disease to a more complex level – that is, that culture is either the origin or catalyst of certain diseases' (Kravitz, 2003: 172). For Kravitz, then, the relationship is symbiotic: neurological disorders reflect and are partially shaped by the fragmented postmodern society in which they occur: 'Culture helps to define disease because of the former's dis-ease, yet disease also contributes to the making of culture' (Kravitz, 2003: 179).

In the most prescriptive literary examples, this relationship becomes a vicious, closed circle. Western society is incurably diseased and finds its choicest metaphors in characters damaged beyond hope. Ian McEwan's *Saturday* (2005) resorts to what Marco Roth calls 'stark biological determinism' (Roth, 2009) in its employment of the antagonist Baxter's Huntington's chorea as a metaphor, variously, for extremism, irreconcilable class division and random thuggery. Much less about Baxter's experience of the disease than the threat it poses to Henry Perowne, the man who is able to diagnose it (and metaphorically to defuse the threat through his diagnosis), *Saturday* provides an apt example of the dangers Susan Sontag identifies.[1]

It would be wrong to argue that metaphors are intrinsically bad, however. First, the syndrome metaphor can serve to place symptoms such as those of the Touretter on a spectrum of *all* human behaviours and thus break down the perception of certain neurological conditions as aberrant and completely outside a medically or culturally sanctioned norm. When Lionel has his sexual encounter with Kimmery, for example, we discover that she has her own gentle tic, the repetition of 'okay' (Lethem, 1999: 221). Secondly, it should not be forgotten that words are metaphors and to deny the metaphorical capabilities of the novel in order to pursue a documentary recording of the real experience of neurological disorder would be to deny the possibilities of the form and the ethical opportunities provided by the deliberate 'mistakes' Lethem speaks of. Yet the particular mistake he makes in *Motherless Brooklyn* flirts with an ahistorical outlook that risks undermining the anti-amnesia stance common to most of his writing. This is because in addition to Lionel's condition, a metaphor for Brooklyn and for the 'disordered reactivity' (Sussler, 2008) which characterises Lethem's creativity, the borough is also employed metaphorically. As part of the underlying debate between competing urban regions, and between old and new and past and present, Brooklyn (specifically Court Street) comes to stand for contact with the past, for a healthy appreciation of neighbourhood history. But this apparently laudable sense of history frequently flirts with enervating nostalgia because of the repetitious and retardant effects of Lionel's Tourette's. So Tourette's is the perfect metaphor for Brooklyn as Lethem conceives it, though not exactly in the way he intends: it demonstrates how metaphorical messages can become obscured and destabilised.

Previous critics have also noted the ways in which New York as a whole complements and contributes to Lionel's condition. Bent Sørensen's reading of the 'Tourettic city' (Lethem, 1999: 113) is consistent with his equation of Tourette's and other neurological conditions with the postmodern. New York becomes for him a spatial embodiment of postmodernity's dismantling of epistemological certainties:

> Take this bumbling detective type, and set him loose in a confusing world such as New York City at the end of the 20th century, and the ensuing interpretation of this world through the lens of his Tourettic mind sets the scene for a non-epistemological devolution of the crime in question: clues become indistinguishable from his own symptoms; the disorder infects the sequentiality and causality of events, and leads to order becoming contingent and at best temporary; ultimately, to the

Tourette's sufferer, the whole of New York, from its subway system to its social hierarchies, resembles a Tourettic body, always in motion, never going anywhere with teleological certainty. (Sørensen, 2004: 4)

New York, seen in this way, becomes a set of symptoms revealing contemporary culture's profound dis-ease and disruption. Where I disagree with Sørensen is in his treatment of 'New York' as a homogenous entity. Throughout *Motherless Brooklyn*, from the moment Lionel declares that he and Gilbert are 'off our customary map' as they track Minna on the Upper East Side (Lethem, 1999: 3), strong distinctions are drawn between Brooklyn and 'citadel Manhattan' (Lethem, 1999: 25), distinctions reprised in *The Fortress of Solitude*. As subsequent remarks illustrate, the two locations are shown to encapsulate different attitudes to history, and therefore to the whole question of amnesia. It is the contradictory impulses of Tourette's, this chapter argues, that threaten to collapse these distinctions and reveal their factitiousness.

In the bravura opening paragraphs Lionel explains, with characteristic mixing of metaphors, these contradictory impulses. Calling himself '[a] downtown performance artist, a speaker in tongues, a senator drunk on filibuster' (Lethem 1999: 1), he nonetheless stresses that in the first instance his verbal tics (like his physical ones) derive from an overwhelming desire to restore order: 'the words rush out of the cornucopia of my brain to course over the surface of the world, tickling reality like fingers on piano keys. Caressing, nudging. They're an invisible army on a peacekeeping mission, a peaceable horde. They mean no harm. They placate, interpret, massage. Everywhere they're smoothing down imperfections, putting hairs in place, putting ducks in a row' (Lethem, 1999: 1). It is only when 'they find too much perfection, when the surface is already buffed smooth' (Lethem, 1999: 1) that his 'little army rebels, breaks into the stores. Reality needs a prick here and there, the carpet needs a flaw' (Lethem, 1999: 2). Although this is Lethem's first novel not to incorporate science fiction, Lionel's outbursts perform precisely the same function as, say, talking animals, intelligent holes in the universe or poetic aliens: they disrupt mundane reality with incongruous, surprising or fantastical elements.

So Lionel is compelled both to smooth imperfections and to ruffle already smooth surfaces. Despite the contrasting motivations, the result is the same: apparent chaos. This is the paradox of Tourette's: in its incessant smoothing over of flaws, its compulsive desire to order, its striving for a discursive precision it can never attain, it reveals language and the world as play and difference. Yet Lionel's narration often insists on enforcing a separation between the two impulses, a separation enacted geographically and indeed ethically in the differences he perceives between Brooklyn and Manhattan, and between the areas of Brooklyn he regards as 'real' or 'authentic' and those that aspire to the glamour of the noisy neighbour across the bridge.

In parentheses, it is interesting to note that the self-allegorising tendencies of many contemporary Brooklyn fictions – Brooklyn allegorised as disappearing spirit of community, as diversity, as local and global in harmony, as knowing, unsentimental nostalgia – similarly require the pitting of periphery against metropolitan centre, and hence the near-demonisation of Manhattan. Such a scheme is evident in Kitty Burns Florey's *Solos* (2004), in which property and interior design choices attest to one's ethical orientation. Manhattan – flashy, homogenising, overly expensive – is associated with anonymous luxury loft conversions (Florey, 2004: 221) and Williamsburg, Brooklyn with the shabby but somehow more honest apartment owned by protagonist Emily Lime. To aspire to own a Manhattan-style loft apartment is to be 'banal, boring, pretentious, untrue to the spirit of Brooklyn in general and Williamsburg in particular' (Florey, 2004: 23). As Elizabeth Gumport rightly points out, such romanticising depictions trade in an aesthetics of authenticity which is blind to economic and class realities (Gumport, 2009).

Lionel Essrog is not averse to such artificial distinctions. At times he engages in a kind of gerrymandering in order to maintain his preconceived notions of what constitutes the essential, authentic Brooklyn; that is, Frank Minna's Brooklyn, centred on 'Court Street, where it passed through Carroll Gardens and Cobble Hill' (Lethem, 1999: 56). Thus Brooklyn Heights, one of the borough's most upmarket areas, is 'secretly a part of Manhattan' and 'everything east of the Gowanus Canal' is rejected as 'an unspeakable barbarian tumult' (Lethem, 1999: 56). Most revealingly, the 'elegantly renovated' Boerum Hill Inn (Lethem, 1999: 238–9) caters for 'a Manhattanized clientele of professional singles too good for bars with televisions ... The dressed-up crowd at the inn gabbled and flirted every night of the week until two in the morning, oblivious to the neighborhood's past or present reality, then slept it off in their overpriced apartments or on their desks the next day in Midtown.' (Lethem, 1999: 239). Nomenclature is central to the oppositions Lionel constructs in these passages. 'Gowanus' signals the pre-gentrification neighbourhood, whereas 'Boerum Hill' comes laden with the cultural, economic baggage of the post-gentrification, bourgeois Brooklyn which becomes the focus of *The Fortress of Solitude*. 'Manhattanized' as a pejorative term is similarly freighted: in Lionel's personal schema to be 'Manhattanized' is to be 'oblivious to the neighborhood's past or present reality'; it is to indulge too enthusiastically in an ahistorical drive toward incessant newness, to be reduced, consciously or unconsciously, to homogenised desires under global consumerism. It is, to return to Lionel's metaphors of Tourette's, to engage in the smoothing over of difference and imperfection.

Court Street, on the other hand, corresponds to the disruptive compulsion of Tourette's, that which 'teaches you what people will ignore and forget' (Lethem, 1999: 43). In contrast to Manhattan, it consistently fails to make things glossy and new, and therein, for Lionel, lays its virtue: 'Minna's Court Street was the old Brooklyn, a placid ageless surface alive underneath with talk, with deals and casual insults, a neighborhood political machine with pizzeria and butcher-shop bosses and unwritten rules everywhere. All was talk except for what mattered most, which were unspoken understandings' (Lethem, 1999: 55). Just as the 'deals and casual insults' erupt Touretically through Court Street's 'placid ageless surface', so the past refuses to lie down and die despite the present's best efforts. In the form of talk – specifically 'tugboating', the Minna boys' term for taking a story too far, for narrative excess (Lethem, 1999: 52) – memories constantly intrude on a Brooklyn which itself feels the hand of bourgeoisification at work in areas such as Park Slope and Boerum Hill. As the author has expressed it elsewhere, Brooklyn is 'permanently unsmoothed over' (Zeitchik, 2003: 37). Following Lionel's schematic division, then, one might argue that Brooklyn operates as the rebellious Id, Manhattan as the Ego, the latter mediating between individual desires and the homogenising demands of the global marketplace. Lionel exemplifies the demands of the Id: his is talk that refuses to lay dormant, that prefers to emerge 'on the fly, out on the pavement, between beats of action' (Lethem, 1999: 70). More than anyone, he has learnt to tell his story walking (Lethem, 1999: 70), to find a voice that echoes the restless trafficking between past and present he sees in the streets immediately around him.

But only in the streets immediately around him, for Lionel's 'Brooklyn', evidently, is restricted to a specific section of Court Street, the territory of Frank Minna and his Minna Men. His vision is, to use the term in its specifically Lethemite sense, an amnesiac one, in that it works hard to reduce the world to a tiny zone of activity, a mini-utopia which excludes contiguous groupings. Manhattan, obviously, is 'off the map' and anathema; Maine is 'off the page' (Lethem, 1999: 264) and even Greenpoint, another part of Brooklyn, falls outside his cultural jurisdiction: 'Brooklyn is one big place, and this wasn't our end of it' (Lethem, 1999: 20). Inspired and nurtured by Frank Minna and Court Street, Lionel's verbal tics are thus revealed as an idiosyncratic form of cognitive mapping; they give him an identity and a defined role within Minna's tiny sphere of operation. However, they also trap him in his fixations on the past, on his surrogate father figure, on the spuriously 'authentic' Brooklyn he has defined for himself. The discovery that his sense even of Frank's 'small world' is 'diminished, two-dimensional' (Lethem, 1999: 231) and that the Minnas' criminal activities also take in Manhattan, Maine and even, indirectly, Japan, severely disturbs Lionel's nostalgic conceptions of Court Street as the centre of the world but it also offers him a chance to escape from these conceptions in much the same way Pella Marsh escapes from her ancestor-worship on the Planet of the Archbuilders.

One of the reasons Lionel is able to map so effectively his Tourette's and his Brooklyn is because condition and place alike exist both materially and symbolically. As Ronald Schleifer argues, one of the most distinctive features of Tourette's is its apparent breaking down of 'the strict distinction between language and motor activities' (Schleifer, 2001: 564). Combining tics and jerky movements with linguistic compulsions such as echolalia and coprolalia, it is (and here Schleifer quotes from the work of Oliver Sacks) 'situated "partway between meaningless jerks or noises and meaningful acts" at the "interface of mind and body,"' and 'seems to take up the very materiality of language and underlines its materiality even as it also preserves it *as* language' (Schleifer, 2001: 567). Schleifer is highlighting the performative nature of much Tourettic discourse. Sudden ejaculations, curses and vocal tics are '"primal cries" in which the distance between signifier and signified, between sound and import, does not exist' (Schleifer, 2001: 571). Their meaning is simply their utterance. Yet the fact that they are invariably context-specific and unique to the speaker invests them with a kind of intentionality. This is why Lionel's ticcing is invariably so funny; as he admits: 'Speech was intention, and I couldn't let anyone else or myself know how intentional my craziness felt' (Lethem, 1999: 47). His verbal tics hover between physical compulsion and a kind of contextual appropriateness. This is what Schleifer means when he says that Tourette's highlights the materiality of language while retaining its status as language: it is physical and symbolic simultaneously.

For several reasons, then, the often-repeated 'Eat me!' (Lethem, 1999: 2) is an entirely appropriate coprolalic outburst for a condition that proves all-consuming for Lionel as he attempts to consume and model the world. (He admits to relating everything to his condition, such that counting tics becomes a tic in itself, resulting in 'meta-Tourette's' (Lethem, 1999: 192).) Food is a repeated metaphor because it emphasises the materiality of the condition. For example, one of the most persistent symptoms is what Lionel dubs his 'echolalia salad' – taking a phrase and repeating it, then gradually modifying it, until it is radically transformed. In this way 'Zendo', for example, becomes: '*Don't know from Zendo, Ken-like Zung Fu, Feng Shui master, Fungo bastard, Zen masturbation, Eat me!*' (Lethem, 1999: 4). Given this tendency, Lionel's declaration that '[f]ood really mellows me out' (Lethem, 1999: 2) deserves close scrutiny because it implies an uneasy truce between material consumption – of the White Castle mini-burgers which are his favourites at the beginning of the novel (Lethem, 1999: 2), the skinny frankfurters from the 'Papaya Czar' (Lethem, 1999: 160), the kosher 'chicken schwarma' sandwiches he craves at the end (Lethem, 1999: 302) – and metaphorical consumption. Most importantly, food, along with other things like Prince's music (Lethem, 1999: 128), allows him to externalise his symptoms. Lionel is only able to relax when he can 'let [his] syndrome live outside [his] brain for once, live in the air instead' (Lethem, 1999: 128).

Benedict Anderson's 'imagined community' (Anderson, 2006: 6) is a familiar concept: it reminds us that places and communities depend on an uneasy truce between their status as geographical, material spaces and as subjective, linguistic constructs. Brooklyn is taken to stand for so many things in recent novels, including Lethem's, that Brooklyn authors have become peculiarly self-conscious and explicit about its geographical specificity and its overlapping symbolic value. Audrey, the narrator of Lynne Sharon Schwartz's *Leaving Brooklyn*, refers to the borough as 'a state of mind or perception' (Schwartz, 1990: 16). Michael Stephens' Brooklyn in *The Brooklyn Book of the Dead* (1994) 'lend[s] itself more to the imagination than facts' (Stephens, 1994: 23). Myth and history, physical reality and intentionality, compete Touretically in these texts.

So if Lionel imagines and identifies with Brooklyn more passion-
ately than with Manhattan, it is because he insists on seeing in its be-
guiling combination of elegance and chaos, concreteness and myth,
a mirror of and contributor to his own condition. The eruptive fragments of the past are comforting to Lionel as an orphan, an individual
detached from a sense of familial history and mourning the loss both
of his parents and his replacement father figure Frank Minna. As Lionel puts it, 'we orphans were idiots of connectivity, overly impressed
by any trace of the familial in the world' (Lethem, 1999: 74). (At one
point in the novel Lionel goes as far as to dial the numbers of all the
Essrogs in the phone book in an attempt to locate possible relatives,
but he never speaks to any of them, other than to spout random tics
down the line (Lethem, 1999: 69).) In moving incessantly between
past and present, between myth and facts, Brooklyn allows a glimpse
of those longed-for connections.

Oliver Sacks, in *An Anthropologist on Mars*, implies the existence
of just such a temporal aspect in Tourettic tics and utterances: 'Tics
are like hieroglyphic, petrified residues of the past and may, indeed,
with the passage of time become so hieroglyphic, so abbreviated, as
to become unintelligible (as "God be with you" was condensed, col-
lapsed, after centuries, to the phonetically similar but meaningless
"goodbye"' (Sacks, 1995: 81). In effect, tics function as stored-up fragments of the past which are employed either to make sense of or to
destabilise the present. In *Motherless Brooklyn*, it has been argued, the
temporal transitivity underlying Lionel's Tourette's is reflected in the
temporal and spatial negotiations of Brooklyn itself. The statement
'[w]e learned to tell our story walking' (Lethem, 1999: 70), which is
rehearsed in the very last line of the novel as an entreaty to the reader,
attests to the perception of a Brooklyn constantly in motion and under
negotiation, like Lionel's language; a place where past and present are
constantly interacting; where people immigrate and emigrate; where
whole chunks of the neighbourhood can change colour and class in
the blink of an eye while retaining some essential quality innately
'Brooklynite'.

The storing-up quality of Tourette's and Brooklyn presents its own
problems, however. Like the borough, Lionel's condition is tenacious and stubborn; it simply will not leave things alone or forget
'the intolerable, the incongruous, the disruptive' (Lethem, 1999: 43).
While it may well be instructive, Tourette's becomes intolerable for
this very reason. And when Lionel is disillusioned and honest enough

to acknowledge it, so does his neighbourhood: 'Ordinarily I savored Brooklyn's unchangeability, the bullying, Minna-like embrace of its long memory. At the moment I yearned to see this neighborhood razed, replaced by skyscrapers or multiplexes. I longed to disappear into Manhattan's amnesiac dance of renewal' (Lethem, 1999: 179). In this episode, Lionel is being bullied by Tony, one of the other Minna boys whom he suspects of being connected with Minna's murder. It is at moments like these, moments of high stress, sadness and loneliness, when Lionel wishes that Brooklyn's memory were not quite so long, when he wishes it could be more like Manhattan and aspire to continual rejuvenation through willed amnesia.

Lionel and Brooklyn's Tourettic inability to let go is the most ambiguous and problematic of their metaphorical tendencies. The smoothing and the disrupting impulses of Tourette's may have a common endpoint – a kind of chaos. Yet it is chaos which, as Lionel suggests, runs the risk of becoming retrogressive or even ahistorical because in the end it is unclear whether the potentially destabilising relationship between past and present is truly dialectical. In fact, it is likely that Lionel's Tourettic tics and echoes reveal a desire to freeze (or in Oliver Sacks' terms petrify) a particular period in time, which results in a destruction of historical sense altogether. In Fredric Jameson's terms (and here the metaphors of neurological disorder become unavoidably mixed) Lionel's Tourette's is schizophrenic, in that it defeats reference and reduces sentences to isolated signifiers: 'With the breakdown of the signifying chain, therefore, the schizophrenic is reduced to an experience of pure material signifiers, or, in other words, a series of pure and unrelated presents in time' (Jameson, 1991: 25–6). With this breakdown and with the waning of 'our lived possibility of experiencing history in some active way' (Jameson, 1991: 21) comes an inability to represent the present as history and a recourse to modes of representation dominated by nostalgia.

Lionel suffers from precisely this problem after Minna's death: his is an idealised Brooklyn always on the verge of obsolescence, 'an everyday life that already felt nostalgic' (Lethem, 1999: 230). Lionel's incessant tinkering with language thus attests to a desire not to change or move forward, to complete the mourning process, but to change back and thus maintain a nostalgically conceived past situation in the present (when Minna was still alive, when Lionel's Brooklyn was not motherless). Seen in this way, linguistic play offers only the illusion of transitivity and vehicularity. As Oliver Sacks asserts: '[Tourette's sufferers are] *no* nearer for not being still. [They are] no nearer to anything by virtue of motion; and in this sense, motion is not genuine movement' (Sacks, 1987: 16–17).

Because Lionel's idealised Brooklyn is so inextricably linked to Lionel's condition, because it is in a sense internalised and created by his verbal and motor tics, it precludes the possibility of externalising his Tourette's for long enough that he can reflect on his loss and move on. Lionel's Court Street is yet another temporary utopia in Lethem's work, but one which the protagonist tries to make permanent to the detriment of his future well-being. As he admits soon after Minna's death: 'If I didn't stem my syndrome's needs, I would never clear a space in which my own sorrow could dwell' (Lethem, 1999: 127). Brooklyn cannot appease or quell the demands of his syndrome because it is too closely associated with it; therefore it cannot provide the 'space' he needs. Too bound up in his personal myths and symbols, too imprinted with icons of Minna, Lionel's Brooklyn ends up simply feeling too small. Lionel himself becomes, in Bennett Kravitz's words, 'a self-fulfilling prophecy' because 'his symptoms emanate from specific cultural and social contexts' (Kravitz, 2003: 175) from which he is reluctant to depart, partly due to his guilt over Minna's murder. And guilt, as he says, also has a Tourettic quality, always wanting to 'reach into the past to tweak, neaten, and repair' (Lethem, 1999: 284).

All of which imbues the climactic episodes in Maine with added significance. They take place in a chapter called 'Auto Body', which refers not only to Lionel's overnight stake-out outside the storefront and to his pursuit of Tony and the murderous giant along the freeways to Maine, but also to his motor compulsions. At the moment he crosses the bridge at Portsmouth into Maine, however, he determines to jettison the automatic body and become a creature of pure intentionality: '[I] focused everything I had left on the drive, on casting off unnecessary behaviours, thrusting exhaustion and bitterness aside and making myself into a vehicular arrow pointed at Musconguspoint Station' (Lethem, 1999: 262).

When he leaves the car and contemplates the ocean, he experiences a terrifying yet liberating moment of the sublime. Tacitly acknowledging that Brooklyn is a text of his own creation, or a map drafted through his own tics and obsessions, he says: 'Waves, sky, trees, Essrog – I was off the page now, away from the grammar of skyscrapers and pavement' (Lethem, 1999: 264). The 'loss of language' he experiences, the 'great sucking away of the word-laden walls I needed around me' (Lethem, 1999: 264), forces him to 'reply in some new tongue, to find a way to assert a self that had become tenuous, shrunk to a shred of Brooklyn stumbling on the coastal void' (Lethem, 1999: 264). What he does, remarkably, is deliberately to shout some of his recurring tics ('Bailey!', 'Eat me! Dickweed!') across the ocean, culminating in an ironic yet hugely significant proclamation of ownership: 'I claim this big water for Essrog!' (Lethem, 1999: 265). Though he in no sense owns this water, the reassertion of his non-Tourettic self as his Brooklyn self dissipates suggests strongly that a more permanent departure from the borough will be beneficial to him, by relieving him of his fixation on the past. The vastness, the openness gives him the space to mourn properly, to externalise his symptoms away from the claustrophobic meaningfulness of the borough.

Just after his ocean epiphany, another episode increases the sense that Maine is a place where Lionel can externalise his condition. Although Frank Minna once gave Lionel a book on Tourette's, a book that was of no real use to him (Lethem, 1999: 81), nobody else in Brooklyn seems to recognise Lionel's behaviour as a neurological condition, preferring instead to regard him as crazy, his tics as a performance or 'routine' in keeping with Brooklyn's pervading sense of mischief (Lethem, 1999: 123). Yet in Maine, Lionel meets with an old man called Foible who instantly and without judgement states 'You got a touch of Tourette's syndrome there, son' (Lethem, 1999: 270). This simple act of recognition is an additional aspect of the radical de-contextualisation Lionel experiences here, and another invitation to get out of Brooklyn.

After defeating the giant and piecing together the full story with Minna's wife Julia, Lionel does of course return to Brooklyn (Lethem, 1999: 303). Before he leaves, however, he flings the detritus of the case – his and Julia's guns, his cell phone, Minna's pager – into the ocean in a symbolic act of catharsis and consignment of the past to the past (albeit one partly driven by physical compulsion). In a typical moment of tragicomic bathos, he is forced to throw away one of his shoes, too, in order to honour the number that happens Tourettically to be haunting him that day – five (Lethem, 1999: 303). Yet the absurd image of Lionel driving 'with [his] gas-pedal-and-brake foot clad only in a dress sock, back to Brooklyn' (Lethem, 1999: 303), only partially hides the deeper resonances of the incident. For Lionel has, in a sense, left part of himself behind in the ocean that defeats his language.

Back in Brooklyn, the remaining Minna Men still work together as a detective agency and in the closing paragraphs, Lionel indulges in some final observations on the nature of the detective genre. Throughout the novel, he has shared with the reader these kinds of observations, such that his meta-Tourette's is matched by a meta-generic consciousness on a par with Lethem's. There is a solicitous assumption of a constellated community in which Lionel and the readers participate, shown, for example, by the sharing of quotations from the work of Raymond Chandler (Lethem, 1999: 205). However, his final comments on the genre, where he reflects melancholically on his performance as a detective and on his losses and disappointments, point to its unsuitability to a man already inclined toward nostalgia:

> Assertions are common to me, and they're also common to detectives. ... And in detective stories things are always *always*, the detective casting his exhausted, caustic gaze over the corrupted permanence of everything and thrilling you with his sweetly savage generalizations. This or that runs deep or true to form, is invariable, exemplary. ... Assertions and generalizations are, of course, a version of Tourette's. A way of touching the world, handling it, covering it with confirming language.
> Here's one more. As a great man once said, the more things change, the harder they are to change back. (Lethem, 1999: 307)

Seen in this way, detective fiction in *Motherless Brooklyn* succumbs to the same temptation as it does in *Gun, With Occasional Music*: to attribute such importance to the past, to remembering, that a sense of historical evolution is sacrificed to a contrived sense of timelessness.

Moreover, Lionel's observations in these paragraphs reveal another aspect of the tension discussed earlier in this chapter: the 'everyman' syndrome. The detective's urge to generalise, one shared by Lionel's Tourettic self and, as he perceives it, by Brooklyn, has a dangerously ahistorical quality but also the potential to reduce individuals to representative figures, or metaphors for the 'human condition'. About 'Bailey', the subject of so many of his verbal tics, Lionel speculates: 'Maybe Bailey was everyman, like George Bailey in *It's a Wonderful Life*' (Lethem, 1999: 10). As an 'imaginary listener' (Lethem, 1999: 10), this everyman performs a similar function to the reader of the novel, meaning that Lionel's narrative solicitousness reads like an attempt to create a metaphorical, representative reader figure to collude with his speculations and generalisations. Thus in the final paragraph the figures of 'Bailey', 'Ullman' (the lawyer murdered early on without ever appearing in the story, and phonologically related to 'all men'), and indeed the reader, assume a paradoxical status: they are the 'ghosts' who 'never even get into your house they are so busy howling at the windows' (Lethem, 1999: 311), unknown individuals who stand for every person we will never know and never be able to know. At a textual level, Lionel's way of dealing with this epistemological gap, achieved partly through his Tourette's, partly through his chosen genre and partly through his neighbourhood, is to assume complicity with and sympathy for his observations on the part of others.

One of the dangers of *Motherless Brooklyn*, then, derives precisely from the irresistible pleasures of its narration. Of course, the simple fact of having a first-person narrator with a neurological disability is a positive thing, in that it forces the reader to question the structures of normativity which usually prevail in wider society. But for all the Tourettic narrator defamiliarises the world in the first instance, his desire to generalise, to smooth, to keep things as they were risks undermining the *ostranenie* the novel initially promises. As Linda Fleissner says, the tic becomes 'a mode of mimesis' (Fleissner, 2009: 391) of an eccentric and ticcish world (Court Street, Brooklyn) that Lionel finds comforting and familiar and about which, by and large, he wishes the reader to feel likewise. He might momentarily shake it up, but his desire is to conserve. And although Lionel, as we have seen, does on occasion question his own assumptions, and does at the end hint at a revised outlook, our identification with him is so strong that it is difficult not to assume a desire on the part of the author for readers to subscribe to similar prejudices (about Brooklyn and Manhattan, for example). As Chapter 6 demonstrates, the same danger lurks in the first part of *The Fortress of Solitude*, but Lethem finds a means in the second part of averting it.

Yet there are ultimately signs that Lionel's restricted outlook might be changing. The Minna Men call themselves detectives, but they have no clients, and so instead operate as a proper car service for the first time. Lionel's investigative impulses, having been the means by which he could attempt to arrest time and keep reaching into the past, have been banished, and he now engages in an activity – driving – that at least symbolises real mobility, a desire to move on. The fact that he takes a trip to JFK Airport at the end of the novel also connotes a broadening of horizons (Lethem, 1999: 310). As Bent Sørensen suggests (Sørensen, 2006: 6), Lionel's new-found love of the chicken sandwich sold at the 'kosher-food stand called Mushy's, run by a family of Israelis' (Lethem, 1999: 310) hints at a reconnection with the Jewish roots signified by his surname (the esrog being a citrus fruit used at the harvest festival of Sukkoth), and thus with a community that crosses neighbourhood, city and national boundaries. Thus Lionel's closing demands to Bailey, to Ullman and to the reader apply equally well to him as he looks for a way out of the tiny utopian world he has inhabited up to now: 'Put an egg in your shoe, and beat it. Make like a tree, and leave. Tell your story walking' (Lethem, 1999: 311).

Notes

1   Other notable 'neuronovels' include Mark Haddon's *Curious Incident of the Dog in the Night-Time* (2003) (autism), Richard Powers' *The Echomaker* (2006) (facial agnosia, Capgras syndrome), Rivka Galchen's *Atmospheric Disturbances* (2008) (Capgras syndrome again), Matt Ruff's *Set This House in Order* (2003) (DID) and John Wray's *Lowboy* (2009) (paranoid schizophrenia).

6

Mixed media: graffiti, writing and coming-of-age in *The Fortress of Solitude*

'He'll be with children who'll never learn.' (Lethem, 2003: 20)

Jason Picone compares the author of *The Fortress of Solitude* (2003) to its protagonist, Dylan Ebdus, and says: 'Much like Dylan, who cannot escape the confines of 1970s Brooklyn even after moving to 1990s California, Jonathan Lethem is always staying home' (Picone, 2004: 29). Despite Lionel Essrog's exhortations at the end of *Motherless Brooklyn* to 'Put an egg in your shoe, and beat it. Make like a tree, and leave. Tell your story walking' (Lethem, 1999: 311), the first part of *The Fortress of Solitude* returns us, in dreamily descriptive, nostalgic prose, to the streets of his Brooklyn childhood. Indeed, so close are the territories of the two books and so similar the themes (Dylan becomes 'motherless' as early as p. 63 when Rachel Ebdus runs away) that Picone is right to assert that '*Motherless Brooklyn*' might well have served as the title of its successor (Picone, 2004: 29).

It is Picone's closing remarks, however, that deserve particular scrutiny: 'Lethem has surpassed his award-winning effort here, mostly by eschewing his prior genre-writing, dragging whatever scraps he needs from the world of the fantastic into the realm of the literary' (Picone, 2004: 29). The facile dissociation of genre and literary merit is a critical error any number of Lethem's reviewers have made (and as previous chapters have shown the distinction is untenable), but it is particularly revealing in this context. If Picone misleadingly suggests that *Fortress* represents Lethem's coming-of-age, the moment when he finally puts his juvenile generic extravagances behind him, then such a suggestion is likely to be prompted (consciously or otherwise) by the two linked, ironic coming-of-age narratives that form the backbone of the novel. Dylan Ebdus's transition to adulthood, marked roughly halfway through the novel by the abrupt change from the 'Underberg' section to his 'Liner Note' on the music of Barrett Rude Junior and the Distinctions (a change that has divided critical opinion), is bound up in Gowanus's renaming and reorientation as Boerum Hill, a coming-of-age itself freighted with cultural, racial and economic issues and ethical dilemmas. As Matt Godbey says: '*Fortress* is part of a body of works that I call the fiction of gentrification, a literary genre that has emerged from and in response to the redevelopment of United States cities since the 1960s' (Godbey, 2008: 132).[1] Whether Godbey is right to label it a 'genre' is open to debate, but the important point is that the novel's central relationship between Dylan Ebdus and his mixed-race friend Mingus Rude personalises and intensifies the insoluble questions of race, class, authenticity and memory which bedevil the gentrifying process.

Godbey is correct to argue that *Fortress* is partly about 'the constructed nature of gentrified landscapes and the way these constructions complicate the relationship between place and identity' (Godbey, 2008: 132). Although his value judgements are dubious, Picone is also right to assert that the novel does not stage the sometimes playful (as in *As She Climbed Across the Table*), sometimes deadly serious (as in *Girl in Landscape*) genre collisions seen in earlier works, even if, in essence, it takes the form of a bildungsroman with one fabulistic element, the magic ring given to Dylan by the dissolute, hospitalised superhero Aaron X. Doily, aka Aeroman (Lethem, 2003: 149). Doily, like 'Super Goat Man', the college teacher and former superhero who fails to save a drunken student falling from the college clock tower in one of Lethem's short stories (Lethem, 2004: 136), represents the failure of an American myth of the heroic individual and in so doing joins the roll call of 'Depressed Super Heroes' Lethem analyses on his website. Though one would not wish to make too much of the symbolism, he might also be seen as another version of the 'falling man' figure which became especially resonant after September 11 2001: he interrupts Dylan's first attempt to scrawl a graffiti tag by falling from the roof onto the ground next to him (Lethem, 2003: 101). The ring, which gives Mingus the power of flight and Dylan the power of invisibility, becomes a metaphor for teenage anxieties, the fetishisation of youthful experience and, given the difference in the abilities it bestows on its users, for Dylan's worries about racial identity. When one considers these metaphorical significances, it is clear that the ring, though fantastical, is perfectly at home in a coming-of-age narrative.

However, this chapter argues that there is another, more fruitful way of looking at this novel 'generically' which is connected in specific ways to the novel's ambiguous comings-of-age: to Dylan's character development, to Gowanus's gentrification and transformation into Boerum Hill and, one can speculate, to Lethem's development as a writer. Rather than bringing together literary genres such as detective fiction, science fiction and the campus novel, Lethem here counterposes three distinct forms of writing: graffiti tagging, properly known as 'writing' (Rahn, 2002: 5) and the dominant influence over Dylan and Mingus's youth; music journalism (Dylan's eventual career); and of course the novel which includes both – Lethem's *The Fortress of Solitude*. To these three forms one can add the comics that lend the novel its title (the Fortress of Solitude being Superman's hideaway) and to which Dylan is first exposed at the house of Isabel Vendle, the woman depicted as the prime mover of Gowanus's gentrification (Lethem, 2003: 39–41). Studying the complex relationships between these forms of writing allows us to see how Dylan (and Lethem) map and negotiate precious childhood experiences in adulthood and at least attempt, in deeply ambiguous ways, to move on from them.

Of all these forms, it is graffiti writing that exerts the strongest emotional pull on Dylan and thus constitutes the greatest obstacle to his maturation and his attempts to write his youth out of his system. Its importance is revealed in the title of the first part: 'Underberg's' is the name of the shop 'on the other side of Flatbush ... a region of lack' (Lethem, 2003: 186) where the precious Garvey Formula XT-70 Violet industrial ink can be purchased, and where neophyte taggers like Dylan can catch a glimpse of some real writers. And the fact that the cover of the 2005 Faber edition is adorned with tags which surround the name of the novel and its author suggests that there is a complex relationship between literary authorship and the more subterranean power of the name in graffiti writing, as we shall see. Graffiti, more than the other cultural phenomena in *Fortress*, seems to promise the 'authentic' (that is, black) experience Lethem's white, middle-class creative types like Dylan so crave (Greenwald, 2010). Yet so often they end up not truly immersed in that experience, but only in anxious 'proximity' to it (Greenwald, 2010).

This argument depends on two key terms which have become particularly germane to Lethem's writing from *Fortress* through *Omega the Unknown* (2008), *Chronic City* and *They Live* (2010b). The first is 'ekphrasis', commonly defined as 'the verbal representation of visual representation' (Heffernan, 1993: 7). *Fortress* is full of detailed descriptions of visual art, from the graffiti tags and pieces that decoratively mark the territory of Dylan and Mingus's Brooklyn to the hand-painted individual frames of celluloid Abraham Ebdus produces daily in his own Fortress of Solitude, the attic studio (Lethem, 2003: 9). Crucial to the understanding of how ekphrasis is used in the novel is its essential ambivalence about the visual image. As Peter Wagner says: 'Ekphrasis, then, has a Janus face: as a form of mimesis, it stages a paradoxical performance, promising to give voice to the allegedly silent image even while attempting to overcome the power of the image by transforming and inscribing it' (Wagner, 1996: 6). To put it another way, ekphrasis proclaims literature's power even as it demands that one give attention to the alternative mode of expression being portrayed, a visual mode that might initially seem to have the potential to disrupt or defeat the representational power of the written word.

The second key term, which includes the first, is 'remediation'. Although I am not, like them, interested in new digital media in this context, I draw on Jay David Bolter and Richard Grusin's understanding of remediation as a refashioning, repurposing or appropriation of one medium by or within another. If a modern digital medium such as the Internet fully exploits remediation in its incorporation of photographic, cinematic, televisual and literary elements, Bolter and Grusin are nonetheless keen to emphasise the technique's long history. Examples they provide include paintings of Biblical tales (Bolter and Grusin, 2000: 44), as well as 'medieval illuminated manuscripts, Renaissance altarpieces, Dutch painting, baroque cabinets, and modernist collage and photomontage' (Bolter and Grusin, 2000: 34). In each case, the remediating form functions 'in a constant dialectic' with that it remediates (Bolter and Grusin, 2000: 50) rather than erasing or transcending it. And, crucially for this argument, a similar dialectical relationship is at work between 'the logic of transparent immediacy' (Bolter and Grusin, 2000: 21) which dictates that the viewer or reader immerse him or herself in the represented world to the extent that the medium is forgotten, and 'the logic of hypermediacy' (Bolter and Grusin, 2000: 31), which deliberately foregrounds representational media. The authors state: 'Like other media since the Renaissance – in particular, perspective painting, photography, film, and television – new digital media oscillate between immediacy and hypermediacy, between transparency and opacity' (Bolter and Grusin,

2000: 19). Inevitably, this oscillation results in a paradox: that the more a medium claims to offer 'a more immediate or authentic experience' than its predecessors (Bolter and Grusin, 2000: 19), the more it exposes its own status as representing medium.

Lethem's *Fortress*, like Dylan's 'Liner Note', is an attempt to remediate childhood experience by extensively employing ekphrasis in its fascination with graffiti, in particular. But if one accepts Bolter and Grusin's analysis of remediation, and indeed Peter Wagner's view of ekphrasis, then Lethem and Dylan's attempts cannot help but be fraught with paradox. Even as they describe in gorgeous detail the intense visual experiences of 1970s Brooklyn, they highlight yet again the inescapability of language which is a constant worry in all of Lethem's work. Moreover, remediation's play of 'transparency and opacity' means that no matter how sincere an engagement with the past acts of remediation might appear to be, they are always exposed as means of hiding in plain sight – a simultaneous celebration and displacement of the past. In Dylan's case this is intimately bound up in guilt over his rejection of Mingus and the attendant racial anxiety he feels – 'the guilt of Dylan's whiteness' (Lethem, 2003: 86) – an anxiety also intrinsic to gentrification, of course. Thus remediation is another way of articulating (but also obscuring) the bigger questions of traumatic loss at the heart of all Lethem's writing and it is, as this chapter goes on to argue, racially inflected throughout the novel. Indeed, one of the most pressing questions arising from Lethem's treatment of Dylan and Mingus's lives, and the forms of writing with which they are respectively associated, is whether he 'risks being an apologist for a white America that let Dylan successfully slip out of a bad upbringing but tightened its nets for Mingus and placed him in jail' (Picone, 2004: 29).

Fortress is not in any overt sense a 'post-/11' text, it should be stressed, and does not include the obvious symbols of New York's destruction found in *Chronic City* such as Laird Noteless's fjord (another example, as Chapter 7 demonstrates, of traumatic ekphrasis). Yet there are symbolic nods to the catastrophe, in particular the gigantic tower of the Brooklyn House of Detention that is the setting of one of the book's most significant episodes (Lethem, 2003: 274). More important than such symbols, however, is the way *Fortress* depicts cultural, emotional, political and chronological rupture of the kind brought about by the attack on the Twin Towers. Not only is this enacted in the novel's 'structural split' (Cohen, 2009: 178), when the third-person narration of the first part makes way, after Mingus shoots his grandfather (Lethem, 2003: 292), for Dylan's first-person narration, but it is also seen in the numerous acts of remediation. The terrorist attacks on the US were hypermediated events, after all, and an unavoidable part of the ongoing processes of mourning and analysis has been their endless remediation. So Lethem's account of Dylan's error-strewn coming-of-age is partially an allegory of how a culture remediates its own traumatic losses. Furthermore, Lethem's collaboration with Karl Rusnak on the resurrection of the cult Marvel comic series *Omega the Unknown*, to which Lethem makes explicit reference in the novel, equating it with Dylan (Lethem, 2003: 83–4, 93), sees *The Fortress of Solitude* itself remediated; the chilling final sequence, as we shall see, tries to escape language in ways the novel and its protagonist cannot.

Right from the outset, Dylan's Brooklyn is characterised by two recurring motifs which anticipate the racial anxieties at the heart of the novel: colour and spatial division. The very first image positively pulses with colour:

> Like a match struck in a darkened room:
> Two white girls in flannel nightgowns and red vinyl roller skates with white laces, tracing tentative circles on a cracked blue slate sidewalk at seven o'clock on an evening in July. (Lethem, 2003: 3)

Their 'sky-pink hair streaming' behind them in 'the orange-pink summer dusk' (Lethem, 2003: 3), these new arrivals to the predominantly black neighbourhood play in front of Dylan, himself a part of the white bohemian influx, and some slightly bewildered Puerto Rican men, remnants of the 'old' Gowanus soon to be transformed forever. Deliberately dreamy and literally rose-tinted, the opening scene of the novel, which finishes bathetically with the line 'white people were returning to Dean Street. A few' (Lethem, 2003: 4), carries all of the ironies and ambiguities associated with gentrification and with nostalgia as an impulse. For the rollerskating girls may be 'the new thing, spotlit to start the show' (Lethem, 2003: 4), but they also signify a return, a looking back to an earlier time when more white people did indeed populate Dean Street. Rather than an idyllic vision of a childhood utopia, then, the moment ostensibly being romanticised in technicolour here is one which reminds us of nothing more than the perpetuity of change. As Samuel Cohen says, emphasising the role of 'contingency', *Fortress* '[sees] the past as ever-changing' (Cohen,

2009: 181) so that the nostalgic tone of the opening scene immediately undermines itself: if nostalgia attempts to freeze a utopian past moment, the moment itself always seems to evade capture.

Soon after the white girls' appearance, when Dylan's mother Rachel encourages him to play out front with Marilla, an older black girl, Dylan recognises the 'setup', the way his mother is 'working the block' and trying idealistically to encourage interracial friendships (Lethem, 2003: 5). By the simple expedient of a piece of chalk, Marilla shows Dylan how untenable the friendship is, and how the spatial demarcations of childhood gaming index racial divisions in wider society: 'Marilla had a hoop and some chalk. The walk in front of Marilla's gate – her share of the irregular slate path was her zone – marked. This was Dylan's first knowledge of the system that organised the space of the block. He would never step into Marilla's house, though he didn't know that now. The slate was her parlor. He had his own, though he hadn't marked it yet' (Lethem, 2003: 5).

Time and time again in 'Underberg' one sees these spatial, racial and cultural divisions redrawn, and often literally. So what Dylan calls the 'second world' of the block (the first being his troubled home life), is 'an arrangement of zones in slate, and the peeling painted fronts of the row houses – pink, white, pale green, various tones of red and blue, always giving way to the brick underneath – those were the flags of undiscovered realms which lay behind and probably determined the system of slate zones' (Lethem, 2003: 13). Dylan's expertise at drawing the pavement skully boards depends on his knowledge of 'the dynamics of space and sound, the quality of privacy and access ... a whole series of subtle aesthetical distinctions' (Lethem, 2003: 21). (That Barrett Rude Junior's band is called The Subtle Distinctions only serves to reiterate just how obsessed this novel is with differences, some blatant, some nebulous and hard to articulate.) At Public School 38, where he is 'one of three white children in the whole school' (Lethem, 2003: 24), Dylan sketches 'utopian skully boards' in his exercise book (Lethem, 2003: 24) with fabulous shapes and angles. The implication is clear: the zones of childhood space, just like the factitious demarcations of urban space undergoing gentrification, are yet more versions of the mini-utopias or FSRs into which Lethem's characters are so prone to shutting themselves. As Dylan grows older, the divisions are only exacerbated and more explicitly racialised. In fifth grade, for example: 'You met zones everywhere. The schoolyard was neighborhoods: black, black girl, Puerto Rican,

basketball, handball, left behind. Through the Cyclone fence someone had brushed the word FLAMBOYAN in white paint on the stone
wall, along with a square box for a strike zone' (Lethem, 2003: 63).
'FLAMBOYAN' signals the graffiti that will become increasingly
vital to Dylan's Brooklyn identity, and it also connotes the 'explod-
ing bomb of possibilities' (Lethem, 2003: 56) that is Mingus Rude,
whom Dylan meets for the first time in fifth grade. It is almost inevitable that Dylan becomes immersed in graffiti culture after meeting
Mingus because, as previous examples have shown, he already interprets his world in visual terms, as a drawn environment that needs
in some way to be claimed by him and the subcultures to which he
aspires. But more than this, the narrative of 'Underberg' insists on
seeing and describing people pictorially. In seventh grade Dylan sees
'[b]odies ranged like ugly cartoons, as though someone without talent
was scribbling in flesh' (Lethem, 2003: 118). Mingus's limping gait is
'a cartoon squiggle or bass line come to life' (Lethem, 2003: 124); the
band of funksters leaving Mingus's house is 'a slice of human graffiti'
(Lethem, 2003: 156); the groups that meet at Underberg's to boost
paints are 'like a form of human scribbling' (Lethem, 2003: 188). The
eyes of Robert Woolfolk, the ghetto kid who routinely menaces Dylan
throughout the novel, have 'that same scribbled quality' (Lethem,
2003: 64). Significantly, it tends to be the black, or in Mingus's case,
mixed-race characters who are presented in these terms. When Dylan
goes to college and describes himself as 'a cartoon of Mingus', he is
referring only to his fake Brooklyn schtick, his pretence at blackness,
and his 'self-loathing' (Lethem, 2003: 389). In graffiti terms, he's still
a 'toy', not a writer, just as Arthur Lomb, the other white kid with
whom Dylan shares a love of comic books and an outsider's yearning,
turns himself into 'a Mingus-puppet' (Lethem, 2003: 190).

There are a number of reasons why this peculiarity of the narration
is both curious and problematic. First, it is clear that by rendering
each literary character as 'character', in the sense of drawn figure, the
narrator is attempting the imbrication of style and selfhood essential
to the graffiti tag and, as Douglas Wolk argues, equally essential to the
expressiveness of 'art comics' (Wolk, 2007: 30). Secondly, the tendency to describe people and places as graffiti or cartoons, this incessant
meshing of word and image, is symptomatic of a narrative expressly
about the desire to remediate childhood experience which is itself always-already remediated. For if one accepts that 'Underberg', though
written in the third person, is largely from Dylan's perspective, one

also has to acknowledge the chronological displacement at work. A story of Dylan's youthful discovery of graffiti, comics and abstract visual art is told in terms he could not possibly have fully understood at the time of his discovery; they are retroactively ascribed, seen through the distorting prism of adulthood (as all memories are, of course). Conversely, this speaks of an adult life 'overwhelmed' by childhood obsessions (Lethem, 2003: 319). On the one hand, such a move militates against nostalgia once again; it shows that the authenticity Dylan craves in Dean Street, the elusive 'real', was never there, or was at least always a construction. On the other hand, it implies a continuing resistance to the realities of racial separation and economic change, a desire to reduce such matters to pop representations, to appreciate their style, their form, not their political urgency. This is made most apparent, as we shall see, in the section of 'Prisonaires' which purports to fill in the details of Mingus's story after the shooting.

From the moment Dylan meets Mingus, through their shared adventures in tagging, their subsequent estrangement and their contrasting adulthoods, the desire which dominates their lives is the desire for 'a name' and the sense of locatedness, recognition and identity it instils. The use of names, which is inflected in different ways corresponding to the different forms of writing depicted and narrative voices employed, is ultimately the bravest and also potentially the most problematic aspect of Lethem's novel. By examining the evolutionary trajectories of Dylan and Mingus's names in *Fortress*, one learns something about the cultural and political shifts attendant on the change of Gowanus' name, and, one might add, about the mixed feelings Lethem has about becoming a 'name' in the literary mainstream.

When Dylan first meets Mingus, his neighbour shows him some comics, 'tenderly handled to death, corners rounded, papers browned' (Lethem, 2003: 55), which he has carefully labelled to show ownership: 'MINGUS RUDE was written in slanted ballpoint capitals on each first interior page' (Lethem, 2003: 55). Though there is a comic gravitas about these capitals, the slanting of the characters predicts the stylised lettering of the graffiti tags which soon follow (and the name itself is surely funky enough, anyway). Before long, Mingus is embracing hip hop culture and baffling his white friend with invented street monikers for him such as 'D-Man', 'John Dillinger', 'D-Lone' and 'Lonely D' (Lethem, 2003: 58). These last tags are poignantly prescient in that they unwittingly predict the loneliness Dylan will come to experience precisely because he cannot fully be integrated into the graffiti subculture, personified by Mingus, he finds so authentic and so attractive. In short, Dylan never has his own tag, only those imposed upon him. Mingus's, at least, derive from affection; others, like 'white boy', emerge from the widening racial gap exemplified by the ritualised act of 'yoking', the more-or-less playful mugging of white kids by black kids (Lethem, 2003: 84–5).[2] Still others, like 'mole-boy' (Lethem, 2003: 83), are retroactively applied in the act of narration in an attempt to reproduce the adolescent white boy's fear and desire to wrap himself up, to render himself invisible to the marauding black kids around him. This is precisely what the ring does for him in adult life when he pathetically tries to reproduce Mingus's ring-inspired aeronautical heroics as 'Aeroman' (Lethem, 2003: 411).

In essence, what is at stake in the relationship between Dylan, Mingus and their various names is authorship, and it is negotiated across different media in different sections of the novel. As graffiti subculture begins to supersede the comics over which Dylan and Mingus initially bond, one witnesses a shift in the status of authorship. As Douglas Wolk says, before 'art comics' achieved a greater marketplace status, the 'mainstream' comics, dominated by Marvel and DC, were filled with material from artists and writers who did not own their work, who were of secondary importance to the plots, the characters (chiefly superheroes) and to the house style (Wolk, 2007: 27–8). Though the iconic, cartoonistic qualities of comics and their characters encourage powerful readerly identification (McCloud, 1993: 36), there is, despite interactions between comics fans at conventions and specialist stores, an intensely private quality to this identification, something Wolk's analogy with Superman's Fortress of Solitude makes explicit (Wolk, 2007: 72). When Mingus unveils his new tag – 'DOSE' – what is revealed is the potential for a longing for secret identities to be united with public recognition and the reclamation of urban space. It is no coincidence, then, that the tag draws on the graphic style of comics: Mingus 'wrote DOSE in angled block letters. Then he drew it again in a clumsy balloon font, the D and O barely distinguishable, the E swollen so its three digits overlapped – faint mimicry, it seemed to Dylan, of a Marvel Comics sound-effect panel' (Lethem, 2003: 72). 'Tags and their invisible authors', we learn later, 'were the next skully or Marvel superheroes, the hidden lore' (Lethem, 2003: 78). They provide a chance simultaneously to be superhero and author, and to be both publicly lauded and off the official radar. Character and author become thrillingly synonymous as graffiti writers communicate across the city and 'the invisible [autograph] the world' (Lethem, 2003: 93).

Cooper and Chalfant's classic work *Subway Art* highlights the cultural centrality of the name in graffiti:

> The name is at the center of all graffiti art. The writer usually drops his given name and adopts a new one – a new identity. He can make it up, inherit an established name from an old writer, become part of a series such as Take One, Take Five, and so on. Some names are chosen for the esthetic possibilities in the combination of letters they contain. Others are chosen as puns, such as Ban II or Dis I. (Cooper and Chalfant, 1984: 45)

And, as Gregory J. Snyder observes, there is 'a narrative to a wall that goes beyond individual tags claiming space. Numerous tags on a wall provide writers with the opportunity to tell stories about the exploits of their peers' (Snyder, 2009: 69). As well as being a fun means of 'urban exploration' (Snyder, 2009: 85), the tag underpins the sense of community, of belonging, of identity through secret communication. As Dylan recognises: 'A tag was a reply, a call to those who heard, like a dog's bark understood across fences ... the world was all secret names, you only needed to uncover your own' (Lethem, 2003: 93). The problem for Dylan in 'Underberg' is that he does not uncover his own secret name. Instead, with his adolescence left behind, he puts his real name – 'D. Ebdus' – to the liner note which begins the second half of the novel (Lethem, 2003: 295).

This is important because there is a fundamentally different attitude to authorship in graffiti, at least in its purest, street-level state before zines and gallery exhibitions created a commercial 'global community of writers' (Snyder, 2009: 35), than that which pertains in, say, the publishing industry. There is a crucial difference between the author's name on the book cover and the writer's name on the wall or the subway car, a difference which acquires huge significance in the latter stages of *Fortress*. Unlike literary 'style', which seems to exist at one remove from the name attributed to it, the style of the tag achieves absolute consanguinity with its author because it *is* its author. As graffiti writer Sonik succinctly declares: 'The framework of style is the framework of yourself' (Sonik, 2001). Crispin Sartwell says something similar, but in more scholarly and overtly political terms:

> In graffiti, the name and the act of dubbing is seized and simultaneously undermined. Most graffiti artists dub themselves with the name they

use in their work. In part, this is an attempt to undermine the use of names in the legal system and modes of surveillance: to create a persona that worms its way underneath the forms of textual power. The idea is simultaneously to be hard to identify by power and massively famous outside it: to manufacture an unofficial name that does not appear on the birth certificate or other documents and then to broadcast it as far as can possibly be (to king a line for instance, or go all-city) in a culture underneath the official one. And the means of broadcast is not, essentially or initially, publication or the infinitely reproducible abstract textual form, but in a perfectly concrete inscription: a version of the name that is completely space and time-bound, unlike our imagination of published text, which floats free of all dimensionality. (Sartwell, 2003)

Sartwell's thoughts echo those of Dick Hebdige, who sees a subculture's challenge to hegemony happening at the level of signs, and 'expressed obliquely, in style' (Hebdige, 1979: 17). Hebdige's belief that subcultural style is more about the process of meaning than meaning itself is particularly applicable to graffiti, which is as much about the 'signifying practice' (Hebdige, 1979: 118), the ideological implications of getting the stylised name up and where the name goes up, as what the name might actually mean.

Dylan makes no 'concrete inscription'; he does not succeed in getting his name up. For Dylan to have no name is for Dylan to have no style, no secret identity, no real voice in the neighbourhood. Mingus, on the other hand, is doubly successful in this regard. Not only does the magic ring allow him to become 'Aeroman', a secret identity which is theoretically interchangeable with Dylan but in practice never is (Lethem, 2003: 239), but also Aeroman's special powers allow Mingus to get his tag up in an unprecedented manner. This is most evident in the key scene in 'Underberg', occurring as it does more or less at the centre of the novel in narrative terms and absolutely at the centre in thematic terms, functioning as a symbolic distillation of the social, racial and aesthetic discourses at work in this sprawling and complex text.

One February afternoon in 1981 Dylan is trudging along Atlantic Avenue. As he passes Smith Street, he comes across a man pointing at the Brooklyn House of Detention (the tallest structure in the borough). This man's mouth is 'hung open in some kind of *look, up in the sky, it's a bird, it's a plane* gesture of astonishment' (Lethem, 2003: 274). Dylan looks up, and what he sees blows him away: there on the jail tower is 'a brazen impossibility, the biggest tag in the history of tagging ... Four letters: D, O, S, E' (Lethem, 2003: 274). This 'master-piece' acquires an air of almost religious mystery through its sheer magnitude, aiming 'to shock the viewer's brain with the obvious question: *How the fuck DID it get up there?*' Moreover, Dylan's desire for exegesis, '[p]uzzling the message in the four letters. Puzzling whether it *was* a message' (Lethem, 2003: 274) is intensified by his feelings of complicity and guilt. After all, he has been allowed in the past to piggy-back on the more confident Rude's identity by replicating the 'DOSE' tag himself, thereby 'losing his funkymusicwhiteboy geekdom' and spreading the word (Lethem, 2003: 138).

There is a different kind of guilt at work here, too. For most of all, graffiti is racially inscribed for Dylan. He realises that Mingus has used their magic ring to spray the House of Detention. Racked with guilt at his own imminent departure, and with jealousy of his friend's confidence and success with the ring, Dylan/the narrator muses: 'Someone's betrayed someone but you can't say who./Someone's flying and it isn't you' (Lethem, 2003: 274). His anxieties about race, difference and social acceptance in Gowanus are all laid bare and intensified in the brazen image of the giant tag in which he has played no part. Despite their earlier close friendship and symbolic sharing of the DOSE tag, the supersize writing on the prison wall announces the moment of separation between mixed-race Mingus and white Dylan, a separation confirmed a few pages later when Dylan goes to Mingus's house to ask for the ring back, and is yoked by his friend. At this point, the narrator numbly declares: 'Mingus had let him hear it: their difference, finally' (Lethem, 2003: 286). For a short while, the magic ring gave Dylan hope of integration and acceptance. After he survives unhassled at a block party, for example, the narrator muses: 'Maybe the ring has made him *black*. Who can say?' (Lethem, 2003: 168). But the yoking at the hands of Mingus puts an end to such fantasies of integration, as do the endless yokings in the street: 'Dylan was sick of it, the racial rehearsal. He'd been identified as a whiteboy a thousand times and there was nothing more to learn' (Lethem, 2003: 241). Mingus is 'DOSE' and 'Aeroman'; Dylan is still just 'Whiteboy'.

Evidently, there is much to detain the reader here (the pun being absolutely intentional). In fact, the giant tag on the jailhouse wall is precisely an image of graffiti's potential, within the literary text and in Dylan's adolescent world, to detain the reader, to arrest his or her attention, to leave him or her staring at the sky, open-mouthed, as if expecting Superman, and, ultimately, to disrupt the literary text itself. As Janice Rahn stresses, a 'tagger' only becomes a 'writer', strictly speaking, when 'he or she has developed an individual style within the tradition of hip-hop ... has developed painting skills to a level where the community accepts his or her presence and work' (Rahn, 2002: 5). With this outrageous 'claim', 'dwarfing Mono's and Lee's old bridge stunt' (Lethem, 2003: 274), Mingus/DOSE forces the whole community to recognise his skill, power and presence, and in so doing becomes a 'writer' long before Dylan becomes a writer.

But the giant tag is also a sad prophecy, given that Mingus ends up drifting between various jails after shooting his grandfather. Graffiti's history has long involved the interplay of artistic expression and (perceived) criminality: Joe Austin argues that anti-graffiti media campaigns participated in racist constructions of problem youths as responsible for New York City's social ills (Austin, 2001: 36). Jeff Ferrell argues that a clean, blank wall represents order and is a key element of what he dubs the 'aesthetics of authority' (Ferrell, 1996: 178). What is curious about the House of Detention scene is that despite graffiti's transgressive capabilities, the reclamation of the very hegemonic spaces in which and by which it is proscribed, it serves as the simultaneous reinscription and identification of criminality in DOSE the perpetrator. With a minatory sense of predestination, the tag indelibly marks Mingus's identity with the inevitability of incarceration. Thus 'to tag' is both to assert oppositional identity in public spaces and, in the end, to be held to account for that assertion.

At the precise moment Mingus/DOSE gets a name and becomes a writer, then, he is doomed to estrangement from his childhood friend and from mainstream society. The ekphrasis operative in the description of the giant DOSE tag is traumatic: it betokens loss, division, betrayal and social injustice. But the trauma is all Mingus's, even if, in fact precisely because, the narrative construction of *Fortress* is supposed to follow Dylan's coming-of-age (as Gowanus gentrifies and becomes Boerum Hill) and his inability fully to come to terms with and move beyond his adolescence. Many critics have bemoaned Lethem's decision to leave behind the dreamy magic of Dylan's childhood for the bitterness and dysfunction of his adult relationships. Ron Charles complains that '[t]he book's structure begins to creak and break apart' as soon as we leave 'Underberg'; 'the novel never regains the breathtaking verve of its childhood section' (Charles, 2003). John Leonard says that 'everything goes wrong about two thirds of the way through' (Leonard, 2005). What these reviewers fail to appreciate, and what

Samuel Cohen does understand, is that the relatively unsympathetic adult Dylan is a necessary evil; his immaturity, his bitterness, even, stem from his refusal to deal with his past, 'resulting in the present's seeming always less real, less present, paradoxically, than the past' (Cohen, 2009: 179). As he admits to his girlfriend Abby, his adult life has been 'overwhelmed' by his childhood (Lethem, 2003: 319). The fact that 'Underberg' seems to overwhelm the rest of the novel is an appropriate enactment of Dylan's dilemma.

But in the transition from 'Underberg' to 'Liner Note' and then 'Prisonaires' Dylan has at last acquired a name, one which gives him a certain amount of control over the 'rude' and unruly elements of the past that continue to haunt him. Looking at the title of 'Liner Note' is revealing: 'BOTHERED BLUE ONCE MORE: The Barrett Rude Jr. and the Distinctions Story/Notes by D. Ebdus' (Lethem, 2003: 295). Whether or not it eventually proves therapeutic, Dylan's redaction of 'the story' is a devious act of remediation and of appropriation. His name, now officially sanctioned, allows him to re-author Barrett Rude and, by association, Mingus, Court Street and the 'authentic' Gowanus of his youth. When he writes '[t]he voices of Barrett Rude Jr. and the Subtle Distinctions lead nowhere, though, if not back to your neighborhood. To the street where you live' (Lethem, 2003: 306), he is filtering all his anxieties and jealousies through music journalism, the form of writing accessible to him and which gives him a recognisable name. It is an integral part of his attempt 'to hide in books, Manhattanize, depart' (Lethem, 2003: 431).

What is more, Lethem lets him take over the narration of *Fortress of Solitude* so that he is given privileged access to another form of writing, and therefore doubly empowered. This is why I maintain that the real trauma belongs to Mingus. Dylan narrates his time at Camden College, his move to California, his return to Brooklyn and his search for his lost mother in the first-person. Mingus, on the other hand, has no such privilege. Samuel Cohen is wrong to state that there is 'a long section of the book given to us from Mingus' point of view' (Cohen, 2009: 175); rather the aftermath of the shooting, the years of drifting between prisons and crack houses, are narrated in a kind of free indirect discourse in Chapters 13 and 14. It is as if Lethem cannot quite bring himself to foster the same level of identification with Mingus as he does with Dylan. Moreover, Mingus is referred to as 'Dose' throughout these chapters, as if the graffiti tag on the House of Detention has marked him for life, as if the secret identity that made

him special in the fantasy world of childhood has forever marginalised him in the shabbier real world of adulthood.

Given that Mingus is destined to remain as 'Dose' when Dylan ma-
tures into 'D. Ebdus', it is appropriate that graffiti continues to act as
symbolic marker of the differences between them in the second part
of the novel. It undoubtedly continues to hold a unique and discomfiting status for Dylan. The second part can be seen as a chronicle
of his futile attempts to remediate his youthful obsessions through
journalism and first-person narration of the novel. Like many Lethem
characters, he believes that cluttering his world with language might
distract him from direct consideration of his problems and culpabili-
ties. But graffiti is always a sticking point for him; it is the most powerful representation of his childhood, and yet the one that resists his
attempts at remediation, partly because he has never really had the
skill or the courage to come up with a distinctive tag name of his own,
and partly because it symbolises the world he deliberately abandoned
to go to white, liberal Camden College. Instead it continues to exist
at the margins of his life, a kind of ghost, an image just under the
surface of things, like the 'phantom DOSE' that remains even after
the House of Detention wall is scrubbed (Lethem, 2003: 274). As he
says upon returning to Dean Street after his spell in California: 'I saw
meanings encoded everywhere on these streets, like the DMD and
FMD tags still visible where they'd been sprayed twenty years before'
(Lethem, 2003: 429).

As an adult, it is graffiti that continues to stand for racial difference
in Dylan's eyes. The opening scene of his first-person narration takes
place in his California apartment, where he is having an argument
with his black girlfriend, Abby. Tellingly, Dylan declares: 'I loved having a black girlfriend, and I loved Abby, but I was no trumpet player'
(Lethem, 2003: 312). When she confronts him with some previously
undeclared truths, the imagery he evokes takes him all the way back
to Brooklyn, which is precisely one of the problems – Dylan's obsession with his past – that Abby has identified:

> 'I said to myself, Abby, this man is collecting you for the color of your
> skin. That was okay, I was willing to be collected. I liked being your nig-
> ger, Dylan.' Ouch. The word throbbed between us, permitting no reply
> from me. I could visualize it in cartoonish or graffiti-style font, glowing
> with garish decorations, lightning, stars, halos. As with the lick, I could
> appreciate the *form*. (Lethem, 2003: 319)

He visualises racial difference as graffiti and, once again, reduces it to a matter of style. Later still, when he goes to visit Mingus in jail, Dylan comments: 'There, we were sealed from one another by a Plexiglas window covered with minute scratchiti, and allowed to converse on telephones' (Lethem, 2003: 442). Yet again, the invisible barrier between Dylan the white boy and Mingus the black boy is inscribed with graffiti markings, returning again to mark difference. Races, the scene seems to say, are never transparent, never comprehensible and never compatible. Dylan and Mingus are separated by their race, by Mingus's criminality, by cultural referents they have attempted to but failed to share.

The distance appears insurmountable. So what if, as Jacob Siegel contests, 'Lethem espouses a vision of essentialist racial difference?' Can the novel, in Siegel's words, 'be read as the account of a white heart breaking when it learns that a qualitative difference in humanity separates it by an unbridgeable gap from its black love?' (Siegel, 2005). The unequal distribution of narrative authority seems to support such a reading. Similarly, the fact that Mingus once again becomes 'Dose' in jail arguably serves to reinforce the idea of graffiti, and possibly blackness, as criminality.

However, it is more complex than this. While it would be simplistic to argue that Lethem is just 'telling it like it is', that is, enacting at the level of narrative voice the unequal opportunities afforded to whites and blacks in the US, the choices Lethem makes in the second half of *Fortress* constitute his bravest rejection of the desire to fabricate and live in mini-utopias because they resist the construction of blackness itself as a utopia, a construction that tends to ignore social realities. Blackness, and predominantly black culture such as graffiti and hip-hop, is for Dylan one of the 'middle spaces' of utopian arrested time (Lethem, 2003: 510) yearned for by Rachel and Abraham, by Dylan and, for a while at least, by Mingus. These middle spaces derive from dreams of endless summers in 'a place where Mingus Rude always grooved fat spaldeen pitches, born home runs' (Lethem, 2003: 510). They are destroyed by, among other things, the economic modalities of gentrification (Lethem, 2003: 510) and, of course, by simply growing up.

For Dylan, the fact that Mingus is only 'black. Sort of' (Lethem, 2003: 72) by virtue of having a white mother briefly promises another liminal middle space floating between the strict oppositions of black and white, a utopian melting pot. His realisation that socially and culturally Mingus will always be considered black and endlessly perform that role effectively disabuses him of another fantasy of the middle space. Appropriately enough, it is in Chapter 13, when the reader learns about Mingus's life after the shooting, that the most heartbreaking deconstruction of the dream occurs:

> But the stories you told yourself – which you pretended to recall as if they'd happened every afternoon of an infinite summer – were really a pocketful of days distorted into legend, another jailhouse exaggeration, like the dimensions of those ballpoint-crosshatched tits or of the purported mountains of blow you once used to enjoy … How often had that hydrant even been opened? Did you jet water through a car window, what, twice at best? Summer burned just a few afternoons long, in the end. (Lethem, 2003: 473–4)

Dylan is incapable of such perspicacity until the very end of the novel. Most of the time, he is the child who never learns.

As the novel comes to a close, Dylan is travelling back east with his father after a fruitless attempt to locate Rachel Ebdus, aka 'Running Crab' (she too aspires to a secret identity). They drive through a blizzard, listening to the music of Brian Eno, while Dylan reflects, with an astuteness that suggests he may finally have come of age, on the untenability of nostalgia, freezing time and creating closed fantasy worlds. These discrete realms of imagination, he realises, must give way to history, change over time and uncertainty. Crucial to this new understanding is his father's unfinished celluloid painting: 'Abraham had the better idea, to try to carve the middle space on a daily basis, alone in his room. If the green triangle never fell to earth before he died and left the film unfinished, it would never have fallen – wasn't that so? Wasn't it?' (Lethem, 2003: 510–11). Art, like life, is an ongoing negotiation or process and it is best to remain, like the green triangle, forever 'in the middle of half-completed motions and in the middle between confusion and certainty' (Cohen, 2009: 184), resistant to closure and to the temptations of retreat into romantic utopias. As Samuel Cohen says (Cohen, 2009: 184), *Fortress* resists a happy ending (we never know if Dylan makes up with Abby or if his relationship with his father improves long-term) and finishes with the image of the drive through the blizzard into an uncertain future that serves to show that the past was also never a place of safety or certainty, but was always changing.

Abe's is a silent, wordless art and as such offers an alternative to Dylan's endless talking and writing. The irony *Fortress* shares with many of Lethem's novels is its own status as novel, where language cannot be avoided; the celluloid painting, ethically at the heart of the text, can nonetheless only be endlessly re-described. Once again, ekphrasis enacts the problem of remediating experience and in so doing becomes part of the problem. It is noteworthy that in the last line of the book Dylan refers to himself and his father as 'two gnarls of human scribble, human cipher, human dream' (Lethem, 2003: 511), as if he is not quite prepared to shake off his old habits of evasive remediation.

As a footnote, it is useful to draw some connections between *Fortress* and the text with which it has a lot in common, *Omega the Unknown*. In light of the argument above, one might instinctively feel that Lethem's desire to resurrect the comic that he openly admits inspired *Fortress* (Lethem and Rusnak, 2008) is a retrogressive step. After all, in returning to a Marvel strip that 'pushed all [his] buttons' in the 1970s (Lethem and Rusnak, 2008), he appears to be fetishising childhood cultural artefacts in the same way Dylan Ebdus does. Moreover, if *Fortress*, as has been suggested, worries about Lethem's coming-of-age as a writer and about the power and guilt associated with gaining 'a name', then the front cover of *Omega*, emblazoned with the line '[b]y the Award-winning author of *Motherless Brooklyn* Jonathan Lethem' reads like an unabashed celebration of his newfound canonical status. Echoing Douglas Wolk's thoughts on the shift from mainstream to art comics, Ray Davis says that 'movie and comic book studios have been caught between allegiances to genre, characters, and performers, and allegiances to the "masterwork" as singular artifact and "auteur" as infallible genius' (Davis, 2009: 71). The cover of *Omega* appears to make its allegiances clear.

But to make these claims is to forget a number of important aspects of *Omega*. First, it is a collaboration and, although he gets top billing, Lethem has to share credit for its success with Karl Rusnak, artists Farel Dalrymple and Paul Hornschemer and, of course, the original creators of the strip, Steve Gerber and Mary Skrenes. Thus *Omega* can be seen as a logical extension of the open acknowledgement of influence and reference that characterises Lethem's work from *Amnesia Moon*, with its heavy debt to Philip K. Dick, to 'The Ecstasy of Influence'. So while Lethem's intervention reinvents a mainstream comic as a 'graphic novel' or 'art comic', it also deliberately popularises the work of the auteur.

Secondly, *Omega* references *Fortress* even as it has so obviously influenced that novel, so that their relationship becomes a cyclical one of interdependence. The two texts share a great deal: a geeky, slightly alienated protagonist who loses his parents (admittedly they are robot parents in the comic) and has a lot to learn about popular culture; a black buddy for the white kid; and, of course, the presence of superheroes decidedly on the wane. Both are twisted, melancholic coming-of-age tales. But the partial remediation of the novel by a medium with a fundamentally different attitude to visual images and the written word is highly significant. As Scott McCloud argues, in comics words and pictures have a relationship of interdependence, frequently operating 'hand in hand to convey an idea that neither could convey alone' (McCloud, 1993: 155). Indeed, McCloud goes further and argues that a word should be considered simply the most abstracted possibility on a spectrum of abstraction from reality which contains 'realistic' images and cartoonified images (McCloud, 1993: 47). If one accepts this reasoning, then it is a mistake even to regard comics as combinations of words and pictures. They require an entirely different critical vocabulary.

Experts like McCloud and Wolk are better equipped to supply that vocabulary. My point is that in remediating *Fortress* as comic, Lethem is striving for a way 'to bypass the master tropes of figurative language' (Singer, 2008: 274) which define the novel as a form and which are at the root of Dylan's, and many other characters' difficulties in deciphering and representing the world. Language, as Marc Singer says, has come to be seen in structuralist and post-structuralist discourse as a series of substitutions of symbols resulting in an endless deferral of meaning (Singer, 2008: 274). Comics, on the other hand, exploit their unique figurative strategies to construct literalised metaphors which have the potential, at least, to circumvent that deferral and engage in a more direct mimesis. As earlier chapters have shown, Lethem is fond of concretised metaphors in his novels and short stories and this, one might speculate, is partly due to his passion for comic art. However, Singer is also right to argue that *Fortress*, for all its sensitivity to comic book culture, is guilty (like other contemporary 'comic-book novels') of using comic book tropes simply as metaphors for, among other things, adolescent angst. And '[a]s Lethem's protagonist learns that these metaphors cannot fully signify their objects, they become exhausted, thus reconfirming rather than overcoming the inadequacies and absences of symbolic representation' (Singer, 2008: 275).

The remediation of *Fortress* in *Omega* can therefore be seen as evidence of what Singer dubs 'a counter-linguistic turn' (Singer, 2008:

274). Indeed, the remarkable final chapter of *Omega*, in which an utterly decrepit and homeless Omega the Unknown is wheeled underground to take his place in a bizarre exhibit of exhausted superheroes, is almost totally devoid of words. Lethem is a writer, first and foremost, and will always be bound to language, but *Omega*, like the texts examined in Chapter 7, signals the desire of someone who has only recently achieved widespread acclaim as a novelist to reach out to other media where language either does not figure, or where it behaves differently, in a less obfuscatory manner. Both *You Don't Love Me Yet* and *Chronic City* rely on remediation and engagements with other media to explore themes such as collective loss and the decline of reality.

Notes

1   Earlier examples of Brooklyn gentrification novels would include Paula Fox's *Desperate Characters* (1970) and L. J. Davis's caustic *A Meaningful Life* (1971).

2   Lethem's essay 'Yoked in Gowanus', from the collection *Everything but the Burden: What White People Are Taking from Black Culture* (2003) goes into more detail.

7

'Hiding in plain sight': reality and secrecy in *You Don't Love Me Yet* and *Chronic City*

In Chapter 4 it was noted that a feature of the novel in all its abundance is the misleading opportunity it appears to afford for interpretive success. 'Come and get me', it seems to say (it is no coincidence that Frank Kermode dubs reading for the obvious primary sense 'carnal' (Kermode, 1979: 9)), before closing the door and taking refuge in its own secrets. That so many scholars are still analysing Henry James stories is testament to the texts' continued determination to deceive and to keep their secrets. If we do not make allowances for this, Kermode implies, if we continue trying to impose definition or force conformity, texts make fools of us all.

So if one ventures that *You Don't Love Me Yet* (2007a) is 'about' secrecy, is one merely being suckered by the text? Is that precisely what it wants everyone to think? Another reader could very easily retort, 'well yes, it is obviously about secrecy: where's the secret in that?' After all, this is a novel which opens with a clandestine act of lovemaking in an art installation (Lethem, 2007a: 5) and ends with two gnomic slogans playing with the idea of secrecy. One is worn on a T-shirt and declares, 'NOBODY KNOWS I'M SUICIDAL' (Lethem, 2007a: 223) and the other, the final line of the novel, has a character state '[y]ou can't be deep without a surface' (Lethem, 2007a: 224). In between, the action revolves around a nameless LA rock band whose 'secret genius' songwriter, the deeply sensitive but hapless Bedwin (Lethem, 2007a: 165), is suffering writer's block until the bass player, Lucinda, privately offers him some lyrical ideas for a song called 'Monster Eyes' (Lethem, 2007a: 22–3). The song is destined to become a brief underground hit, but unbeknown to Bedwin, Lucinda has plagiarised the words from the mysterious 'Complainer', an enigmatic stranger who regularly calls her at the 'complaint line' she is working for the conceptual artist Falmouth Strand. (Another secret, then: the complaint line is 'a sort of theatrical piece … A fake office that needs fake office workers to answer real telephone calls' (Lethem, 2007a: 4).) When the Complainer, whose real name is Carl, joins the band, the narrator observes: '[t]heirs was a band whose secret genius had a secret genius, a conspiracy huddled around a confusion' (Lethem, 2007a: 165). Unfortunately, Carl's disruptive influence and his tendency to reveal the secrets of the lyrics (Lethem, 2007a: 150) eventually pull the band apart. From this synopsis it is clear that Lethem intends to make no secret of his subject matter.

So once again, for a critic to observe that *You Don't Love Me Yet* is about secrecy is unwittingly to cast himself in a similar role to that of the first subject in Jacques Lacan's famous 'Seminar on "The Purloined Letter"'. That is, one which 'sees nothing and deludes itself as to the secrecy of what it hides' (Lacan, 1988: 32). In presuming to say something new about the text – that it is all about secrecy – the critic assumes the blindness of previous readers and narcissistically assumes that he is not likewise 'seen' by a more perspicacious interpreter, one that 'sees that the first two glances leave what should be hidden exposed to whomever would seize it' (Lacan, 1988: 32). Put simply, what the critic cherishes as the big revelation has been there for everyone to see all along.

But this might be precisely the point. Lethem's novel owes an obvious debt to Edgar Allan Poe's tale partly because of its preoccupation with the predicaments of *open* secrets. For example, just as the Minister famously steals and then hides the purloined letter in full view, thus evading the scrupulous searches of the police with their 'realist's imbecility' (Lacan, 1988: 40), so Lucinda's attraction to Bedwin toward the end of the novel prompts this comment: 'The band's secret genius was also Lucinda's, hiding in plain sight.' He is 'the answer to the question she'd only just formed': in other words, the revelation of this particular 'secret' depends only on her way of seeing, her desire for the perceived secret (Lethem, 2007a: 203). Of course, as is the way with secrets, once Lucinda reveals this one to herself, Bedwin's attractiveness almost immediately disappears (four pages later, in fact). Thus there is a paradox in Carl's assertion that the quality of a secret should be judged 'by its telling' (Lethem, 2007a: 168); just as someone is put in a position to judge the secret's quality, it ceases to be a secret.

'Hiding in plain sight', as it is in so many Lethem texts, is this novel's key motif, and as the example above demonstrates, it is intimately bound up with intersubjectivity's structuring through desire. It is nowhere better exemplified than on Carl the Complainer's T-shirt, emblazoned with the slogan 'NOBODY KNOWS I'M SUICIDAL'. This statement's effect is not dissimilar to the familiar paradox 'Everything I say is a lie'. For the signifiers to maintain any kind of sense, the mental image they conjure, the signified, must by necessity be false. In fact it is evident that the content of such a statement, like the content of the purloined letter, is unimportant. As Leo Bersani and Ulysse Dutoit explain, '[w]hat the secret is – or whether a secret even exists – is irrelevant to the intelligibility given to a relation by the mere appearance of a secret' (Bersani and Dutoit, 1998: 16). Fascination is produced by the possibility of the secret, not the secret itself.

What expressly fascinates about this ridiculous T-shirt is the apparent frankness of the admission, coupled with the lingering suspicion that, despite its self-negating quality, there remains an enigmatic, elusive, indeed secret surplus, something important we are not being told. It may simply be a symptom of interpretive paranoia, but the very boldness of the declaration tempts one to try and 'rediscover a secret to which truth has always initiated her lovers, and through which they learn that it is in hiding that she offers herself to them *most truly*' (Lacan, 1988: 37). What is the secret behind the non-secret? My contention – and this also applies to the virtualised world of *Chronic City*, as demonstrated in the second part of this chapter – is that the question can only be answered properly with reference to the specific historical, cultural, economic and technological context in which Jonathan Lethem is writing.

Jacques Lacan's 'Seminar' does not take into account such a context in its discussion of Poe's tale. Neither should one expect it to, of course. What it does is reaffirm 'the primacy of the signifier over the subject' (Muller and Richardson, 1988: 67) by exploring the way in which participants in the narrative are repositioned in relation to the 'pure signifier' of the letter (Lacan, 1988: 32). By so doing, it appoints the narrative as a model of Lacanian psychoanalytic theory. Inadvertently, perhaps, Lacan's writing also highlights the problematic gender prescriptions at the heart of Freudian and post-Freudian psychoanalysis through its designation of 'the attributes of femininity and shadow' as 'propitious to the act of concealing' (Lacan, 1988: 44).

Nonetheless, in preparation for a discussion of *You Don't Love Me Yet* and *Chronic City* it is rewarding briefly to consider the extent to which Poe's cultural, historical and economic milieu might have influenced his creation of a story about privacy, the thrill of secrecy and the fear of/desire for revelation. For example, in its structuring of unspoken contractual relations between people, relations founded shakily on secrets the contents of which are never actually redeemed, the letter functions as an allegory of the promissory paper economy. Such an economy, which began to supersede the 'gold standard' model in early nineteenth-century America, dissolves the certainties of material exchange and submits to abstract notions of credit, speculation and debt. As the financial panic of 1819 illustrated, it has the potential to provoke intense anxiety about economic and, according to David Anthony (2005) in his excellent reading of Washington Irving, masculine identity and status. It does so precisely by means of an open secret: everyone knows that the paper itself is worthless, that the power and status it confers upon the user is apparitional, yet disbelief must be suspended (and the secret undeclared) for fungibility to persist. Exchange society relies on the collective maintenance of the secret and the endless deferral signified by the 'promise to pay'. The content of the purloined letter is in itself similarly worthless, and the threat derives from a 'promise to pay', that is, to make good the letter's supposed potential.

The feeling that another person might at some point redeem or reveal one's innermost secret, the 'promise to pay', is linked not only to the paper economy, but also the ontological anxieties of the democratic individual. For it is another open secret that, while clinging on to the notion of an inviolate, secret inner core of identity, the democratic individual is nonetheless like everyone else (even in this clinging on), is, in fact, part of 'the mob'.[1] While 'The Man of the Crowd' deals with 'the *loss* of 'private' self-interest, or the inability to be let alone' in the city streets (Renza, 2002: 66), 'The Purloined Letter' exploits images of violated chambers and letters to allegorise the ease with which the inner core of selfhood is exposed as a myth. All characters in the tale, and by implication everyone in wider society, share this desperate need to maintain a sense of secrecy and distinguish themselves from others, to observe but not be observed. In the 1840s, when there was the highest level of immigration in proportion to the USA's total population (over four million immigrants arriving between 1840 and 1860), this must have seemed increasingly difficult (statistics taken from Foner, 2006: 417).[2]

It is no coincidence, then, that the Minister's downfall hinges on the moment he is distracted by a gunshot and 'the shoutings of a mob' outside his window (Poe, 1971: 347). At the moment he observes the public, he is most closely observed, his secret replaced with another and his myth of inviolability secretly destroyed. As José Liste Noya argues, the relationship between private and public in discussions of secrecy is riddled with paradoxes: 'The secret, after all, in its conventional senses, would seem to need to make public its hermetic privacy. One must know that a secret exists; otherwise there is no secret' (Liste Noya, 2004: 242). Thus he can state that in the world as represented by certain authors (his examples are Henry James and Don DeLillo) 'the sphere of the public is built up through the proliferation of secrets, seemingly the most undemocratic of hierarchical devices' (Liste Noya, 2004: 242). The question, and it is one applicable to Lethem's latest novels, is whether there exists a truly democratic secret whose very existence remains a secret, one that cannot be represented publicly.

These brief musings on Poe are intended to show how historical context shapes the very patterns of secrecy and power within which human subjects interact. Lethem's world is very different from Poe's, of course. Whereas Poe's text obliquely raises anxieties about intimacy and extimacy at a time of mass immigration and urbanisation, Lethem writes within and about a twenty-first century western world in which mass culture, particularly television, aestheticises notions of secrecy and exposure themselves. It is a truth widely acknowledged by enthusiasts and curmudgeonly antagonists alike that the predominant cultural phenomena of the late twentieth and early twenty-first centuries are 'celebrity' and 'reality'. From the proliferation of reality TV shows, beginning with true-life series like *Cops* in the US and culminating in the global success of *Big Brother*, to the increased popularity of celebrity autobiographies and prurient gossip magazines such as *Now*, popular culture is dominated by texts promising the continual revelation of secrets. A pornographic fantasy of total availability and total access to the real is on offer; hidden cameras make voyeurs of us all, and in so doing perform the neat trick of making celebrities appear more 'normal' while transforming ordinary members of the public into instant celebrities. Nobody has any secrets any more, or at least, none which are not on the verge of imminent exposure. Most significantly, secrets are commodities: they are there to be sold and consumed, and if this sounds like a form of blackmail, it has become a distinctly Gramscian, consensual form.

Before this argument spills over into polemic, it is important to note that things are not quite as simple as the overview above suggests.

Total availability is of course a fantasy. Reality culture functions, with the help of producers, editors and executives, by means of a complex interplay between the real and the false, the hidden and the revealed. As Randall L. Rose and Stacy L. Wood argue, reality TV 'represents a sophisticated quest for authenticity within the traditionally fiction-oriented paradigm'. However, 'within the apparent obsession with authenticity lies a postmodern paradox. Although authenticity is desired and earnestly promoted, consumers of reality television revel in the ironic mixture of the factitious and the spontaneous' (Rose and Wood, 2005: 284, 286).

In their considerably more polemical book *Shooting People*, Sam Brenton and Reuben Cohen dub the placement of real people in unreal situations, typical of so much reality TV, 'situationism' (Brenton and Cohen, 2003: 46). Citing empirical research by Annette Hill (2005), they contend that despite viewers' expectation of some inter-penetration of the real and unreal, there is nonetheless 'deep suspicion ... towards the "real" nature of behaviour captured in reality shows and docusoaps'. They continue:

> Viewers overwhelmingly believe that people overact for the camera, and part of the appeal of the reality TV experience is waiting for the mask to slip, in moments of stress and conflict, revealing the concealed 'true self' or 'real face' of a contestant. In their hunger for occasions when anger flares and performance gives way to authenticity, we see the audience's fascination with a gaudy, demonstrative self- hood, and a boundless curiosity for the shadowplay of false and real selves. (Brenton and Cohen, 2003: 51)

What this situationist shadowplay serves to exaggerate, then, is the tension between privacy and secrecy which, regarded in broader philosophical terms, is a tension between ontology and representation. 'Reality' texts necessitate a destruction of privacy in which viewers and contestants willingly collude, while maintaining desire for the revelation of the secret self. As Sissela Bok argues, secrecy 'serves as an additional shield in case the protection of privacy should fail or be broken down', the difference in this context being that it does not guard 'against unwanted access' (Bok, 1983: 13) but actually invites and aestheticises that access.

The open secret, then, is partly that there are still secrets and partly that the whole postmodern artificiality of it all threatens to implode at any time. Precisely because the technology-enabled aesthetic of access to the private actually exacerbates the distance between selfhood and the representation of it, the Baudrillardian idea that simulation has completely superseded reality increasingly looks unsatisfactory. The level of invasive representation one sees in reality television is now such that one can no longer embrace the idea that all we have are representations, so that at the point of highest artificiality the possibility of the real is reinvigorated. In its own paradoxical way, then, 'reality' culture does, after all, signal a renewed engagement with reality. These are the kinds of paradoxes *You Don't Love Me Yet*, historically situated in an early twenty-first century hypermediated 'reality' culture, sets out to investigate and exploit. Dismissed by many critics[3] and regarded by the author himself as a deliberately 'cavalier gesture' (Peacock, 2009) after the intense mining of childhood experience in *Fortress of Solitude* and *The Disappointment Artist*, it is nonetheless a novel with serious points to make about secrecy, aesthetics, language and reality.

As the earlier synopsis shows, music is central to the story and to its epistemological implications. Lethem's passion for music has long been evident in the essays on his website (on subjects such as The Clash), his editorial work and, of course, his treatment of soul groups and fans in *The Fortress of Solitude*.[4] Unlike *Fortress*, which uses music partly as an illustration of the way Dylan attempts to remediate his adolescent experience, its successor is a full-blown rock and roll novel. As such, it is in the author's opinion flirting with disaster from its very inception: 'everyone agrees rock and roll novels are all bad, and I think I managed to help confirm this impression' (Personal Interview, 2009). The lowly status of the genre derives partly from writers' ill-advised desire to depict 'fake famous' groups, which is why Lethem's novel features a band whose members all have mundane day jobs (lead singer Matthew works in the local zoo, for example, which allows Lethem to contrive the subplot involving the kidnapping of a disaffected kangaroo called Shelf, just like Kimmery's cat in *Motherless Brooklyn*), and partly from the bald fact that 'you never believe the songs could be good, and you never believe the lyrics would be ... you never believe the career' (Personal Interview, 2009). *You Don't Love Me Yet* sincerely wants us to believe in the songs, the lyrics and the short-lived career: its failure is what concerns us in the following analysis, and what that failure reveals about language and other art forms, and about the unique condition of music as a truly democratic secret.

Key to this analysis is the chapter in which the band first performs in public, and the generic shift that occurs here, so it is necessary to set the scene first. It is only happy accident bordering on farce that allows the band to play at all. Originally, promoter Jules Harvey and artist Falmouth Strand conceive of 'a happening' in 'a rather large loft' structured around certain rigid prescriptions designed to make it the antithesis of normal loft parties (Lethem, 2007a: 39). As Strand explains: 'the rule is you can't bring anyone you know. And you have to wear headphones. You have to listen to whatever you prefer to dance to, your own mix. If people don't have their own headphones we'll provide them at the door ... What I want is a sea of dancing bodies, each to their own private music' (Lethem, 2007a: 39). This 'Aparty' (Lethem, 2007a: 39), though ridiculous, is in its own playful way a secretive dystopia: it exploits and exacerbates the isolationism and retreat which have been concerns for Lethem since his debut novel and are themselves exacerbated, one might speculate, by aspects of contemporary technology and culture such as the internet and reality TV. Conceived of as conceptual art, it aestheticises the breakdown of community and makes it seductively, dangerously cool.

Crucially, Harvey and Strand have no interest in the band's music for their Aparty. Referred to in business terms as 'your little consortium' by Strand (Lethem, 2007a: 39), the band is then coldly reduced to superficial generic elements by Harvey: 'Attractive people playing and singing in the classic format: guitar, drums, singer, etcetera' (Lethem, 2007a: 39). To add further insult, the group is initially required to play 'very quietly, with nobody paying any attention' (Lethem, 2007a: 39). However, when the invitation 'becomes exponential' and there are not nearly enough tape players and headsets for all the people who have wandered along (Lethem, 2007a: 95), Harvey and Strand make a desperate decision: the band will play live and audible, the Aparty will become a party and later 'a show' (Lethem, 2007a: 106), and Strand's 'important art' (Lethem, 2007a: 100) will for the moment be supplanted by 'something more spontaneous' and organic (Lethem, 2007a: 101). Needless to say, something special transpires: the band rocks.

Though the jacket blurb describes it as a parody of the romantic comedy, *You Don't Love Me Yet* provides perhaps the clearest example of the tendency in Lethem's work after *Girl in Landscape* not to stage exuberant generic collisions and not to strive so hard to bring the fantastic into the everyday. For this reason, the change of generic discourse from novelistic to mock-journalistic that occurs as soon as the band hits the stage is particularly deserving of scrutiny, marking as it does the moment at which Lethem suspends his role as narrator of a story and temporarily becomes (in the manner of Dylan Ebdus) one of the '[s]uper-high-functioning' and frequently 'self-reinforcing' rock critics Perkus Tooth so despises in *Chronic City* (Lethem, 2009a: 15). Unashamedly pretentious, written mostly in the present tense in an attempt to recreate the spontaneity, the experience of 'being there', the eight pages describing the gig are structurally and hermeneutically at the centre of the novel and form a testimony to music's transforming power, its unique status as a highly symbolic form imbued with a dynamic structure that 'can express the forms of vital experience which language is peculiarly unfit to convey' (Langer, 1953: 32). Lethem's prose, if one accepts this idea of music's qualities, has to be pretentious, in the sense that it pretends to do what it cannot possibly do. And by abandoning the novelistic stance in this section, the author tacitly admits from the outset that the novel is not up to the task. It rapidly becomes apparent that his Greil Marcus impression also falls short.

For the crowd assembled outside, the first strains of the band's music appeal precisely for their reassuringly generic qualities: 'a general drift was discernible, twice through a verse, building to a chorus: hey, everyone knows how this works, knows it in their bones, even if unable to articulate it exactly: rock 'n' roll' (Lethem, 2007a: 103–4). Moreover, hearing the band indistinctly from the street reinforces the paradoxical framing of difference and similarity at the heart of genre production: 'It's what makes this band sound alike to any other that makes them intriguing, at this distance: they could be the Beatles, heard from the street. Or, just as easily, the Beards' (Lethem, 2007a: 104). Immediately, a constellated community is established: the transition from 'atonal clatter' to 'sensible conjunction' (Lethem, 2007a: 103) inspires a concomitant move from isolated individuals to something resembling a crowd, and finally to an audience (Lethem, 2007a: 106) united in appreciation of the show. As this movement is enacted, the entering of the building to avoid 'missing the set' (Lethem, 2007a: 104) acquires a metaphorical power; the guests exit the freight elevator in a quest for the 'inside' of the music, for its occulted realities, for knowledge of its secrets, which include the identities of the players. The reader's privileged position with regard to the backstory of the gig is temporarily suspended at this point: placed within the audience, he or she reads only about 'the band', rather than Bedwin, Lucinda, Denise and Matthew. It is as if the reader has entered the loft on the same voyage of discovery.

Yet the improvised stage lighting serves as another metaphor and instantly rejects the revelatory expectations of the first: 'Without footlights to provide underlighting, the band appears mysteriously remote, silhouettes draped in indigo as they confer with one another and their set list, nodding, perhaps mumbling a word or two, but inaudible above the low crackle and drone of speakers, broadcasting nothing but their own electronic readiness' (Lethem, 2007a: 104). From this sentence on, the critique of the performance is characterised by prolix, ostensibly insightful analysis of the songs consistently undermined by modality, vagueness, images of obscurity and a tension between revelation and concealment. For example, 'The Houseguest', the first song the newly assembled audience hears, simultaneously 'liberates some element of rageful self-pity his own temperament usually quashes' in the vocalist, while transforming him into 'a performer with a series of false faces to wear, urgent charades to put across' (Lethem, 2007a: 105). The 'raw quatrain' of the persistent chorus contains 'the sole words a listener could distinguish with any confidence, and certainly the only ones that matter' (Lethem, 2007a: 105). Whether or not the critic-narrator's rather pompous certitude has an ironic edge, it only serves to intensify the suspicion that the band, their songs and the narrator are collaborating to conceal, and to increase the desire to know what the rest of the song contains.

Desire is crucial to the gig's success. Not only the sexual desire excited merely by performance, that which makes 'about a hundred men watching ask themselves why they've never had the eyes before to see they ought to have asked the drummer or the bassist on a date' (Lethem, 2007a: 106), but also the more profound and complex constitutive relationship of desire based on the unattainable real, the mystery or secret the music seems always on the brink of elucidating. This real is referred to throughout the passage as the 'something' and its elusiveness is, of course, the attraction: 'This band's got something, and some of the something they've got is the allure of an enclave at odds within itself and yet impenetrable to others, its members exchanging small gestures of disaffection within their troupe that makes others crave to be included in the fond dissension' (Lethem, 2007a: 107). The band is, in other words, another version of the FSR or subcultural mini-utopia, trying to remain closed but enticing to others. A similarly desirable aspect of this 'something' is 'the mystery of authorship' (Lethem, 2007a: 107): during 'Temporary Feeling' the narrator wonders, without ever providing answers, 'If a heart's revealed here, whose? ... Is the song a fiction, or a cover version, or the lament of someone hiding in plain sight? Who's moving the mouth' (Lethem, 2007a: 107).

Given his openness about influence, his belief that quotation is 'native to the creative act' and intertextuality 'basic to language' (Lethem, 2010d), these are questions of relevance to Lethem's work as a whole (not that he in any way keeps faith with a rigid distinction between originality and borrowing), but the collective desire for answers during the gig, the yearning to be included in the band's private affiliations, tells us a great deal about the specific structures of desire in the audience's wider historical context. The band and its music function like the Lacanian *objet petit a* in that they are essentially produced by specific modes of desire: 'the object *a* is an object that can be perceived only by a gaze "distorted" by desire, an object that *does not exist* for an "objective" gaze,' Slavoj Žižek explains, 'since it is *nothing but* the embodiment, the materialization of this very distortion' (Žižek, 1992: 12). And as Žižek knows, there is nothing innate about desire; from birth we are taught how and what to desire by culture.

With these ideas in mind, we can begin to formulate the fundamentally romantic, emancipatory notion of rock music Lethem promulgates in this section and in the novel as a whole. As we have seen, a 'reality' culture reinvigorates notions of reality; what it does not do is convince anyone that reality is actually present or available in docusoaps, gossip magazines and *Big Brother*. What the description of the gig strongly suggests is that in contrast live music possesses an essence, a real, a genuinely exciting and reanimating secret, and that an atomised and thoroughly mediated culture redoubles the desire to access that secret. That nobody can actually gain access, that 'there is always a disparity between the experience of music and the way in which we imagine or think about it' (Cook, 1990: 135) is precisely the point. No matter how commodified or 'sold-out' the band might actually be, no matter how technologically 'hypermediated' (Bolter and Grusin, 2000: 42) the performance, at the point of reception live music has a direct, unmediated and absolutely ineffable emotional connection. In this it is inherently more democratic than reality TV, for example, which is always-already mediated. Music, in other words, remains a secret from everybody, and a more than ever attractive and

necessary one, Lethem suggests, in a western society prone to the artificial fetishisation of secrets and the pretence of constant revelation.
After the tumultuous second airing of the band's 'perfect song'
(Lethem, 2007a: 110) called 'Monster Eyes', a pleasing paradox is enacted when the audience members begin to interpret the lyrics: 'this
song's about you and me and the dangerous way we feel sometimes!
It's about all of us! But it's about me most of all, each listener thinks.
It's most particularly about dangerous me' (Lethem, 2007a: 110). Unlike Dylan Ebdus, who persists in regarding the music of his childhood
as exclusively pertinent to his childhood and nobody else's, the revel-
lers have embraced the democratic paradox inspired by the music,
one which underlies all Lethem's work and informs his genre experiments: that we become most like others when we immerse ourselves
in our private subcultural concerns. Thus when the gig ends and people start donning the headphones and 'dancing asynchronously in the
zone before the stage' (Lethem, 2007a: 110), the communal experience of the gig makes their actions a knowing parody of Falmouth
Strand's Aparty, not an endorsement of its ethos: 'No one's quite so
apart as Falmouth might have envisioned, and the artist himself may
well have quit the scene in disgust' (Lethem, 2007a: 111). Touched
by the secrets of the music, the audience has achieved a healthy and
dynamic compromise between individual and collective.

Lethem's is a romantic vision of the power of rock and roll. And his
attempt to harness it in words, characterised by modal verbs, questions and a mood of provisionality, is patently a failure, as he admits:
the novel 'wants to be a pop single and you don't hear the music'
(Personal Interview, 2009). As Chapter 6 argued, ekphrasis, always
double-edged, always aware of the limitations of forms of representation, serves traumatic experience well. Dylan's failures of remediation
read more honestly than the adoption of the journalistic persona in
the middle of *You Don't Love Me Yet* and its more optimistic efforts
to make the music present. Yet this novel, in its slight way, does have
something to say about contemporary American culture and the desire to grasp again the visceral excitement of live, communal experiences.

Chronic City reprises ideas from *You Don't Love Me Yet* – secrecy,
reality, the opportunities for transcendence of banal everyday life in
music and visual art – but moves the action back to the Eastern Sea-
board. Rather than Brooklyn, however, the setting for *Chronic City* is

Manhattan. As the title suggests, something is seriously wrong with Manhattan, and has been going wrong for a long time. Given that 'CHRONIC' is also the name of a powerful brand of marijuana which tends to get the main characters 'devastatingly high' (Lethem, 2009a: 20), it is clear that Lethem intends his Manhattan to be an hallucinatory (or indeed hallucinated) place, a kind of dope mirage where reality deliquesces and time stands still (somewhere between 9/11 and the recent economic collapse).

Though much of the novel's action concerns, in Lethem's words, '[c]onversation and hanging out and friendship' (Barber, 2009), such ordinary lived experiences assume a renewed urgency and significance in an urban space 'made universal by the Internet – a hyper-urban chaos freed from the constraints of both geography and conventional notions of what's real' (Barber, 2009). Partly because 'the whole world dreams of Manhattan' and has those dreams nourished by popular culture, and partly because of the city's infatuation with 'concepts' such as money, exchange, success, Manhattan has achieved, according to Lethem, 'a maximum amount of unreality'. It is 'the dry run for the virtual century we're living in now' (Lethem, 2010c). Or, to put it another way: 'The way people function inside an impossible city like New York City is a precursor to the contemporary problem of how to live under total globalization and media overload' (Barber, 2009). In this derealised environment the novel's main characters – narrator and child star Chase Insteadman; former purveyor of guerrilla criticism in the form of 'rants on posters' (Lethem, 2009a: 7) and obsessive cultural curator Perkus Tooth; ghost writer Oona Laszlo; former radical and now 'major villain' in the Mayor's office Richard Abneg (Lethem, 2009a: 32); and Richard's girlfriend Georgina Hawkmanaji, 'the Hawkman' – form what Lethem calls 'a kind of counterculture ... trying to ignore the gigantic, gaping holes in reality that are arising again and again' (Lethem, 2010c). These holes, it becomes clear, are both metaphorical and material ones.

Evidently, then, *Chronic City* is consistent with earlier texts in its dedication to subcultural identity. In fact, when one considers Perkus's deeply-held conviction that '[t]he horizon of everyday life was a mass daydream – below it lay everything that mattered' (Lethem, 2009a: 13), it is clear that the novel takes the meaning of *sub*culture quite literally. This idiosyncratic subculture, haunting the Upper East Side's privileged dinner party circuit and with Perkus at its heart, is motivated by no less than a desire to reinvigorate reality itself, a desire believed to be sated by rock music in *You Don't Love Me Yet* and here, momentarily, by the enigmatic and transfixing appearance of the chaldrons, vase-like creations sought after on Ebay and regarded by Perkus and his companions as 'a door' into a place of beauty and essences (Lethem, 2009a: 142). One of the biggest disappointments they experience is the discovery that the chaldrons only exist virtually, as treasures to be traded by elite gamers in a online site called (in an obvious parody of Second Life) 'Yet Another World' (Lethem, 2009a: 331). They are simply commodities, and not even real ones.

Considering this over-arching anxiety about the decline of reality, symbolised by the tragedy of the chaldrons, one might argue that Lethem has chosen the perfect narrator and the perfect genre for the novel. Once the child star of a sitcom called *Martyr and Pesty*, Chase now lives, with a knowing reference to the narcotic after-effects of Chronic, on '*residuals*' (Lethem, 2009a: 28) and drifts comfortably through Manhattan's glittering social scene. His name connotes the pursuit of roles, and Perkus perspicaciously says upon first meeting him that '[t]hey [the Manhattanites] watch you like you're still on television' (Lethem, 2009a: 11). Perkus is referring specifically to Chase's daily chronicled romance with Janice Trumbell, 'the American trapped in orbit with the Russians, the astronaut who couldn't come home' (Lethem, 2009a: 10). Later, at a Park Avenue dinner party, Chase demonstrates sufficient self-awareness to admit how 'bogus' his story becomes in such a glamorous and tawdry environment: 'I might love Janice, yes, but what I showed these people was a simulacrum, a portrayal of myself' (Lethem, 2009a: 35). Chase's doomed romance with Janice, like the chaldrons, turns out to be a fake: he has become 'the ultimate Method actor' (Lethem, 2009a: 441), losing himself inside a role he has come to regard as his real life, forgetting that it was all the idea of some 'obnoxious young producers' he once met (Lethem, 2009a: 441).

'Chase' suggests another pursuit: that of Perkus Tooth. As a fading celebrity hovering around the margins of the city's elite, Chase almost immediately perceives in Perkus's chosen discursive method – the yoking together of diverse and obscure political and cultural artefacts from J. Edgar Hoover to Chet Baker in order to prove some kind of conspiracy or explanatory story (Lethem, 2009a: 12) – a route into an exciting secret reality. 'Where Perkus took me, in his ranting, in his enthusiasms', Chase observes, 'was the world inside the world ... Perkus was the opposite of my astronaut fiancée – my caring for him could matter, on a daily basis' (Lethem, 2009a: 27). To Chase, Perkus becomes friend, antagonist, constant worry and – though a peculiarly unstable and dissolute one – hero. Therefore *Chronic City* can be considered a contemporary participant in a genre dubbed by Lawrence Buell 'observer-hero narrative' (Buell, 1979: 93); other examples include *Moby Dick, The Great Gatsby* and *The Good Soldier*.

The observer-hero narrative, Buell argues, emerged during the Romantic period as a result of 'the popularity of a number of forms and techniques which juxtapose divergent psychic universes' (Buell, 1979: 104). Examples include the Gothic motif of the psychological double; 'the Richardsonian formula of allowing the protagonist ... to fall from a secure, conventional life into the clutches of a fascinating but demonic villain' (Buell, 1979: 104); and the admiration for mentor figures frequently expressed by protagonists of the bildungsroman (Buell, 1979: 106). Wherever the genre comes from (and Buell spends rather too much time on its literary evolution and its status as a viable genre), it is characterised by the interdependence and inseparability of the observer and hero, despite the latter's 'more intensely focused and more romantic' worldview and greater charisma (Buell, 1979: 93), and the observer's tendency to live vicariously through the hero, even if he disapproves or is suspicious of the hero's behaviour (Buell, 1979: 96). The observer is the narrator, and because the reader is closer to him in terms of narrative, and may also be closer to him in terms of sharing a more conventional worldview, there is always a barrier, 'more or less opaque, between reader and hero' (Buell, 1979: 99). However, the observer's motives for narrating in the first place – as an act of mythology, satire or even vengeance – mean that '[t]he reliability of the witness ... may vary as much as the stature of the hero' (Buell, 1979: 98). Thus the observer-hero narrative is the perfect means of emphasising the unavailability of an objective, unfiltered reality, the loss of traditional heroes, and the modern concern with 'subjective consciousness as a literary subject' (Buell, 1979: 103).

The observer and the hero are symbiotically connected even if, as is often the case, the observer comes to reject the hero's passions and obsessions. (Chase eventually concedes that Perkus's conspiracy theories, though discomfiting, are 'ludicrous' (Lethem, 2009a: 448).) When Chase and Perkus engage in some impromptu 'cavorting', the connection is made explicit: Perkus claims that Chase is the body and he the brain (Lethem, 2009a: 143). There are two ways to interpret this claim – one romantic, one more traumatic in nature. In the soothing glow of the on-screen chaldron, Chase indulges in the 'notion of a gestalt identity alive among us. The chaldron's door might open to a place where selves dissolved and merged' (Lethem, 2009a: 143). However, if one agrees with Timothy Melley that trauma results in a 'profound sense of self-division' (Melley, 2003: 106), then one might be more inclined to read the observer-hero relationship as revealing of rupture, of the divided self which derives from the need both to experience trauma and to bear witness to traumatic experience.[5] In a sense, the yearning for gestalt, for integration and wholeness and the fragmentation of self are merely different symptoms of the same thing: Chase's desire for a meaningful identity within a cohesive society causes him to fixate on Perkus, whose paranoid rantings see everything as deeply meaningful and presuppose a totalising secret conspiracy to explain a New York that has come to feel unmoored from reality, but which only serve to reduce the world to an FSR of his own devising. (*Chronic City* in this way forms the bridge between *Amnesia Moon* and the later New York novels.) Both men, observer and hero, are dealing with personal traumas that have become embroiled in universal, or at least city-wide suffering.

But what exactly is the trauma? As Lethem observes, 'ordinary events become suffused with dread' in the novel; 'something is wrong but it no longer has a name' (Lethem, 2010c). There is an unmistakable air of menace and melancholia throughout, exemplified by some of the novel's more surreal elements such as 'the gargantuan escaped tiger ... ravaging sections of the East Side' (Lethem, 2009a: 22), the fog enveloping lower Manhattan (Lethem, 2009a: 173), the snow falling in August (Lethem, 2009a: 463) and even the childish nostalgia brought about by the chocolate smell that mysteriously hangs over the city one November (Lethem, 2009a: 173). Perkus, we discover, is an orphan, yet 'the celebrated master of Eastern medicine', Strabo Blandiana (Lethem, 2009a: 76), offers an explanation for Perkus's crippling 'cluster headaches' (Lethem, 2009a: 16) that has less to do with his orphanhood and more to do with New York's pervasive sense of loss: 'You mourn a loss suffered by the world. Something in living memory, but not adequately remembered. You see it as your sole responsibility to commemorate this loss' (Lethem, 2009a: 79).

Although Perkus dismisses Strabo's treatments as 'innocuous and charming' and 'Victorian' (Lethem, 2009a: 93), to the reader it is obvious that for all his expensive quackery the doctor has correctly identified the problem. He has instantly diagnosed in Perkus the willed amnesia at the heart of *Chronic City*, the deliberate avoidance of the event which more than any other has shaped attitudes to New York City in the twenty-first century – the 2001 attack on the World Trade Center. In a virtualised urban space full of ultimately meaningless distractions – Janice Trumbell's (admittedly heartbreaking) letters to Chase from space, the chaldrons, Yet Another Life – symbolic hints of a catastrophe that cannot be directly discussed are all that are permitted. The closest Chase's narration comes to explicit acknowledgement is in his analysis of the chocolate smell's tranquilising effects: 'a chocolate mystery reminded us that we all dwelled in Candyland, after all ... So much for the deliberate terrors advancing on our shores, let alone our complicity with any wider darkness. We were, it turned out, a whole island of crimeless victims, survivors of nothing worse than a cream pie in the face, which, hey, tasted pretty good!' (Lethem, 2009a: 174).

Elsewhere, Chase fails to match this perspicacity by failing to interpret what are, to the reader, the blindingly obvious symbols displayed before him. Gazing at the Gothic church spire from his apartment window, where another more modern tower dominates the view (Lethem, 2009a: 67), he admires the aerial acrobatics of a flock of birds, the species of which, along with the name of the church, he does not bother to find out. Admitting at least that the birds are 'carefree, and I'm not' (Lethem, 2009a: 68), Chase senses a mystery that might explain life in New York City, but cannot, or will not, penetrate it. When, in the most obvious symbolic contrivance, a passenger plane passes by the two towers, Chase once again fails to make a connection: 'A planeload of people on their way to somewhere from somewhere else, having as little to do with birds or tower as birds or tower have to do with each other. I am the only witness to their conjunction. The privilege of my witnessing is limited to that fact: there's nothing more I grasp ... if relation exists, I don't fathom it' (Lethem, 2009a: 68).

From this scene it is easy to understand why Lethem claims that *Chronic City* 'is about not thinking about 9/11'. As he explains it, this avoidance, a kind of ellipsis echoed in the periods of deep withdrawal Perkus experiences when his migraines are at their worst (Lethem, 2009a: 26), has to do with the complex relationship between personal and public reactions to the catastrophe (this is much the way Strabo Blandiani sees it, in fact). Immediately after the attack, Lethem states, the tragedy felt 'very personal' to New Yorkers, who experienced 'a very, very intense intimate despair'. However, when George Bush and Dick Cheney were re-elected, the personal yet communal despair of New York City residents was 'appropriated for a giant political purpose' (Lethem, 2010c).

This political co-option happened in tandem with the cultural appropriation lamented by Leon Wieseltier, when 'the managers of meaning, the anchors and the reporters and the commentators' set to work on shaping the representations of an event that had previously 'bested every representation of it'. According to Wieseltier, September 11 was then inevitably changed into 'September 11' (Wieseltier, 2002: 38). Transformed into convenient symbols of heroism, defiance and the American drive to reinvention by media representations that tend to celebrate not the event but their own coverage of it, the towers become public property in an egregious way. Rather than encouraging a truly democratic mourning process, whereby the individual imagination is allowed to construct a personal image of the event which co-exists with the disparate images of others (what Wieseltier evocatively calls 're-privatiz[ing] the wound' (Wieseltier, 2002: 38)), the media creates a spectacle which imposes a false sense of televisual community over and above national, urban or familial communities. It is no wonder that the city, according to Lethem, 'shifted back into an attempt to forget this event or displace it' and that the characters in *Chronic City* are 'stoned on media confusion' (Lethem, 2010c). The 'WAR-FREE EDITION' of the *New York Times* (Lethem, 2009a: 74) is only the most blatant attempt to opt out of remembrance of harsh realities and retreat into collective fantasy.

Perhaps, then, Chase's failure to spot the symbolism of his towers, birds and planes is evidence less of his obtuseness than of the paucity of meaning in the symbols themselves. More important than their symbolic value is the sheer physical presence of the elements that comprise the view from his window, and the beauty that derives from the accidental and fleeting constellation of natural world and man-made objects. Similarly, Laird Noteless's gigantic *Fjord* artwork is impressive more for its sheer physical immensity, the way it seems to have been 'hewn out of the earth by unnatural force' (Lethem, 2009a: 109) than for its obvious symbolic connotations. This is not just a metaphor, even if inevitably it will be read as such: it is a gigantic chasm, a piece of work, something that must be appreciated for its material qualities. Again this can be traced back to Lethem's reflections on the terrorist attack of September 11 2001. For him, it was 'very visceral – it literally involved changes in what you were breathing and feeling between your fingertips as these ashes fell on the city' (Lethem, 2010c). Hence *Obstinate Dust*, the monumental novel that appears many times during *Chronic City* as a playful allusion to David Foster Wallace's *Infinite Jest* (1996), testifies obliquely to the enduring material and sensory qualities of 9/11 and its aftermath. Like the towers and the birds, what matters about the dust is its physical existence and how it affects the minds and bodies of New Yorkers. It is appropriate, then, that Chase hurls the 'tubby paperback' into Noteless's *Fjord* as a kind of offering to this 'Obstinate Hole' (Lethem, 2009a: 111). Maybe the gesture is symbolic, but it will also lighten his pockets on the journey home.

Like *You Don't Love Me Yet*, *Chronic City*'s treatment of themes like reality, representation and secrecy is determined by its historical moment. And like its predecessor, it suggests that a media-saturated 'reality' culture, in which people are, like Chase Insteadman, cast in fictionalised versions of their own lives, reinvigorates a desire for reality. Where it differs is in the depiction (or more correctly, non-depiction) of a specific historical event – the terrorist attack on New York City – that has also succumbed to the demands of media culture. It also differs in its choice of alternative. Clearly Perkus's retreat into pot-smoking and networks of arcane cultural references is no solution. The chaldrons, as we have seen, are just an illusion. Neither does Lethem propose, somewhat facilely, that rock and roll might save the day. Instead, he looks, equally romantically, one might argue, to the physical world and to nature for escape. *Chronic City*, most critics agree, concerns virtuality and mediation in a cityscape virtualised more than any other. Yet it is also a novel more fascinated than any other of Lethem's works with physicality, nature, with biology and the body (with the possible exception of his novella *This Shape We're In*, which takes place inside the body of an animal and satirises the way the natural world is regarded as 'a cute, impotent relic' (Lethem, 2000: 54), commodified and turned into theme parks). It is full of ailments, deteriorating bodies and animals – the escaped 'tiger', the polar bear adrift on an ice floe (Lethem, 2009a: 180), the eagles nesting on Richard Abneg's window ledge (Lethem, 2009a: 50) and, most importantly, Ava, the three-legged dog whose apartment Perkus shares after his own apartment block is designated unsafe (Lethem, 2009a: 315). It is also consistently interested in weather and the physical landscape beneath and surrounding the city's extravagant architecture. So while

Strabo Brandiani's psychological diagnosis of Perkus's migraines (the first of his ailments) is a laudable one, another piece of advice he gives seems even more sensible: 'I couldn't help noticing you came here wearing nothing but your dress jacket. You should have a coat in this weather' (Lethem, 2009a: 91).

This switch to the practical and the somatic is typical of a novel which frequently flirts with symbolic or metaphorical interpretations of physical phenomena before forcing us to consider them and appreciate them *as* physical phenomena. When Chase first meets Perkus, for example, he notices the 'undisciplined hazel eye' that seems to 'discredit Perkus Tooth's whole sober aura with a comic jape' (Lethem, 2009a: 3). Throughout the ensuing episodes, the observer is unable to regard the hero's defective eye as anything more than a linguistic challenge, a kind of metaphor: hence his use of a different adjective each time he mentions it: 'bad' (Lethem, 2009a: 4), 'crazy' (Lethem, 2009a: 14), 'distaff' (Lethem, 2009a: 26) and even 'revelatory' (Lethem, 2009a: 218). This last example suggests that Perkus's wandering eye might have the same deconstructive power as that of the narrator of Lynne Sharon Schwartz's *Leaving Brooklyn* (1990): the ability to reveal and unpick the seamless skin of social convention and uncover the contradictions and neuroses beneath. Yet Chase's narrative never elaborates on this metaphorical possibility in the way Audrey's does: Chase's adjectival contrivances merely suggest the inescapability of language and a desire to deflect the awkward physical reality of Perkus's condition. Only the woman at the dog apartments, in a playful reference to Foible's diagnosis of Lionel's Tourette's, has the courage to mention it directly: 'Something wrong with your eye?' Perkus's reply – 'From birth' (Lethem, 2009a: 319) – is accompanied by a smile which suggests relief at finally being given the opportunity to acknowledge his condition for what it is.

In one sense, of course, Chase is right to regard Perkus's manic, paranoid cultural curating as 'Perkus' disease' (Lethem, 2009a: 111), but once again, this metaphorical disease is rendered much less important by his fatal physical disease, the horrific collapse of his internal organs heralded by the crippling hiccoughs that cause him 'to oscillate like his own eye' (Lethem, 2009a: 385) and are rendered typographically as spatial and temporal disruptions within the text. The fact that Ava sympathetically shares these hiccoughs is the biggest clue to Perkus's changed priorities in the latter stages of the novel. Having entered into the 'pair-bonding' he recognises is a fundamental aspect of the animal kingdom (Lethem, 2009a: 219), Perkus devotes most of his time to the intensely physical pleasures of Ava's companionship: sleeping huddled together, feeding, cleaning, taking walks (pleasures Chase enjoys when he takes Ava after Perkus's death). Paying attention to Ava alters his view of the city, too. Rather than esoterically mapping New York through his obscure cultural references, he now navigates by learning 'to which patches of snow-scraped earth Ava craved return' (Lethem, 2009a: 321). (When the Hawkman becomes pregnant, Abneg's world is similarly transformed: he describes with relish her physical changes, the '*milk map*' her body has become (Lethem, 2009a: 420).) New York, so long a conspiracy for Perkus, is becoming a physical space in which he can find true friendship before he dies. Most of all, he learns through Ava just how amnesiac his, and other people's attitudes, are: 'No body – that's *no body* – really believes in the news from beyond the boundaries of their neighbourhood or pocket universe. Manhattan is one of those, you know, a pocket universe' (Lethem, 2009a: 386). From being one of the Lethem characters most inclined to retreat into his pocket universe, Perkus has become, largely through his friendship with Ava, the most succinct and articulate spokesperson for the biggest idea in Lethem's writing.

Throughout this book, reference has been made to Lethem's obsession with the inescapability of language, which is invariably bound up in concerns over the unavailability of reality. As we have seen, *You Don't Love Me Yet* offers rock and roll as a means of escape: its message might be 'shut up and listen'. *Chronic City* offers something different: attention to the natural world, to the transformations of the body, to the workings of the senses. Even in New York, the embodiment of media overload and postmodern fakery, nature intrudes, bodies meet and interact, new lives are created. These things are real and go beyond a language that cannot hope to match them. Thus when Chase looks at the 'wheeling birds' outside his window, 'language dies' (Lethem, 2009a: 124), just as the ocean arrests Lionel's Tourettic impulses. In the novel's final surreal twist, the Dorfl Tower appears to have shifted to the right, obscuring Chase's view a little more (Lethem, 2009a: 467). Chase hopes the view will survive, because by simply being there it frees him, for a while, just to shut up and look.

Notes

1   Jonathan Elmer takes this idea and expertly analyses Poe's ambivalent attitude toward the mob itself: he is 'both critic of and participant in the mass culture of his time' (Elmer, 1995: 11).

2   It is a pleasing fact in the context of this chapter that the first significant Nativist, anti-immigration party in the US was the Know-Nothing Party, so called because it began as a secret organisation 'whose members, when asked about its existence, were supposed to respond, "I know nothing"' (Foner, 2006: 419).

3   Ian Chipman described it, appropriately enough, as 'a b side' in comparison to Lethem's previous novels (Chipman, 2006: 6); Robert Collins said 'this leisurely poke at the vapid appeal of art and rock 'n roll feels as disposable and unconvincing as the easy targets of his satire' (Collins, 2008: 57).

4   In interview with Fiona Kelleghan, Lethem reveals another way in which music is important to him: '*Amnesia Moon* has a soundtrack. It's an album by a band called My Dad Is Dead, called *The Taller You Are, The Shorter You Get*. Every song on that record has a chapter. It's the soundtrack to the book. The book I'm finishing now has a theme song, a song by John Cale called "Dying on the Vine". I can enunciate to some extent why that's the theme song of the book, and also some of it's just mysterious in that emotional way that musical connections can be' (Kelleghan, 1998: 240).

5   Other writers on trauma evoke similar images of split selves. Lawrence Langer talks of 'shifting voices emerging from the same person' in Holocaust testimonies (Langer, 1991: 161). Cathy Caruth regards witness as listening to another voice, or as a wound with a voice (Caruth, 1996: 3).

Conclusion

Anyone who has read 'Five Fucks', 'Sleepy People' (both 1996) or
This Shape We're In might find it surprising that Lethem claims to
be an 'extremely traditional writer' (Personal Interview, 2009). He
is 'so devoted to the traditional means' of 'scenes and characters and
dialogue and paragraph and plot' and although he sometimes makes
'intertextual jokes', he believes there is nothing in his work to 'threat-
en anyone short of the mandarins who just don't want the Fantastic
Four ever to be mentioned inside a novel' (Personal Interview, 2009).
Citing as a specific example the insertion of the 'Liner Note' into *The
Fortress of Solitude*, Lethem insists that such a manoeuvre should not
lead critics to assume that he is 'some sort of problematic, postmodern bombthrower' (Personal Interview, 2009), only that in the context of Dylan Ebdus's coming-of-age he has chosen the most appo-
site means of showing his protagonist hardening himself against his
adolescent emotional attachments even as he appears to be indulging
them. Thus the 'Liner Note' is less postmodern formal experimentation than simply the most expedient way of representing the adult
Dylan's tendency to 'hide in plain sight'.

Lethem has a point. *Fortress* provides only the most famous and
critically acclaimed example of how, in the end, for all their cartoon-
ish flights of fancy and their fabulistic qualities, Lethem's novels
and short stories are dedicated quite straightforwardly to simple and
timeless themes: the search for, or lack of community, 'the yearning to feel connected to the people around you' (*Front Row*, 2004)
and the damaging consequences of disengagement from communities or, equally dangerously, over-investment in secluded, amnesiac
utopias. Even a short story like 'Five Fucks', which was nominated
for a Nebula Award in 1997, is only superficially experimental. Its
subject is obsessive coupling of the type studied by Cynthia Jalter in

As She Climbed Across the Table: after each sexual liaison between the unnamed male and female characters, time is mysteriously lost and elements of the familiar world disappear (Lethem, 1996: 158). As an extended metaphor for the introspection attendant upon new and intense relationships, it makes itself almost too clear, but its more recondite satisfactions lie in the gradual degradation of the female protagonist's world and the generic shifts through which it is enacted. 'Five Fucks' starts out with simple dialogue as the couple reflect on their first night together, but rapidly mutates into a freakish meditation on sexual desire and amnesia, encompassing detective fiction (the woman hires a gumshoe called Pupkiss, the only other recurring character, to find out what has happened to her missing life), a fairy tale involving protagonists recast as two rampant giants, and finally a de-evolutionary descent into a twisted sci-fi monologue. In this last section the female protagonist is reduced to 'a bright pink crablike thing, some child artist's idea of an invertebrate' (Lethem, 1996: 170), painstakingly building a wall from grains of sand to keep her copulatory 'nemesis' at bay (Lethem, 1996: 170).

Yet none of these genres is experimental in itself and, despite the destabilising modal shifts, the story adheres almost doggedly to a conventional narrative thread (the doomed romance) and retains absolute faith in the roundedness and legibility of its characters, whatever form they take. Calling its male protagonist 'E.' constitutes a bluff, a playful gesture towards a postmodern abandonment of traditional literary expectations, without ever actually abandoning them in the manner of John Barth or Mark Z. Danielewski. What creates the familiar Lethemite sense of estrangement and irony is merely the collision of these disparate genres and, as was argued in Chapter 1, it is debatable that there is anything uniquely postmodern about such a move.

Andrew Hoberek suggests that 'the embrace of generic forms' (Hoberek, 2007: 240) by authors such as Lethem and Michael Chabon is one of the symptoms of what has become known as the 'post-postmodern' in contemporary fiction. Unlike Thomas Pynchon, for example, whose appropriation of the detective story and political conspiracy thriller for *The Crying of Lot 49* (1967) serves what Hoberek calls a postmodern 'metadiscursive' purpose (Hoberek, 2007: 238) and is partly an ironic disavowal of those genres by a highly 'literary' writer, Lethem, even at his most meta-generic, appreciates the literary and cultural value of popular genres in themselves. As this study has insisted, following Rick Altman's work in *Film/Genre*, this is partly because he sees in genres and in the tendency of critics rigidly to demarcate genre boundaries a model of the ways in which human beings form mini-utopias or subcultural groupings based on a misplaced sense of 'authenticity' and, at their most amnesiac, refuse to entertain the possibility of difference, of contiguous or overlapping groupings.

What would be at stake, then, were a literary scholar to venture by way of conclusion that Lethem might be regarded as a post-postmodern writer, rather than simply the 'extremely traditional' writer he proclaims himself to be? Before I adduce the evidence for such a claim, it is necessary that I declare my interests as a critic. If Altman's work on the processes of genrification teaches us one thing, it is that the attribution of labels is never disinterested and is always politically, economically and ideologically freighted. Since the time of Horace, genre works have been 'pressed into the service of broader institutional goals' (Altman, 1999: 6). Altman summarises the emergence of melodrama in the eighteenth and nineteenth centuries to show how new forms arise through hybridisation of established ones (in this case tragedy and comedy) but also how the heated political debates surrounding melodrama's ascent suggest that 'critics once understood their role as far more active and interventionist' (Altman, 1999: 5) than those who, to this day, prefer to adhere to an Aristotelian approach which codifies pre-determined categories rather than accepting ongoing transformations. To read Altman's work, then, is to be forced into self-reflexivity, to recognise one's personal, professional and institutional motivations as both literary critic and passionate fan of certain genre productions. And as Thomas Beebee claims, genres are above all the way texts get *used* by readers: they have both professional and emotional use-value (Beebee, 1994: 14). No reading, this one included, can be considered 'pure' or external to the work and to the historical context of the reading moment.

So if I wish to argue for the post-postmodernness of Lethem's writing, especially his most recent novels, I am aware that I am applying yet another label, and partaking of an instinct for categorisation (or product differentiation) that Lethem's work, and to some extent this book, have tried strenuously to discredit. In finding myself entangled in a paradox partly of my own creation, I hope at least that this study has demonstrated the paradox inherent to genrification itself – that categories are there to be disrupted but can only be disrupted by acceptance of their stable-enough existence at a particular historical moment – and has strived not to 'eradicate contradictions' (Altman, 1999: 175) in Lethem's work but to celebrate them for their ethical possibilities. Yet the fact remains that immersed as I am in the study of contemporary American fiction, alive to critical movements, my sense of Lethem as a post-postmodern writer derives partly from the influence of one of my own constellated communities: the innumerable literary scholars in other departments whose collective efforts have raised the recent profile of post-postmodernism as an idea, and whose approbation I seek as fellow panellists at conferences and as reviewers of my work. Moreover, it is important to remember that the critical essay, as Ralph Cohen (1988) notes, is itself a literary genre with its own complex history: this is just another reason why scholars have some professional investment in the idea of stable-enough disciplines and categories, especially at a time when higher education faces such challenges.

But the evidence for my claim is surely there. In *Fortress* and *Chronic City*, for example, one finds many of the post-postmodern characteristics succinctly summarised in Stephen J. Burn's introduction to his recent monograph on Jonathan Franzen. Beginning with the straightforward observation that recent American mainstream literary fictions have tended to be less formally experimental than works by exponents of high postmodernism (Burn, 2008: 18), Burn goes on to state that works coming 'after' postmodernism (and quotation marks are employed for reasons that become clear soon), nonetheless 'look back' to postmodern culture and theories, such that post-postmodern fiction effectively 'dramatises its roots within pomo' (Burn, 2008: 19). In *Chronic City* Perkus Tooth's paranoid belief that Manhattan is 'a simulation of itself' created for 'some purpose' (Lethem, 2009a: 448) locates his ravings within an exaggerated Baudrillardian postmodernity where reality has all but absconded and aesthetic beauty, in the shape of the chaldron, is just another fake concept, a virtual representation. Yet from this late capitalist despair there emerge glimmers of hope and reality, or rather, a reinvigorated sense of a complex reality comprised of myriad interconnecting lives and able to incorporate the multiple simulations of a media-saturated culture.

Perkus is a postmodern subject. He epitomises the 'encyclopedic drive' of much postmodern textual production (Burn, 2008: 20); he feels himself trapped in representations, and is maniacally dedicated to the curation of those representations, but he comes to find meaning and fulfilment in the simplest of things: his intimate relationship with a dog. Moving from stoned, paranoid disquisitions on popular culture to the affection he shares with Ava, Perkus's character undergoes a conventional temporal development. And, with the introduction of Perkus's twin sister June in the final chapter (Lethem, 2009a: 460), Lethem adopts the analepsis characteristic of much post-postmodern fiction (Burns, 2008: 24), a technique which emphasises temporality and frees the individual from an amnesiac-arrested present. Moreover, as Chapter 7 argued, the very physicality of Perkus and Ava's relationship, exemplified by her missing limb, his deteriorating health and the sympathetic transference of the hiccoughs, evinces a sincere interest in biology, genetic inheritance and neurophysiology (Burns, 2008: 25) Lethem first revealed in *Motherless Brooklyn*, and one shared by recent fictions such as *The Corrections*. Indeed, the physical and emotional transactions of Perkus and Ava's friendship locate it in the discourse of the post-human, beyond even an idea of art as 'a living transaction between humans' (Foster Wallace, quoted in McCaffery, 1993: 142), where the sovereignty of the human subject is brought into question and relations between humans and animals (as well as humans and technology) acquire a greater epistemological and ethical importance. With Lewis Carroll's *Alice* tales as his first literary influence, Lethem has long had a predilection for including animals in his fiction, but whereas the kangaroo in *Gun, With Occasional Music* is, as Chapter 1 suggested, as much an inter-textual reference as a brute physical presence (likewise the kangaroo in *You Don't Love Me Yet* which shares a name with the cat in *Motherless Brooklyn*), Ava exists primarily on her own terms, less knowingly, and with more emotional investment.

What Perkus, and subsequently Chase, begin to appreciate is that Manhattan cannot be considered a monolithic conspiracy. Although it is full of fakes and simulations, it is not simply a mass of texts to be collated and analysed for signs of a singular nefarious design: it is a complex, living system of interconnected lives carrying on beyond the private obsessions of individuals, but also intricately affecting them. As Claire Carter asks Chase: 'How could a place like Manhattan exist for just one purpose, instead of a million?' (Lethem, 2009a: 448). For Chase, this plural reality is revealed in the myriad pleasurable, material details of everyday living: '[t]he neat pink seam of Ava's surgery scar ... the "milk map" across Georgina's pregnant belly ... the exact flavour of Oona's kisses (or Ava's for that matter) ... the sugar dust on a Savoir Faire almond croissant ... these details could no more have been designed and arranged than Laird Noteless could have thought to include discarded baby carriages and crushed crack vials in his sketches for *Urban Fjord*' (Lethem, 2009a: 449).

Such a realisation mirrors a post-postmodern tendency to eschew recursivity, metanarrative games, and a sense of an unseen author always in absolute control of his or her world despite 'death of the author'-style gestures, in favour of exophoric reference to a world outside the text (Burns, 2008: 20–1; Foster Wallace, in McCaffery, 1993: 142). One can see this tendency in novels such as Jeffrey Eugenides' *Middlesex*, which places its fiction against specific historical backdrops such as the Detroit riots and, once again, *The Corrections*. It is also evident in *The Fortress of Solitude* which, as we have seen, refers outward to the circumstances of Brooklyn's gentrification and to the evolution of graffiti and hip-hop culture in the New York of the 1970s and 1980s, and to a lesser extent in *Chronic City*, which makes use of real newspaper stories about New York.

All these facets of the post-postmodern – the reduction in metafictional strategies, references to the world beyond the text, the revivifying of plot and character – result in what James Wood infamously calls 'the novel of intimacy, of motive, of relation', one which attempts a psychological realism and an 'antique sensitivity' to the vicissitudes of human nature (Wood, 2001: 8). But one should be wary of the connotations of Wood's phrase. He may consider it worthwhile to posit a return to 'traditional' forms of novelistic storytelling, but it would be naive, despite Lethem's similar protestations, to regard Franzen or Foster Wallace or Lethem as traditional or antique, as writers who have consciously returned to earlier modes. As Foster Wallace's essay, 'E Unibus Pluram: Television and US Fiction' makes clear, in a world in which rebellion, knowingness and irony have been absorbed and appropriated by television (Foster Wallace, 1993: 185), the contemporary writer has faithfully to represent human relationships in a mediated world without recourse to enervating metadiscursivity. This, I would suggest, is precisely what Lethem does in *Chronic City*.

Just as one has to be suspicious of terms which suggest a return to 'pre-' postmodern unities, one should also qualify use of the prefix 'post' in 'post-postmodern'. Such easy affixation, in terms like 'postfeminist', in particular, is always dubious because it implies a supercession or negation of what came before rather than a dialectical relationship. Despite the playful title of a recent article – 'PoMo's Wake' (2002) – postmodernism is not 'dead' at all; it is only under renewed scrutiny. So if I suggest that Lethem be understood, for the reasons given, as post-postmodernist, it is with the understanding that 'post-postmodernism' is no more 'after' postmodernism than the detective novel is 'after' the Western. As Andrew Hoberek says: 'if contemporary fiction is indeed post-postmodern, this does not exemplify some singular, dramatic, readily visible cultural transformation – the search for which in fact constitutes a postmodern preoccupation – but grows out of a range of uneven, tentative, local shifts that in some cases reach back into the postmodern period and can now be understood in hindsight as intimations of a new order' (Hoberek, 2007: 241). Post-postmodernism, in other words, despite being hampered by cumbersome and misleading prefixes, inspires a reappraisal of aspects within the postmodern rather than signalling a dramatic historical shift. And it gains validity only retrospectively.

This is important for two reasons. First, the emergence of a descriptive category from localised tendencies precisely parallels the 'diverse system-building paths' leading to genre formation (Altman, 1999: 176), the way that individual textual examples coalesce, in the eyes of constellated communities of consumers, into something more or less solid and recognisable (though still eminently unstable). It reminds us once again that scholarly readers of Lethem's work are as engaged in community-formation as the protagonists of his novels and short stories and the fans of the genres he enlists. Secondly, the fact that critical terms, like genres, inevitably emerge after the event has implications for the whole question of periodisation. Not only is it impossible to make truly meaningful statements about the contemporary moment but, as Adena Rosmarin argues, the decisions about genre each critical reader makes in the moment of consumption depending on his or her 'need' (Rosmarin, 1985: 25) overturn the conventional logic of 'before' and 'after'. Rosmarin's theory, that 'there are precisely as many genres as we need, genres whose conceptual shape is precisely determined by that need' (Rosmarin, 1985: 25) is an extreme one, but it accounts for the central importance of the reader and his or her interested nature in ways that connect it to the work of Altman and help to highlight the challenges inherent in trying to fashion categories for a writer like Jonathan Lethem.

Any conclusions one might reach concerning Lethem's place in the contemporary American literary scene can only be tentative ones, in any case: Lethem is a young writer, a remarkably energetic and prolific one, and one whose need to collapse generic distinctions and deliver the unexpected has inspired this book and shows no signs of abating. It would be no real surprise, therefore, if his next novel eschewed the (post-)humanistic tendencies outlined in this conclusion and opted instead for inward-looking, meta-discursive (and, indeed, post-modern) ruminations on the role of the writer in the manner of Paul Auster's *Travels in the Scriptorium* (2006). One hopes not, but the only thing one can state with any certainty is that Lethem will continue to surprise.

His latest work, to illustrate, is a monograph on John Carpenter's low-budget 'science-fiction-horror' movie (Lethem, 2010b: 9), *They Live* (1988). Although essays such as 'Defending The Searchers' and 'Two or Three Things I Dunno About Cassavetes' (2005) contain moments of incisive film criticism, particularly the latter, these moments are ultimately subservient to the overall revelatory, autobiographical thrust of the essays. Lethem's pursuit of the minor characters in Cassavetes' films, for example, eventually arrives at a series of thinly-veiled admissions: when the author says that 'the purloined letter of Cassavetes' lifework is his own terror of boredom and superficiality, right there at the locus of so much vitality and inspiration' (Lethem, 2005: 121), he is surely referring to himself, hiding in plain sight once again. In the personal anecdote which concludes the piece, Lethem emerges more boldly from the text to proclaim his influences. Leaving the cinema with the unnamed woman who has introduced him to Cassavetes' work, the young author realises that the non-naturalistic staginess of some of the director's scenes should not provoke frustration or disgust. Rather, it forces him to reconsider his own approach to artistic creation: 'life had been revealed to me to be so much more like a series of actor's exercises than I'd ever understood before. This epiphany seemed to me profound enough that I knew I would have to change my life, or at least my art, to account for it' (Lethem, 2005: 122). In *Fortress*, as Dylan plays the role of authentic Brooklyn street kid in Vermont, one sees the results of this epiphany.

If *They Live*, despite Lethem's prefatory personal declaration – 'I genuinely like *They Live*' (Lethem, 2010b: 13) – eschews the soul-searching of the film essays in *The Disappointment Artist*, it is nonetheless an autobiographical work and one which demonstrates consistency with its predecessors in expertly mixing genres. By framing the book as a running commentary not dissimilar to those included almost mandatorily on rental DVDs, complete with timings, Lethem pulls off a neat trick. Although the book cannot actually be read along with the film in real time, its structure encourages the reader to indulge in the illusion of such a reading experience. From one perspective, then, Lethem's *They Live* is less a book about Carpenter's *They Live* than a book about the author's original viewing/reading experience of the film. It is one he wishes to share with us: 'I'm sure I'll watch it again, even after this vigil is concluded. If we meet up, I'll watch it with you. In the meantime, I think you'll have fun with this book – or hey, *without* this book – if you watch it yourself' (Lethem, 2010b: 13). To offer an explicit invitation in this way is to acknowledge that the author is entering various constellated communities as he narrates his reading experience: communities of film buffs, John Carpenter fans, Lethem scholars and students of film criticism.

There is a distinct sense in which this piece of film criticism performs novelistically, like a doubled bildungsroman: the narrative of Nada's awakening to the alien conspiracy overlaps with the story of Lethem's awakening to the film's contradictions and its subtle manipulations of genre. These character trajectories run simultaneously but along opposite courses: Nada is transformed from an 'innocent', a man who unblinkingly claims to 'believe in America' (quoted in Lethem, 2010b: 54) to one who, after donning the 'Hoffman Lenses' that reveal the alien ghouls and their nefarious work (as well as the film's bludgeoning allegory of Reaganite individualism), understands the full horror of the earth's enslavement; while Lethem undergoes his own education, moving from archness to a kind of bemused shock. His early pronouncements are characterised by a knowing, amused but fannish tone: 'this tension between the film's simplicity and strangeness, between its thunderous stolidity and its abject porousness, is probably what compels me most. No offense, but *They Live* is probably the stupidest film ever to take *ideology* as its explicit subject. It's also probably the most fun' (Lethem, 2010b: 16). By the end of the monograph, having reflected in detail on Nada's journey and his martyrdom to the fight against the ghoul overlords, Lethem dwells on *They Live*'s infamous pornographic final shot and says: 'Cue mocking laughter (and an obnoxiously taunting, disco-fied version of the score's blues motif.) We're stranded here, women handcuffed to men, in bed with the pun/chline's verdict: *We're all fucking ghouls*' (Lethem, 2010b: 194).

Clearly the italicised statement refers to the audience's ghoulish delight in the gratuitous sordidness of the last shot, and to our delight in reading about it in Lethem's critique, but if one considers Lethem's work as a whole in light of the thesis proposed in this book, then it begins to resonate in a number of ways. First, enjoyment of the final shot corresponds to the transgressive pleasures offered by genre texts in general; in a sense, the hyperbolic nature of the shot only highlights its function as what Rick Altman calls a 'generic crossroad' (Altman, 1999: 145), a point at which generic pleasures are consciously opposed to culturally sanctioned behaviour. More broadly, this relates to the tortured relationship between representation and reality which is a central concern of Lethem's writing. Caught 'somewhere in the breach between the TV satires and their own longing for authentic contact, *fucking with the TV on,* or *watching TV with the fucking on*' (Lethem, 2010b: 193), the girl and the ghoul together stand as a deliberately excessive portrait of a real, physical world shot through with representations (like the New York of *Chronic City,* or the USA of *Amnesia Moon*), one in which even their sexual behaviour is 'mediated through porn stylistics which have invaded their sexual imaginations' (Lethem, 2010b: 193). Indeed, Lethem argues that the entire film, even after Nada's triumphant destruction of the aliens' broadcast tower, threatens to dissolve into artifice, into a 'kaleidoscopic maze of commercial simulations' (Lethem, 2010b: 193). The implication is that the viewer's enjoyment of such a wholly mediated spectacle would be even more ghoulish than simple voyeurism of the sexual act.

In so crudely bringing human and ghoul together, the final shot ratifies a relativism only hinted at elsewhere in the film, and one giving Lethem's punchline – '*We're all fucking ghouls*' – a significance which resonates back through his other writings. If, as the ghoul cop says to Nada earlier in the film, '[y]ou look as shitty to us as we do to you' (quoted in Lethem, 2010b: 117), then might it not also be possible, despite Nada's immediate scotching of the cop's suggestion, that humans and ghouls could be mutually attracted when the ghoul masks come off? Difference, as Everett Moon, Alice Coombs and Dylan Ebdus know only too well, is something desired even as it threatens and frightens. We are all ghouls first because we cannot stop ourselves trying to peep round the corner into the alien lives of others, and secondly, to adopt an important platitude from a thousand science fiction texts, because to those who live round the corner in their own FSR or mini-utopia, we look just as strange/revolting/enticing as they do to us.

The final shot Lethem therefore sees, punningly, as concerned with the 'embrace' of difference. Its appeal to the author stems from its playful (yet in ethical terms deadly serious) collision of the real and the fantastic, the physical body and the mediated body, the self and the other. In terms of the plot, it signifies the moment at which the ghouls begin to realise that '*the jig is up*' (Lethem, 2010b: 194), that humans no longer need the Hoffman Lenses to recognise the alien presence all around them. However, Lethem's underlying thesis in *They Live* is one applicable to his work as a whole. To don them is to realise, like so many of Lethem's own fictional creations, that the tiny, comfortable, familiar world one has created has been infested by science fiction elements all along, and that refusal to wear the glasses is simply a refusal to accept that the categories of existence to which one has adhered are themselves a blocking out of alternative lives.

But Nada's Manichaean, Hollywoodised understanding of humans and ghouls, even when he has put on the Hoffmans, as good versus evil, beautiful versus ugly masks a deeper understanding that Lethem's analysis of the narrative brings to the surface: the glasses were only ever a metaphor in the first place and might never even have been necessary. After noting Carpenter's apparently unequivocal dismissal of the ghouls' right to exist, the way he dismissively puts 'his 1950s monster-movie foot down' (Lethem, 2010b: 118), Lethem adds a teasing final line: 'Still, Nada never *does* wear his Hoffman Lenses for a look in the mirror' (Lethem, 2010b: 119). The implication is clear: what our meathead protagonist might see there, with or without glasses, and what he undoubtedly sees when he looks at the ghouls, is his own otherness, his own sense of alienation from himself, his own ghoulishness. Throughout his career so far, Lethem has gnawed away at the same problem: how to find fresh ways to reveal the world's strangeness, and the ghoulishness of the characters who inhabit it, without utilising cheap and cumbersome devices like the Hoffman Lenses. Although occasionally he strays close to the employment of gimmicks every bit as cheap as the Hoffmans, an example being the magic ring in *Fortress* which is not always satisfactorily integrated into 'a novel so firmly, even painfully rooted in the real world' (Rehak, 2003: 35), it is nonetheless true that few other contemporary writers are able to provoke genuinely emotional responses to elements that might otherwise be dismissed as 'wacky'. As Melanie Rehak says: 'It has always been one of Lethem's gifts as a writer to make even his most futuristic, postapocalyptic universes and characters as humane and well observed as the city streets he chronicles in *The Fortress of Solitude*. If anyone can make you believe it's possible to fall in love with a void, or that a homeless man can fly and a prison break can be aided by powers of invisibility, it's him' (Rehak, 2003: 35).

This is because, as the preceding chapters have shown, all the bizarre and original techniques and ideas Lethem employs – genre collisions, alien interventions, mixed media, Tourettic narrators, FSRs, interpolated fragments of music and lyrics – address issues that are fundamental and eminently recognisable to any reader: loss and the concomitant yearning for a renewed sense of fellowship and community. Loss takes many forms – the loss of a loved one, of a best friend, of youthful innocence and aspiration, of a fragile conception of reality – but what matters in Lethem's writing is one's reaction to it or, to borrow a metaphor from *They Live*, which glasses one chooses to wear. Is the pain of loss negated if one puts on the rose-tinted glasses which see the past as 'a pocketful of days distorted into legend, another jailhouse exaggeration' (Lethem, 2003: 473), the jailhouse here connoting entrapment in nostalgia, the obsessive, fetishising grasping onto details? Is it better to don a virtual reality mask, like the protagonist of 'How We Got in Town and Out Again' (Lethem, 1996) and block out the real world entirely? Both these approaches are, of course, amnesiac. In the end what is needed is the ability to step outside oneself and beyond one's familiar genres of behaviour and realise that loss, devastating though it may be, provides an opportunity not for immersion in one's personal experience and cultural obsessions, but in the diverse, creative responses to loss offered by others. The most powerful and rewarding 'constellated community' in Lethem's work is the community, in which an infinite number of disparate souls participate, of those who have lost something and wish to make something beautiful of it.

Bibliography

Works by Jonathan Lethem

Authored works

(1994) *Gun, With Occasional Music.* Orlando, FL: Harvest.

(1995) *Amnesia Moon.* Orlando, FL: Harvest.

(1996) *The Wall of the Sky, the Wall of the Eye.* London: Faber and Faber.

(1997) *As She Climbed Across the Table.* London: Faber and Faber.

(1998a) *Girl in Landscape.* London: Faber and Faber.

(1998b) 'Why Can't We All Just Live Together?: A Vision of Genre Paradise Lost'. *New York Review of Science Fiction.* 11.1 (September). 1, 8–9.

(1999) *Motherless Brooklyn.* London: Faber and Faber.

(2000) *This Shape We're In.* New York: McSweeney's Publishing.

(2003) *The Fortress of Solitude.* London: Faber and Faber.

(2004) *Men and Cartoons.* London: Faber and Faber.

(2005) *The Disappointment Artist and Other Essays.* New York: Doubleday.

(2006) *How We Got Insipid.* Burton, MI: Subterranean Press.

(2007a) *You Don't Love Me Yet.* New York: Doubleday.

(2007b) 'The Ecstasy of Influence: A Plagiarism'. *Harper's Magazine* (February). 59–71.

(2007c) 'We Happy Fakes'. *Guardian Books* (1 September). 12.

(2009a) *Chronic City.* New York: Doubleday.

(2009b) 'Procedure in Plain Air'. *The New Yorker* (26 October). 78–83.

(2009c) 'Crazy Friend'. http://jonathanlethem.com/crazyfriend.html, accessed 12 September 2010.

(2010a) 'The Salon', in S. J. Rozan and Jonathan Santlofer (eds), *The Dark End of the Street.* London: Bloomsbury.

(2010b) *They Live.* New York: Soft Skull Press.

Edited works

(2000) *The Vintage Book of Amnesia: An Anthology of Writing on the Subject of Memory Loss.* New York: Vintage.

(2002) *Da Capo Best Music Writing 2002: The Year's Finest Writing on Rock, Pop, Jazz, Country, and More*. Cambridge, MA: Da Capo Press.
(2007) *Philip K. Dick: Four Novels of the 1960s*. New York: Library of America.

Articles
(2003) 'Yoked in Gowanus', in Greg Tate (ed.), *Everything but the Burden: What White People are Taking from Black Culture*. New York: Harlem Moon.
(2006) 'Phil in the Marketplace'. *Virginia Quarterly Review*. 82 (Fall). 24–30.

Collaborative works
Lethem, Jonathan and Karl Rusnak (2008). *Omega the Unknown*. New York: Marvel.

Interviews
Barber, John (2009). 'Jonathan Lethem's in a New York State of Mind'. *Globe and Mail* (25 November). www.theglobeandmail.com/news/arts/jonathan-lethems-in-a-new-york-state-of-mind/article1377124/, accessed 1 December 2010.
Birnbaum, Robert (2004). 'Birnbaum v. Jonathan Lethem'. *Morning News* (7 January). www.themorningnews.org/archives/personalities/birnbaum_v_jonathan_lethem.php, accessed 1 December 2010.
—— (2005). 'Birnbaum v. Jonathan Lethem'. *Morning News* (19 October). www.themorningnews.org/archives/birnbaum_v/jonathan_lethem.php, accessed 1 December 2010.
Front Row (2004), interview with Jonathan Lethem, presented by Francine Stock. BBC Radio 4 (14 January).
Gaffney, Elizabeth (1998). 'Jonathan Lethem: Breaking the Barriers Between Genres'. *Publishers Weekly* (30 March). 50–1.
Kelleghan, Fiona (1998). 'Private Hells and Radical Doubts: An Interview with Jonathan Lethem'. *Science Fiction Studies*. 25.2. 225–40.
Lethem, Jonathan (2005b). 'Jonathan Lethem Talks with Paul Auster'. *The Believer* (February). 49–57.
—— (2010c). 'Jonathan Lethem in Conversation with Tom McCarthy'. London Review Bookshop (7 January). www.lrbshop.co.uk/news/36/Chronic-City---Jonathan-Lethem-in-conversation-with-Tom-McCarthy-.html, accessed 30 November 2010.
—— (2010d). 'Jonathan Lethem on *Chronic City*'. *The Guardian* (30 March). www.guardian.co.uk/books/video/2010/mar/22/jonathan-lethem-chronic-city-fiction.
Peacock, James (2009). 'Negotiations: An Interview with Jonathan Lethem'. *Adirondack Review*. (Winter) www.theadirondackreview.com/JamesPeacock.html, accessed 5 January 2010.
—— (2009). 'Personal interview with Jonathan Lethem'. Brooklyn (25 May).

Schiff, James (2006). 'A Conversation with Jonathan Lethem'. *Missouri Review*. 29.1. 116–34.

Stein, Lorin (2003). 'The Art of Fiction'. *Paris Review*. 166 (Summer). 218–51.

Sussler, Betty (2008). 'Jonathan Lethem'. *Bomb* (2 October). www.bombsite.com/issues/0/articles/3217, accessed 10 November 2009.

Weich, Dave (2003). 'Jonathan Lethem Takes the Long Way Home'. *Powells* (23 September) www.powells.com/authors/lethem.html, accessed 17 July 2008.

Zeitchik, Steven (2003). 'Jonathan Lethem: A Brooklyn of the Soul'. *Publishers Weekly* (15 September). 37–8.

Reviews of Jonathan Lethem's work

Begley, Adam (1999). 'Detective Yarn with a Twist: Tick-Plagued P. I. Sleuths Self'. *New York Observer* (18 October). 15.

Charles, Ron (2003). 'There Goes the Neighborhood'. *Christian Science Monitor* (11 September). www.csmonitor.com/2003/0911/p15s01-bogn.html, accessed 1 December 2010.

Chipman, Ian (2006). '*You Don't Love Me Yet*'. *Booklist* (15 October). 5–6.

Collins, Robert (2008). '*You Don't Love Me Yet*'. *Sunday Times* (15 June). 57.

Deresiewicz, William (2009). 'A Geek Grows in Brooklyn'. *The New Republic* (21 October). 48–53.

Leonard, John (2005). 'Welcome to New Dork'. *New York Review of Books* (7 April). www.nybooks.com/articles/archives/2005/apr/07/welcome-to-new-dork/, accessed 9 November 2010.

Mobilio, Albert (1999). 'What Makes Him Tic?' *New York Times* (17 October). 7.

Secondary works on Jonathan Lethem

Abbott, Carl (2005). 'Homesteading on the Extraterrestrial Frontier'. *Science Fiction Studies*. 32.2 (July). 240–64.

Bredehoft, Thomas A. (1998). 'Cosms and Lacks: Baby Universes in Lethem and Beyond'. *New York Review of Science Fiction*. 11.1 (September). 9–10.

Cohen, Samuel (2009). *After the End of History: American Fiction in the 1990s*. Iowa City: University of Iowa Press.

Davis, Ray (2009). 'High, Low, and Lethem'. *Genre*. 42 (Fall/Winter). 61–78.

Duchamp, L. Timmel (1998). 'Denaturalizing Authority and Learning to Live in the Flesh: Jonathan Lethem's *Amnesia Moon*'. *New York Review of Science Fiction*. 121 (September). 15–17.

Fleissner, Jennifer L. (2009). 'Symptomatology and the Novel'. *Novel: a Forum on Fiction*. 42.3 (Fall). 387–92.

Godbey, Matt (2008). 'Gentrification, Authenticity and White Middle-Class Identity in Jonathan Lethem's *The Fortress of Solitude*'. *Arizona Quarterly*. 64.1 (Spring). 131–51.

Greenwald, Richard (2010). 'Find Myself a City to Live in: Jonathan Lethem's Imagined Metropolis'. *The Rumpus* (25 August). http://therumpus. net/2010/08/find-myself-a-city-to-live-in-jonathan-lethem's-imagined-metropolis, accessed 10 November 2010.

Kravitz, Bennett (2003). 'The Culture of Disease or the Dis-ease of Culture in *Motherless Brooklyn* and *Eve's Apple*'. *Journal of American Culture*. 26.2 (June). 171–9.

Rehak, Melanie (2003). 'Local Color'. *The Nation* (27 October). 33–6.

Rossi, Umberto (2002). 'From Dick to Lethem: The Dickian Legacy, Post-modernism and Avant-Pop in Jonathan Lethem's *Amnesia Moon*'. *Science Fiction Studies*. 29.1 (March). 15–33.

Sheehan, Bill (1998). '*Girl in Landscape* by Jonathan Lethem'. *New York Review of Science Fiction*. 11.1 (September). 14–15.

Singer, Marc (2008). 'Embodiments of the Real: The Counterlinguistic Turn in the Comic-Book Novel'. *Critique*. 49.3 (Spring). 273–89.

General

Altman, Rick (1999). *Film/Genre*. London: BFI Publishing.

Anderson, Benedict (2006). *Imagined Communities*. London: Verso.

Anthony, David (2005). '"Gone Distracted": "Sleepy Hollow", Gothic Masculinity, and the Panic of 1819'. *Early American Literature*. 40.1 (January). 111–44.

Attebery, Brian (2002). 'But Aren't Those Just ... You Know, Metaphors?', in Veronica Hollinger and Joan Gordon (eds), *Edging into the Future: Science Fiction and Contemporary Cultural Transformation*. Philadelphia, PA: University of Pennsylvania Press.

Auster, Paul (2006). *The New York Trilogy*. New York: Penguin.

Austin, Joe (2001). *Taking the Train: How Graffiti Art Became an Urban Crisis in New York City*. New York: Columbia University Press.

Baccolini, Raffaela and Moylan, Tom (2003). 'Introduction: Dystopia and Histories', in Raffaela Baccolini and Tom Moylan (eds), *Dark Horizons: Science Fiction and the Dystopian Imagination*. New York: Routledge.

Bakhtin, Mikhail (2004 [1981]). 'Forms of Time and the Chronotope', in Michael Holquist (ed.), *The Dialogic Imagination: Four Essays*. Trans. Caryl Emerson and   Michael Holquist. Austin, TX: University of Texas Press.

Beebee, Thomas O. (1994). *The Ideology of Genre: A Comparative Study of Generic Instability*. Philadelphia, PA: University of Pennsylvania Press.

Bersani, Leo and Dutoit, Ulysse (1998). *Caravaggio's Secrets*. Cambridge, MA: MIT Press.

Blanchot, Maurice (1959). *Le Livre à Venir*. Paris: Gallimard.

Bok, Sissela (1983). *Secrets: On the Ethics of Concealment and Revelation*. New York: Vintage Books.

Bolter, Jay David and Grusin, Richard (2000). *Remediation: Understanding New Media*. Cambridge, MA: MIT Press.

Brenton, Sam and Cohen, Reuben (2003). *Shooting People: Adventures in Reality TV*. London: Verso.

Brodhead, Richard H. (1993). *Cultures of Letters: Scenes of Reading and Writing in Nineteenth-Century America*. Chicago: University of Chicago Press.

Buber, Martin (2004 [1937]). *I and Thou*. London: Continuum.

Buell, Lawrence (1979). 'Observer-Hero Narrative'. *Texas Studies in Literature and Language*. 21.1 (Spring). 93–111.

Burn, Stephen J. (2008). *Jonathan Franzen at the End of Postmodernism*. London: Continuum.

Carroll, Joseph (1995). *Evolution and Literary Theory*. Columbia and London: University of Missouri Press.

Caruth, Cathy (1996). *Unclaimed Experience: Trauma, Narrative and History*. Baltimore, MD: Johns Hopkins University Press.

Chabon, Michel (1995). *Wonder Boys*. London: Fourth Estate.

Chalfant, Henry and Prigoff, James (1987). *Spraycan Art*. London: Thames and Hudson.

Chandler, Raymond (1973 [1958]). *Playback*. London: Penguin.

—— (2005 [1953]). *The Long Goodbye*. London: Penguin.

Cheyfitz, Eric (1991). *The Poetics of Imperialism: Translation and Colonization from* The Tempest *to* Tarzan. New York: Oxford University Press.

Cohen, Margaret (2003). 'Traveling Genres'. *New Literary History*. 34.3 (Summer). 481–99.

Cohen, Ralph (1988). 'Do Postmodern Genres Exist?', in Marjorie Perloff (ed.), *Postmodern Genres*. Norman, OK and London: University of Oklahoma Press. 11–27.

Cohen, Samuel (2009). *After the End of History: American Fiction in the 1990s*. Iowa City: University of Iowa Press.

Colby, Chris (2006). 'Introduction to Evolutionary Biology'. *Talk Origins*. www.talkorigins.org/faqs/faq-intro-to-biology.html, accessed 12 June 2010.

Cole, Thomas (1836). 'Essay on American Scenery'. *American Monthly Magazine*. 1 (January). 1–12.

Colie, Rosalie (1973). *The Resources of Kind: Genre-Theory in the Renaissance*. Berkeley, CA: University of California Press.

Cook, Nicholas (1990). *Music, Imagination and Culture*. Oxford: Oxford University Press.

Cooper, Martha and Chalfant, Henry (1984). *Subway Art*. London: Thames and Hudson.

Connor, Steven (1995). *The English Novel in History, 1950–1995*. London and New York: Routledge.

Csicsery-Ronay Jr., Istvan (1991). 'Science Fiction and Postmodernism'. *Science-Fiction Studies*. 18.3. 305–8.

—— (2002). 'Dis-Imagined Communities: Science Fiction and the Future of Nations', in Veronica Hollinger and Joan Gordon (eds), *Edging into the Future: Science Fiction and Contemporary Cultural Transformation*. Philadelphia, PA: University of Pennsylvania Press.

Cuddy, Lois A. and Roche, Claire M. (eds) (2003). *Evolution and Eugenics in American Literature and Culture, 1880–1940: Essays on Ideological Conflict and Complicity*. Lewisburg, PA: Bucknell University Press.

Dalton-Brown, Sally (2008). 'Is There Life Outside of (the Genre of) the Campus Novel? The Academic Struggles to Find a Place in Today's World'. *Journal of Popular Culture*. 41.4. 591–600.

Darwin, Charles (1981). *The Descent of Man and Selection in Relation to Sex* (2 vols). Princeton, NJ: Princeton University Press.

—— (2003). *On the Origin of Species by Means of Natural Selection*. Ed. Joseph Carroll. Peterborough, ON: Broadview.

Delaney, Samuel (1994). *Silent Interviews: on Language, Race, Sex, Science Fiction and Some Comics*. Hanover, PA and London: Wesleyan University Press.

DeLillo, Don (1985). *White Noise*. New York: Viking.

—— (1988). *Libra*. New York: Viking.

Derrida, Jacques (1980). 'The Law of Genre'. *Critical Inquiry*. 7.1 (Autumn). 55–81.

Donawerth, Jane (2003). 'Genre Blending and the Critical Dystopia', in Raffaela Baccolini and Tom Moylan (eds), *Dark Horizons: Science Fiction and the Dystopian Imagination*. New York: Routledge.

Eco, Umberto (1992). *Interpretation and Overinterpretation*. Cambridge: Cambridge University Press.

Elmer, Jonathan (1995). *Reading at the Social Limit: Affect, Mass Culture and Edgar Allan Poe*. Stanford, CA: Stanford University Press.

Ferrell, Jeff (1996). *Crimes of Style: Urban Graffiti and the Politics of Criminality*. Boston, MA: Northeastern University Press.

Florey, Kitty Burns (2004). *Solos*. New York: Berkley Books.

Foner, Eric (2006). *Give Me Liberty! An American History*. New York: W. W. Norton & Company.

Frank, Nino (1996). 'The Crime Adventure Story: A New Kind of Detective Film', in R. Barton Palmer (ed.), *Perspectives on Film Noir*. New York: G. K. Hall.

Franzen, Jonathan (2001). *The Corrections*. London: Quality Paperbacks Direct.

Frow, John (2006). *Genre*. London and New York: Routledge.

Fussell, Edwin (1965). *Frontier: American Literature and the American West*. Princeton, NJ: Princeton University Press.

Gill, David (2007). 'The Three Stigmata of Philip K. Dick'. *Article*. (11 October). http://articlejournal.net/2007/10/11/the-three-stigmata-of-phillip-k-dick/, accessed 8 August 2010.

Goehr, Lydia (1993). '"Music Has No Meaning to Speak of": On the Politics of Musical Interpretation', in Michael Krausz (ed.), *The Interpretation of Music: Philosophical Essays*. Oxford: Clarendon Press.

Gold, Steven N. (2004). '*Fight Club*: A Depiction of Contemporary Society as Dissociogenic'. *Journal of Trauma and Dissociation*. 5.2 (July). 13–34.

Guillén, Claudio (1971). *Literature as System: Essays toward the Theory of Literary History*. Princeton, NJ: Princeton University Press.

Gumport, Elizabeth (2009). 'Gentrified Fiction'. *n+1*. 5 (November). www.nplusonemag.com/gentrified-fiction, accessed 14 April 2009.

Harris, Charles B. (2002). 'PoMo's Wake, 1'. *American Book Review*. 23.2 (January/February). 1–3.

Harvey, David (1989). *The Condition of Postmodernity: An Enquiry into the Origins of Cultural Change*. Oxford: Blackwell.

Hebdige, Dick (1996 [1979]). *Subculture: the Meaning of Style*. London and New York: Routledge.

Heffernan, James A. W. (1993). *Museum of Words: The Poetics of Ekphrasis from Homer to Ashbery*. Chicago: University of Chicago Press.

Hill, Annette (2005). *Reality TV: Audiences and Popular Factual Television*. London: Routledge.

Hoberek, Andrew (2007). 'Introduction: After Postmodernism'. *Twentieth-Century Literature*. 53.3 (Fall). 233–47.

Hopkins, Lisa (2004). *Giants of the Past: Popular Fictions and the Idea of Evolution*. Lewisburg, PA: Bucknell University Press.

Jameson, Fredric (1990). *The Political Unconscious: Narrative as a Socially Symbolic Act*. London: Routledge.

—— (1991). *Postmodernism: Or, the Cultural Logic of Late Capitalism*. London and New York: Verso.

Kaplan, Amy (1988). 'Nation, Region and Empire', in Emory Elliott (ed.), *Columbia Literary History of the United States*. New York: Columbia University Press.

Kenyon, J. P. (1980). '*Lucky Jim* and After: The Business of University Novels'. *Encounter*. 54 (June). 81–4.

Kermode, Frank (1979). *The Genesis of Secrecy*. Cambridge, MA: Harvard University Press.

Kowalewski, Michael (2003). 'Contemporary Regionalism', in Charles L. Crow (ed.), *A Companion to the Regional Literatures of America*. Malden, MA: Blackwell.

Kristeva, Julia (1982). *Powers of Horror: An Essay on Abjection*. Trans. Leon S. Roudiez. New York: Columbia University Press.

Kucukalic, Lejla (2009). *Philip K. Dick: Canonical Writer of the Digital Age*. New York: Routledge.

Lacan, Jacques (1988). 'Seminar on "The Purloined Letter"', in John P. Muller and William J. Richardson (eds), *The Purloined Poe: Lacan, Derrida and Psychoanalytic Reading*. Baltimore, MD and London: Johns Hopkins University Press.

LaCapra, Dominick (2001). *Writing History, Writing Trauma*. Baltimore, MD: Johns Hopkins University Press.

Langer, Lawrence (1991). *Holocaust Testimonies: The Ruins of Memory*. New Haven, CT: Yale University Press.

Langer, Suzanne K. (1953). *Feeling and Form: A Theory of Art*. New York: Charles Scribner's Sons.

Levitas, Ruth and Sargisson, Lucy (2003). 'Utopia in Dark Times: Optimism/Pessimism and Utopia/Dystopia', in Raffaela Baccolini and Tom Moylan (eds), *Dark Horizons: Science Fiction and the Dystopian Imagination*. New York: Routledge.

Limerick, Patricia Nelson, Milner, Clyde A. and Rankin, Charles E. (eds) (1991). *Trails: Toward a New Western History*. Lawrence, KS: University Press of Kansas.

Lodge, David (1975). *Changing Places: A Tale of Two Campuses*. London: Secker and Warburg.

—— (1986). *Write On: Occasional Essays '65–'85*. London: Secker and Warburg.

Lutz, Tom (2004). *Cosmopolitan Vistas: American Regionalism and Literary Value*. Ithaca, NY and London: Cornell University Press.

Lyons, John O. (1962). *The College Novel in America*. Carbondale, IL: Southern Illinois University Press.

McCaffery, Larry (ed.) (1992). 'The Avant-Pop Phenomenon'. *ANQ*. 5.4 (October). 215–20.

—— (1993). 'An Interview with David Foster Wallace'. *Review of Contemporary Fiction*. 13.2 (Summer). 127–50.

—— (1993). *Avant-Pop: Fiction for a Daydream Nation*. Boulder, CO: Black Ice Books.

—— (ed.) (1995). *After Yesterday's Crash: the Avant-Pop Anthology*. New York: Penguin.

McCloud, Scott (1993). *Understanding Comics: the Invisible Art*. New York: Kitchen Sink.

McCracken, Scott (1998). *Pulp: Reading Popular Fiction*. Manchester and New York: Manchester University Press.

McEwan, Ian (2005). *Saturday*. London: Jonathan Cape.

McHale, Brian (1987). *Postmodernist Fiction*. London and New York: Routledge.

Melley, Timothy (2003). 'Postmodern Amnesia: Trauma and Forgetting in Tim O'Brien's *In the Lake of the Woods*'. *Contemporary Literature*. 44.1. 106–31.

Meyer, Michel (1995). *Of Problematology: Philosophy, Science and Language.* Chicago: University of Chicago Press.

Miller, Jim (1998). 'Post-Apocalyptic Hoping: Octavia Butler's Dystopian/ Utopian Fiction'. *Science Fiction Studies.* 25.2. 336–61.

Morse, Margaret (1998). *Virtualities: Television, Media Art, and Cyberculture.* Bloomington and Indianapolis: Indiana University Press.

Moseley, Merritt (2007). *The Academic Novel: New and Classic Essays.* Chester: Chester Academic Press, 2007.

Muller, John P. and Richardson, William J. (eds) (1988). *The Purloined Poe: Lacan, Derrida and Psychoanalytic Reading.* Baltimore, MD and London: Johns Hopkins University Press.

Nietzsche, Friedrich (2004 [1882]). *The Gay Science: With a Prelude in German Rhymes and an Appendix of Songs.* Ed. Bernard Williams. Cambridge: Cambridge University Press.

Newton, Adam Zachary (1995). *Narrative Ethics.* Cambridge, MA: Harvard University Press.

Noon, Jeff (1995). *Pollen.* London: Pan.

Noya, José Liste (2004). 'Naming the Secret: Don DeLillo's *Libra*,' *Contemporary Literature.* 45.2 (Summer). 239–75.

Paik, Peter Y. (2010). *From Utopia to Apocalypse: Science Fiction and the Politics of Catastrophe.* Minneapolis and London: University of Minnesota Press.

Palahniuk, Chuck (1996). *Fight Club.* London: Vintage.

Pavel, Thomas (2003). 'Literary Genres as Norms and Good Habits'. *New Literary History.* 34.2 (Spring). 201–10.

Perloff, Marjorie (1988). 'Introduction', in Marjorie Perloff (ed.), *Postmodern Genres.* Norman, OK and London: University of Oklahoma Press. 11–27.

Pinsker, Sansford (1999), 'Who Cares if Roger Ackroyd Gets Tenure?' *Partisan Review.* 66.3 (Summer). 439–52.

Poe, Edgar Allan (1971). 'The Purloined Letter', in *Selected Writings of Edgar Allan Poe.* Ed. David Galloway. Harmondsworth: Penguin.

Pynchon, Thomas (2000 [1967]). *The Crying of Lot 49.* London: Vintage.

Rahn, Janice (2002). *Painting Without Permission: Hip-Hop Graffiti Subculture.* Westport, CT: Bergin & Garvey.

Renza, Louis A. (2002). *Edgar Allan Poe, Wallace Stevens, and the Poetics of American Privacy.* Baton Rouge, LA: Louisiana State University Press.

Ricoeur, Paul (2003). *The Rule of Metaphor: The Creation of Meaning in Language.* Trans. Robert Czerny. London: Routledge.

Roberts, Adam (2006). *Science Fiction.* London and New York: Routledge.

Rose, Randall L. and Wood, Stacy L. (2005). 'Paradox and the Consumption of Authenticity through Reality Television'. *Journal of Consumer Research.* 32 (September). 284–96.

Rosmarin, Adena (1985). *The Power of Genre.* Minneapolis: University of Minnesota Press.

Roth, Marco (2009). 'The Rise of the Neuronovel'. *n+1*. 8 (October). www. nplusonemag.com/rise-neuronovel, accessed 20 September 2009.

Sacks, Oliver (1987). *Awakenings*. New York: Knopf Publishing Group.

—— (1995). *An Anthropologist on Mars*. London: Vintage.

Sartwell, Crispin (2003). 'Graffiti and Language'. www.crispinsartwell.com/ grafflang.htm, accessed 5 November 2010.

Schleifer, Ronald (2001). 'The Poetics of Tourette Syndrome: Language, Neurobiology, and Poetry'. *New Literary History*. 32.3 (Summer). 563–84.

Schryer, Catherine F. (1994). 'The Lab Versus the Clinic: Sites of Competing Genres', in Aviva Freedman and Peter Medway (eds), *Genre and the New Rhetoric*. London: Taylor and Francis.

Schutz, Alfred (1970). *On Phenomenology and Social Relations: Selected Writings*. Chicago: University of Chicago Press.

Schwartz, Lynne Sharon (1990). *Leaving Brooklyn*. New York: Minerva.

Seitel, Peter (2003). 'Theorising Genres – Interpreting Works'. *New Literary History*. 34.2 (Spring). 275–97.

Siegel, Jacob (2005). 'Back to the Fortress of Brooklyn and the Millions of Destroyed Men Who Are My Brothers'. *New Partisan* 1 (18 April). www.newpartisan.com/home/back-to-the-fortress-of-brooklyn-and-the-millions-of-destroy.html, accessed 5 November 2010.

Simms, Karl (2003). *Paul Ricoeur*. London: Routledge.

Snyder, Gregory J. (2009). *Graffiti Lives: Beyond the Tag in New York's Urban Underground*. New York and London: New York University Press.

Sonik (2001). 'Style, Technique, and Cultural Piracy: Never Bite the Hand that Feeds'. www.graffiti.org/faq/sonik.html, accessed 5 November 2010.

Sontag, Susan (1978). *Illness as Metaphor*.

—— (1989). *AIDS and its Metaphors*.

Sørensen, Bent (2004). 'Jewishness and Identity in Jonathan Lethem's *Motherless Brooklyn*'. Nordic Association of English Studies Conference, Aarhus (May).

Stephens, Michael (1994). *The Brooklyn Book of the Dead*. Champaign, IL: Dalkey Archive Press.

Suvin, Darko (1979). *Metamorphoses of Science Fiction*. New Haven, CT: Yale University Press.

Tal, Kalí (1996). *Worlds of Hurt: Reading the Literatures of Trauma*. Cambridge: Cambridge University Press.

Turner, Frederick Jackson (1999). 'The Significance of the Frontier in American History', in Richard W. Etulain (ed.), *Does the Frontier Experience Make America Exceptional?* Boston, MA and New York: Bedford/St Martin's.

Vidal, Gore (1988). *At Home: Essays 1982–1988*. New York: Random House.

Wagner, Peter (ed.) (2003 [1996]). *Icons-Text-Iconotexts: Essays on Ekphrasis and Intermediary*. New York: de Gruyter.

Wallace, David Foster (1993). 'E Unibus Pluram: Television and U. S. Fiction'. *Review of Contemporary Fiction*. 13.2 (Summer). 151–94.

Wegner, Phillip E. (2003). 'Where the Prospective Horizon is Omitted: Naturalism and Dystopia in *Fight Club* and *Ghost Dog*', in Raffaela Baccolini and Tom Moylan (eds), *Dark Horizons: Science Fiction and the Dystopian Imagination*. New York: Routledge.

White, Hayden (2003). 'Anomalies of Genre: The Utility of Theory and History for the Study of Literary Genres'. *New Literary History*. 34.3 (Summer). 597–615.

Wieseltier, Leon (2002). 'A Year Later'. *New Republic* (2 September). 38.

Wolfe, Gary K. (2002). 'Evaporating Genre: Strategies of Dissolution in the Postmodern Fantastic', in Veronica Hollinger and Joan Gordon (eds), *Edging into the Future: Science Fiction and Contemporary Cultural Transformation*. Philadelphia: University of Pennsylvania Press.

Wolk, Douglas (2007). *Reading Comics: How Graphic Novels Work and What They Mean*. Cambridge, MA: Da Capo Press.

Wood, James (2001). 'Tell Me How Does It Feel?' *Guardian* (6 October). 8.

Žižek, Slavoj (1992). *Looking Awry: An Introduction to Jacques Lacan through Popular Culture*. Cambridge, MA: MIT Press.

—— (2006a). *The Parallax View*. Cambridge, MA: MIT Press.

Index

Note: 'n.' after a page reference indicates the number of a note on that page.